Snakes

Their Care and Keeping

LENNY FLANK, JR.

FEATURING PHOTOGRAPHS

BY

BILL LOVE

HOWELL
BOOK
HOUSE

*To my fellow animal lover Julie who helped me
more than she knows. Thanks, Jule.*

Howell Book House
A Simon & Schuster Macmillan Company
1633 Broadway
New York, NY 10019

Macmillan Publishing books may be purchased for business or sales promotional use. For information, write: Special Markets Department, Macmillan Publishing USA, 1633 Broadway, New York, NY 10019.

Macmillan is a registered trademark of Macmillan, Inc.

Library of Congress Cataloging-in-Publication Data
Flank, Lenny.
Snakes: their care and keeping / Lenny Flank, Jr.
    p. cm.
    Includes bibliographical references
    ISBN 0-87605-635-4
    1. Captive snakes. I. Title.
SF515.5S64F38   1998
639.3'96—dc21 97-29225   CIP

Manufactured in the United States of America

Photo credits:
Lenny Flank, Jr.: 4, 14 (bottom), 17 (bottom),
18, 28 (bottom), 62 (top), 86, 116, 120 (bottom), 148, 149
Fred Wilson: 111 (top)
Courtesy of Neodesha Plastics, Inc.: 78

All other photos by Bill Love.

Contents

Preface

About a year ago, I was corresponding with a fellow reptile enthusiast (who usually refer to themselves as "herpers") on one of the various computer mailing lists that are dedicated to the care and breeding of captive reptiles. In one message, he noted that herpers seem to be divided into two distinct groups of roughly equal size. One the one hand are those who view their animals as simply pets and who desire only to obtain and keep as many varieties and color strains as they are able. These collectors, who are sometimes referred to disparagingly as "stamp collectors," usually take little or no interest in the habits or conservation of snakes in the wild—they are solely interested in their captive care.

On the other hand are those who have a deep interest in the natural history of snakes and who view their captives as an interesting way to obtain more information about the lifestyles and habits of these animals. These collectors, who are sometimes chided as "eco-nuts," also have a firm interest in ecology and conservation, and while they are usually quite knowledgeable about the captive care of snakes, they are equally aware of efforts to understand them in the wild.

In response, I noted that this was unfortunate, since these groups have much common ground and much to learn from each other. What was needed, I remarked, was a good source that discussed the hobby of snake-keeping from *both* points of view—giving good care and husbandry advice as well as placing snakes in their proper natural and ecological roles.

This book is the result of that correspondence. I hope that it will serve as a useful and interesting reference for both types of snake keepers, and that it will allow both groups to better appreciate the other. Also, I hope that it entices those who may have only a passing interest in snakes to take up this fascinating and unique hobby. But be warned—snake-keeping is *extremely* addicting. Like potato chips, nobody can stop at just one . . . .

Happy herping!

Acknowledgments

No book is ever the work of a single individual. A number of people played a role in the preparation of this book. I would like to particularly thank Steve Grenard and Rich Zuchowski, two of the best snakers in the United States, who have been kind enough to review manuscripts for me, make helpful suggestions and pass on invaluable information and references. Also, thanks are due to my cyber-friends on the SLITHER Internet mailing list, the rec.pets.herp and sci.bio.herp newsgroups, and the FidoNet CHAMELEON and EVOLUTION echos, who had to put up with innumerable questions and queries from me while this manuscript was being prepared.

Thanks are also due to editor Ariel Cannon, who wields her blue pencil with skill, and to Dominique DeVito, who took a chance on an untested freelance writer.

Finally, I would like to thank Bill Haast and Raymond Ditmars, whose book and TV exploits first sparked my interest in snakes all those years ago. If this book helps spark a similar interest in just one of its readers, then it will have been well worth the effort.

Introduction

The hobby of collecting and caring for reptiles and amphibians in captivity is known as "herpetoculture," from the Greek word *herpeton*—"one which creeps." Although reptiles and amphibians are separate classes of animals and are quite different from each other, the scientific study of both groups has been combined together into one discipline called "herpetology," and reptile and amphibian keepers have been similarly lumped together as "herpetoculturalists." Since the phrase "reptiles and amphibians" is too long and awkward to use in casual conversation, both herpetologists and herpetoculturalists have tried various shorter words to mean the same thing. Reptiles and amphibians are thus sometimes referred to collectively as "herpetofauna" or sometimes as "herptiles," but by far the most common name is "herps." Both herpetoculturalists and herpetologists, in turn, usually refer to themselves as "herpers."

When snake keepers want to impress their friends, they may refer to themselves as "ophiodioculturalists," a tongue-twister that comes from the Greek word for "snake."

Whatever you like to call them, though, snake keepers are growing in numbers by leaps and bounds. When I first started collecting reptiles, about fifteen years ago, herpers were few and far between. Today, it has been estimated that some two million families—around seven percent of the entire U.S. population—keep at least one reptile, usually a snake, as a pet. Breeding and importing reptiles for the pet trade has become a billion-dollar-a-year business. Nearly every state has at least one herpetological society devoted to the care and study of herps, and several national herp organizations have appeared in the past few years. The development of the computer network has been a boon to the herp hobby, and the Internet offers access to dozens of reptile-related web pages and several e-mail lists and newsgroups devoted to snakes and snake-keeping.

PART I

What Makes a Snake a Snake?

Evolutionary History · Basic Biology · Ecology · Taxonomy and Classification

Evolutionary History

Snakes are members of the reptile class of organisms. There are five basic groups, called "orders," of reptiles alive today. The order Chelonia includes the turtles and tortoises. The order Crocodilia includes the

the alligators, crocodiles, caimans and

The long forked tongue of this Savannah Monitor betrays its close evolutionary kinship with the modern snakes.

REPTILE SKIN VERSUS AMPHIBIAN SKIN

Reptiles are most readily distinguished from their amphibian relatives by their thick, scaly skin, which protects the animal from scratches and abrasions much more effectively than the thin, moist skin of amphibians.

Amphibian skin is water-permeable, causing the animal to desiccate if it ventures into dry areas. Because of this, all amphibians are restricted in their habitat to areas that are damp and moist. The scaled reptile skin, however, is waterproof and retains body moisture, allowing the animal to move away from the water onto drier land areas without dehydrating. Because of their waterproof skins, reptiles have been able to establish themselves in a much wider range of habitats than their amphibian cousins. In some arid environments, such as deserts, reptiles can outcompete even mammals and birds, and are the dominant form of life.

gavials. There is only one living member of the order Rynchocephalia (the Latin name means "beak head"), the lizardlike Tuatara, which is found on isolated islands in New Zealand. The Amphisbaenas are slender burrowing reptiles that vaguely resemble snakes. Their biology is very poorly known. The order Squamata (meaning "scaled ones") is divided into two suborders, the Sauria, which contains all of the lizards, and the Serpentes, which includes all of the snakes.

The development of the amniote egg was critical to the success of the reptiles. The amphibian ancestors of the reptiles laid soft, jellylike eggs, which dried out easily and had to be laid in water or damp areas. Unlike the naked egg of the amphibians, the reptile egg is covered by a hard protective shell, which surrounds the embryo with fluids and moisture inside the "amniotic sac." In effect, reptiles managed the problem of reproducing on land by taking a tiny little pond along with them. In a further improvement over amphibians, which first hatch into a vulnerable larval or tadpole stage, embryonic reptiles complete their development inside the egg and emerge as tiny copies of their parents—ready to fend for themselves in the world. The shelled egg is therefore the key to the success of the reptiles, allowing them to invade and establish themselves in a wide range of environmental niches.

Like all other reptiles and amphibians, snakes are "cold-blooded" in their metabolism. The proper scientific term for this is "ectothermic," which comes from the Latin words for "outside heat." In all animals, biological processes are controlled by a class of chemicals known as enzymes, and these enzymes work best at rather high temperatures. In "warm-blooded" animals, the heat released during the metabolism of food is used to warm the body and maintain the proper temperature for these enzymes, no matter what the environmental temperature might be. Mammals and birds are therefore referred to scientifically as "endothermic," meaning "inside heat." A human being, for example, uses internal metabolic heat to maintain a body temperature of close to 98.6°F whether the air temperature is 100°F or 50°F.

Ectotherms, however, cannot produce enough body heat metabolically to maintain their body temperatures at the appropriate level, and must use external sources of heat to keep their internal temperatures sufficiently high. Snakes that live in tropical areas, where the ambient air temperature is usually very close to the preferred body temperature, don't have a problem keeping warm. Snakes from cooler areas, however, are more dependent on outside heat sources. They are typically smaller and darker in color than tropical snakes, allowing them to absorb sunlight and heat themselves more efficiently. By basking for part of the day and thus absorbing energy from the sun, these snakes are able to maintain their body temperatures at levels much higher than the surrounding air temperature, allowing them to remain active even in cool, temperate regions. In the winter, when short days and colder temperatures make it impossible to obtain enough outside heat, snakes

retreat to underground chambers and hibernate, slowing down their metabolic activity and living on glycogen reserves stored in the liver. The snake emerges in the spring when the temperatures get warmer, and it can reach the body temperature necessary to become active.

The fossil history of snakes is very poorly known, as snake skeletons are very delicate and do not fossilize easily. By carefully examining the fossil materials that have been recovered, and by making comparisons of the anatomy of living snakes and their relatives, biologists have been able to reconstruct something of the evolutionary history of snakes. Snakes, like all living things, are the product of the process of evolution, which allows species to change over time in response to environmental factors to produce entirely new species. The engine of evolution is "natural selection," in which those individual animals that possess superior survival traits tend to live longer than others and reproduce, in turn passing those same traits on to their offspring.

The currently accepted scientific model of the evolution of life was first laid out in Charles Darwin's book *On the Origin of Species through Natural Selection.* The Darwinian theory of biological evolution can be summed up in three basic postulates:

1. The members of any particular biological population differ from each other in minor ways and will each have slightly differing characteristics in construction and behavior. This is the principle of "variation." In Darwin's time, nothing was known about genetics, and scientists then had no idea how or why the observed variations within species occurred. Today, we know that they are caused by copying errors ("mutations") within the cell's DNA.

2. These variations can be passed on from one generation to the next, and the offspring of those organisms possessing a particular type of variation will also tend to have that same variation. This is the principle of "heritability."

3. Some of these variations will give their possessor an advantage in life (or help it avoid some disadvantage), allowing that organism to obtain more food, escape predators more effectively, and so on. Thus, those organisms that possess such a useful variation will tend, over the long run, to survive longer and produce more offspring than will other members of the population. These offspring, moreover, through the principle of heritability, will also tend to possess this advantageous variation, and this will have the effect, over time, of increasing the proportion of the population that

possesses this variation. This is the principle of "natural selection."

These three basic principles are combined to form the basic Darwinian model of the evolution of life. The traditional Darwinian outlook holds that small incremental changes in structure and behavior, brought about by the natural selection of variations, will produce, after a long period of time, organisms that differ so greatly from their ancestors that they are no longer the same organism and must be classified as a new species. This process of speciation, repeated over the 3.5 billion year span of time since life first appeared on earth, explains the gradual production of all life's diversity.

Although there are very few paleontologists who are actively studying the evolutionary history of reptiles, some fossil discoveries have been made and a rough outline of the history of these animals has been drawn. According to most paleo-herpetologists, reptiles evolved from the large group of ancient amphibians known as labrynthodonts, which received their name from the distinctive structure of their teeth. In the labrynthodonts, the enamel of the tooth was folded in on itself to form a complex mazelike pattern.

The evolutionary advance that set the reptiles apart from the amphibians was the development of the amniote or shelled egg, which could be laid on land, freeing the reptiles from the necessity of returning to the water to reproduce. The oldest known fossil egg was found in Texas and dates to the lower Permian period of the earth's history, over 275 million years ago. It is not known from which particular group of labrynthodont amphibians the reptiles developed; several different families of ancient amphibians seemed to have been simultaneously developing characteristics similar to those of reptiles.

The oldest fossil that can be definitely recognized as a reptile is a small lizardlike animal known as *Hylonomus*, whose skeletons have been found inside petrified tree stumps in Nova Scotia. During the period of time in which *Hylonomus* lived, the earth was a different place. The continents were joined into one large supercontinent near the equator, known as Pangaea (all earth), and even such places as Antarctica and northern Canada had warm, humid climates with lush tropical forests. Since then, the Pangaea landmass has broken up into a series of "plates" that slowly move atop the earth's mantle, a process known as "plate tectonics." As we shall see, the breakup and movement of these plates has had noticeable consequences for the evolution and distribution of modern snakes.

Hylonomus was a member of a group of very ancient reptiles known as the cotylosaurs, or "stem reptiles," which are believed by paleontologists to be ancestral to all of the reptile families alive today. The cotylosaurs first appeared during the Permian period, the period of time that immediately preceded the rise of the dinosaurs. During the next few million years, the cotylosaurs diverged into three distinct groups of reptiles that are distinguished from each other by their differing skull structures. The earliest of the cotylosaurs were anapsids, which means that they lacked any arches or openings between their skull bones. The anapsids eventually went on to produce the modern turtles. Later, another

GREAT SNAKE FOSSILS

The most complete skeleton of a fossil snake was found in upper Cretaceous rocks in Argentina. Most of the skull was preserved as well as a large number of vertebrae and ribs. The 6-foot skeleton was named *Dinilysia patagonica*, and it shares many anatomical characteristics with the modern boas and pythons (boids), which are usually considered to be the most primitive of the living snakes. Another fossil snake, *Gigantophis*, that was found in Egypt had an estimated length of over 50 feet and is the largest of all the known snakes. It is also related to the modern boids.

group of cotylosaurs developed a single arch in the skull, between the postorbital and squamosal bones, through which the jaw muscles passed. These reptiles are known as synapsids, and they went on to evolve into the modern mammals. The third group of reptiles, the diapsids, diversified to produce the extinct dinosaurs as well as the modern lizards and snakes. Although snakes are not direct descendants of the dinosaurs, they are evolutionary cousins of *Tyrannosaurus* and *Triceratops*. (Modern birds are also descended from diapsid reptiles, and are thus distant evolutionary cousins of the modern snakes.)

One of the earliest snakes to appear in the fossil record has been given the scientific name *Lapparentophis defrenni*. It was found in the Sahara Desert and has been dated to the early Cretaceous period, about 130 million years ago. Although the fossil consisted of only a few back bones and was missing all the ribs and the entire skull, the structure of the vertebrae was characteristic of that of snakes. Recently another fossil, a few million years older than *Lapparentophis*, was found in Spain. This fossil consists of just two vertebrae and has not yet been named.

Another very early snake has been found in marine deposits in North Africa and Europe. This snake, which lived about 100 mil-lion years ago, has been called *Simoliophis*. Although it appears to have been at least partially aquatic, *Simoliophis* does not appear to be related to any of the modern sea snakes, and may not be related to any living snakes. Both *Lapparentophis* and *Simoliophis* appear to have become extinct some time before the end of the Cretaceous period.

Some of the most interesting relics of ancient snakes are fossils of the extinct boid *Paleryx*, found in Germany. Some fossils of this ancient snake still contain the impressions of the scaled skin.

The end of the Cretaceous period (the time when snakes were just beginning to diversify), was marked by one of the largest mass extinctions in earth's history. In an extremely short period of geological time, over three-fourths of the earth's life forms were suddenly and inexplicably wiped out (the largest mass extinction known, at the end of the Permian period, killed almost ninety-six percent of all life on earth). The Cretaceous extinction eradicated all of the dinosaurs as well as many other groups of marine and land animals and plants.

According to the latest theories, the Cretaceous extinction was caused by the impact of an asteroid or comet, which struck the earth near what is now Yucatan, in Mexico. The resulting titanic explosion kicked up an enormous cloud of dust and smoke that pre-vented sunlight from reaching the earth. Without sunlight, photosyn-thesizing plants died and the entire ecological system collapsed. If this theory is true (and there is much evidence to support it), the survival of snakes (and of mammals and birds, for that matter) from the Cretaceous period until today was not the result of natural selection or superior survival skills—it was merely a lucky accident.

Based on fossil finds, as well as on anatomical study of modern reptiles, scientists have concluded that the snakes probably evolved from a family of lizards during the time of the dinosaurs. Snakes and lizards share a number of distinct features in the structure of their skulls; both possess a moveable quadrate bone at the back of the jaw, and both are missing the quadratojugal bone at the rear of the skull.

In particular, the varanoid family of lizards, which includes the monitors, have a very similar skull structure to that of snakes. The most snakelike of the living monitors is the Earless Monitor, a burrowing semiaquatic lizard found in Borneo. The Earless Monitor has movable eyelids, but the lower lid sports a clear window that allows the monitor to see even when its eyes are closed, protecting the eyes from water and dirt. This is very reminiscent of the snake's brille or eyecap, which is formed in embryo when the transparent upper and lower eyelids fuse together. The Earless Monitor also has a number of snakelike features in its skull architecture and, as the name implies, it lacks any trace of an external ear, just as snakes do. The Earless Monitor probably resembles the saurian ancestor of the snakes more than any other living lizard.

Based on these similarities, some herpetologists have theorized that an ancient group of monitorlike lizards began to follow a burrowing way of life, tunneling through loose dirt and sand in search of earthworms and other prey, just as some lizards do today. Over a period of millions of years, these burrowing lizards lost their limbs and their external ears—to streamline their bodies and help them burrow more easily—and also replaced their eyelids with a clear brille to protect their eyes while digging. At about the time that the dinosaurs reached their apex, one group of these burrowing lizards gave up its subter-

The varanid family of lizards, which includes the Nile Monitor, is believed to be the closest living relatives of snakes. Snakes evolved from lizards about 130 million years ago.

ranean lifestyle and emerged to the surface, where it developed a new legless mode of locomotion and rapidly diversified to invade a large number of ecological niches. Today, we classify the various descendants of these legless lizards as snakes.

The "burrowing ancestors" theory has, however, come under attack. Several herpetologists have pointed out that the *Dinilysia* skull does

not show many features adapted to a burrowing existence. Some biologists have theorized that the snake's unique features are the result of a largely aquatic or semiaquatic lifestyle, as illustrated by the Earless Monitor. In this interpretation, the lack of ears, the covered eyes and the long, limbless bodies allowed the first snakes to move efficiently through water or wet marshy areas in search of prey. It was only later that snakes moved from an aquatic environment to invade the dry land. During the time that snakes developed, the varanoid group did contain a number of semiaquatic and marine species, including the giant Mososaurs.

The "aquatic ancestors" theory received a big boost in early 1997, when paleontologists reexamined a fossil skeleton that had first been

The oldest fossil snakes closely resemble modern boas and pythons. (Columbia Boa Constrictor)

uncovered near Jerusalem in 1978. The skeleton, found in marine deposits almost 100 million years old, showed a light skull attached to a long vertebral column, with two small legs attached to the rear pelvic girdle. It was identified at the time as a marine lizard and was named *Pachyrachis problematicus.*

In 1997, though, a pair of Australian paleontologists reexamined the *Pachyrachis* fossil and, after comparing it bone for bone with snakes (particularly the skull structure), concluded that it was not a lizard at all, but a very primitive snake. And because it seemed to depict a snake in the process of evolving from an aquatic lizard and losing its legs, the fossil gave support to those who theorized a marine varanoid origin for snakes.

In any case, the first modern terrestrial snakes to appear seem to have been relatives of the living boids, or boas and pythons. The earliest known fossil boid is *Madtsoia madagascarensis,* from the late Cretaceous era. The early boids were large, heavy-bodied snakes with a rather primitive and heavy skull structure. The living boas and pythons all have tiny clawlike toes protruding from either side of their cloaca—these are the remnants of the legs that their ancestors once had, and are thus an evolutionary relic, tying the snakes directly to their lizard ancestors. Some fossil pipe snakes from the late Cretaceous period have also been found in Wyoming and New Mexico.

After the dinosaurs disappeared, the boids were the dominant snake family on earth, becoming widespread and very diverse. About 36 million years ago, however, a group of smaller, faster snakes that competed with the boids for food and living space appeared. These were the colubrids, the family that many people think of today as typical snakes. The earliest colubrid families found in the fossil record include the water snakes and the racers.

The colubrids were unable to outcompete the boids and remained a small group of snakes until about 20 million years ago, when the continental plates began to reach their present positions. As the tectonic plates moved away from the equator, the climate cooled dramatically, and the boids, unable to cope with the lower temperatures, disappeared from many areas and were greatly reduced in number and diversity. The colubrids quickly moved into the empty environmental niches that had been occupied by the boids, and soon dominated the snake world. Today, the colubrids make up over two-thirds of all the living species of snake.

One family of the colubrids, however, added a new twist to the snake's survival arsenal. About 15 million years ago, snakes with a number of greatly enlarged teeth at the rear of the jaw began appearing in the fossil record. These teeth had shallow grooves running down one side. Today, such snakes are referred to as *opisthoglyphs* or "rear-fanged" snakes. In the rear-fanged snakes, the enlarged teeth are used to pierce the skin of prey after it has been seized and partially

Snakes have grown extremely popular as pets in the last few years. (corn snake)

swallowed, allowing venom (composed of highly modified saliva) to flow out of the Duvernoy's gland and dribble down the grooved teeth into the wound. Because it is difficult for these snakes to inject their venom until after they have partially swallowed their victim, it is unlikely that the snakes' venom apparatus was originally developed as a defensive weapon. More likely, it appeared as an effective way of quickly killing and subduing food. A large number of rear-fanged snakes are still alive today.

Shortly after the opisthoglyphs appeared, another group of snakes with a more refined venom apparatus emerged. These snakes are known as *proteroglyphs,* and are classified as the elapids. Instead of having fangs at the rear of the jaws, the proteroglyphs have short, fixed fangs that have migrated (by reducing the size of the maxillary bone) to the front of the mouth, where they can be used to bite and strike at enemies as well as food. The

VIPER DEVELOPMENT

About 10 million years ago, the most highly specialized of the snakes appeared, according to the fossil record—the *solenoglyphs,* commonly known as vipers. In the vipers, the fangs are extremely long, much larger than in the elapids. In fact, they are so long that the snake cannot close its mouth if they are erected. Thus, the solenoglyphs use a rotating maxillary bone to fold the fangs up against the roof of the mouth, where they are ready to spring into position when the snake bites. A short time after the vipers appeared, a group known as

the pit vipers developed a number of heat-sensitive pits on the front of the face, which they used for finding their warm-blooded prey at night (this feature has also been independently developed by the venerable boid family). Finally, just a few million years ago, a group of pit vipers developed a structure at the end of their tail, made up of interlocking pieces of unshed skin, which could be loudly rattled and used as a warning device against predators. The rattlesnakes are generally thought to be the most specialized of all the living snakes.

grooves in the fangs have become deeper and meet at the edges to form a hollow tube. These hollow fangs are connected to venom glands in the cheeks, which can inject venom through the fangs like hypodermic needles when the snake bites. Living descendants of the elapids include the cobras and the sea snakes.

The fossil record of snakes, however, is patchy and incomplete. Newer techniques using molecular biology may give us a more complete picture of snake evolution. Using methods such as immunological responses and DNA-DNA hybridization, the precise genetic "distance" between living species can be determined, and a rough picture of when and in what order they evolved can be drawn. The study of snakes using DNA techniques is still in its infancy, but has already revealed a few surprises. Although new fossils such as *Pachyrhachis* seem to indicate an aquatic origin for snakes, DNA testing has indicated that the primitive burrowing snakes—the thread snakes and blind snakes—are the oldest of the modern snakes. Thus,

Rattlesnakes are the most highly evolved of the living snakes. (Prairie Rattlesnake)

the question of the origin of snakes is still wide open. Preliminary results also indicate that the vipers are not, as formerly thought, the most recent of the snakes, but instead diverged from the ancestral boid stock at about the same time as the elapid/colubrid branch. If this finding is confirmed, it means that fossils of these early vipers have yet to be found. It also means we have to completely rethink our view of how the venom apparatus in snakes evolved. One possibility is that the vipers descended from a branch of fanged colubrids similar to modern rear-fanged serpents, such as the hognose snakes. Much work remains to be done on the evolution of snakes.

CHAPTER 2

Basic Biology

The anatomy of snakes is so similar to that of lizards that the two groups are classified scientifically into one order, called Squamata. In fact, the lifestyles of lizards and snakes are so alike that several families of modern lizards, including

This Eastern Glass Lizard is not a snake but is very similar to snakes in appearance and habits.

anguids (the "glass lizards") and some of the skinks, may be difficult for most people to distinguish from snakes. The glass lizards, in particular, are remarkably similar to snakes—they share corresponding habitats and over time have come to possess the same limbless body form, a coincidence referred to by biologists as convergent evolution.

Nevertheless, because of its unique evolutionary history, the snake's anatomy is different in many ways from that of most other animals, including lizards. The snakelike legless lizards all have eyelids that can open and close; snakes do not. Legless lizards also possess an ear hole on either side of the head; snakes do not have any external ears and are deaf to airborne sounds. Finally, all snakes

have a single row of enlarged scales running along the belly; in legless lizards, the belly is covered with numerous rows of tiny scales.

Snakes' Anatomy

The snake's anatomy differs from that of other vertebrates in many other interesting ways, each a response to some particular problem faced by the animal as it lives and reproduces.

Skull

Because a snake does not have chewing teeth and also has no limbs to help it hold or tear prey, it has no choice but to swallow all of its food whole. In response to these specialized feeding habits, the bones in the snake's skull have become heavily modified.

The bones of the snake's skull are loosely connected by flexible ligaments. The jaw joint can be dislocated from the skull to produce an enormous gape, and the two halves of the jawbone can also spread widely apart at the chin. The lower jaw, which is made up of a single bone in mammals, is composed of several separate bones in snakes, each of which is capable of moving independently of the others. The quadrate bone in snakes is long and narrow, and possesses a joint at each end, allowing the jaw bones to move very far apart from each other. Because of the loose arrangement of the skull and jawbones, an average snake can swallow a food item that is up to three times the diameter of its head.

During the feeding process, the brain is protected by a bony box at the rear of the skull. As in all reptiles, the snake's brain does not

This python skull illustrates the light construction, sharp curved teeth and loose bone structure found in these animals.

completely fill its cavity in the skull, but is cushioned by fluids and connective tissue.

Jawbones

Each of the bones in a snake's upper and lower jaws can move independently of the others. As the prey is swallowed, the pair of toothed bones in the roof of the mouth move alternately back and forth, gripping the prey and pulling it into the throat. This allows the snake to move forward and engulf the prey, in effect "walking" over its food. Once the prey has been swallowed, muscular contractions in the throat carry it down to the stomach. After the prey has been swallowed, the snake will yawn widely once or twice to help put its jawbones back into place.

The jawbones of a snake have also been adapted to another role—that of hearing. Although snakes lack external ears and are almost completely deaf to airborne sounds, they do have an arrangement in their jawbones that allows them to ascertain low-frequency vibrations such as footsteps. In reptiles, the lower jaw is made up of a number of different bones, and the jaw joint is formed between the quadrate bone in the skull and the angular bone in the jaw. In mammals, in contrast, the lower jaw is made up of a single bone, the dentary, which articulates with the squamosal bone in the skull to form the jaw joint. Reptiles have a single bone in the middle ear, the stapes, while in mammals, there are three bones in the middle ear: the malleus, incus and stapes (also known as the hammer, anvil and stirrup).

The fossil record shows that during the evolutionary transition from reptile to mammal, the jaw joints shifted from one pair of bones to another, freeing up the rest of these bones to form the auditory bones in the mammalian middle ear. This process is best depicted in the fossil reptile *Diarthrognathus,* which clearly exhibits two functional jaw joints, one between the quadrate and articular bone as in reptiles, and another between the dentary and squamosal bones as in modern mammals.

During the evolutionary move from reptiles to mammals, several of the bones in the jaw, including the quadrate and articular, became progressively smaller and more specialized in transmitting vibrations. Eventually these modified jawbones became the middle ear bones found in modern mammals. Thus, the changes that occurred in the reptilian jawbones were not a functional change but merely an improvement in a function that these bones already had (and that, in modern snakes, they still have).

In snakes, as well as the early reptiles, the stapes bone in the middle ear is pressed up against the quadrate bone in the skull. Thus, any vibrations that are picked up by the skull or skeleton are carried through the quadrate bone to the stapes, and thence to the inner ear and auditory nerve. Thus, snakes can "hear" using their jawbones—although the range of frequencies they can sense is very limited, and the sense of hearing is closer to feeling vibrations rather than full-fledged sounds.

Teeth

In most snakes, all of the teeth are the same size and shape; snakes do not have the differently shaped incisors, canines and molars found in mammals. Venomous species have specially modified fangs for the injection of venom, and some of the arboreal boids have elongated teeth at the front of the jaws, which they use to pierce the feathers of the birds they feed on. Snake

LOTS OF TEETH!

Snakes have many more teeth than do humans and other mammals. Most species have over 200 teeth, which are found in two rows along the roof of the mouth as well as around the rims of both upper and lower jaws. Unlike those of mammals, a snake's teeth are not set in sockets; instead, they are attached to the sides of the jawbones, an arrangement known technically as *pleurodont* teeth.

teeth are relatively long and curve backwards toward the throat, helping to hold struggling prey while it is being killed and swallowed. Snakes cannot use their teeth to chew. The teeth puncture the prey as it is being swallowed, allowing saliva to enter the food and begin the process of breaking it down for digestion. Most snake saliva is specifically designed to quickly break down the body tissues of that species' preferred prey. The venom found in vipers, cobras and other poisonous species is highly modified saliva that begins breaking down cell walls and digesting the prey before it is even swallowed.

As the snake grows, its teeth continuously fall out and are replaced. This ensures that the teeth are always sharp, and that broken teeth are quickly replaced. Even the hollow fangs of the venomous species are periodically shed and replaced by a fresh set.

Eyes

The anatomy of the snake's eye differs from that of most other vertebrates. Snakes have no eyelids, but instead have a hard clear scale called the "brille," "spectacle" or "eyecap" that covers and protects the eyeball.

Other vertebrates are able to focus a sharp image on the retina of their eyes by using special muscles to change the shape of the lens. In snakes, however, these muscles are absent, and the snake can only focus an image by moving the whole lens back and forth. As a result, snakes have extremely poor vision and cannot separate stationary objects from the background. They are, however, very sensitive to movement. Most snakes also lack

POOR JUDGES OF DISTANCE

Because the eyes of snakes are located on the sides of their heads, it is very difficult for them to focus both eyes on the same point. This lack of binocular vision means they cannot judge distances very accurately. Many times, when a snake is stalking prey, it will sway its head back and forth a few times to help it triangulate the proper distance.

the muscles needed to swivel their eyeballs and can only look in a different direction by turning their whole head.

In nocturnal snakes, such as pythons, the pupil of the eye most often consists of a narrow slit, like the eyes of a cat. This allows the pupil to open very wide in dim conditions to gather as much light as possible. The eyes in nocturnal species also tend to be larger, so they can gather more light. Diurnal snakes, such as garter snakes, usually have round pupils that can be contracted to tiny pinpoints to regulate the amount of light entering the eye.

The back of the snake eyeball is lined by the retina, which transforms incoming light into electrical signals, sending these to the brain through the optic nerve. Snake retinas have both "rods," which produce black and white images

Snakes cannot chew their food and must swallow their prey whole. (albino Burmese Python)

A snake's eyes have no eyelids but are covered and protected by a hard, clear scale called a brille or eyecap. (python)

under low-light conditions, and "cones," which give color vision in sufficient light. (Boids have fewer cones than colubrids, and hence presumably have less vivid color vision.) Unlike most other animals, snakes have no "fovea" or focusing point where the image is sharpest; obviously, this severely limits their ability to detect shapes and forms.

In a few snakes, the nose is long and narrow and has deep grooves running along the side, which improves the forward vision. These snakes, most of which are arboreal hunters that prey on fast-moving lizards, usually have elongated horizontal pupils to improve their binocular vision. In most of the burrowing snakes, in contrast, such as the thread snakes and blind snakes, the eyes are almost non-

functional and are completely covered by translucent scales. Although these snakes can sense light and dark, they cannot form an image and cannot detect shapes or movement. A few species of burrowers have opaque scales over their eyes, blocking out all light. These snakes thus have no sense of vision at all, and depend completely on their sense of smell and touch to gain information about their surroundings.

Jacobson's Organ
Because snakes have such poor eyesight, they depend largely upon their sensitivity to chemical signals to locate their prey and to find breeding partners. The inside of the nasal cavities contains a number of chemical sensors, but the

bulk of a snake's chemical information comes from the Jacobson's organ, a twin structure in the roof of the mouth. During the development of the snake embryo inside the egg, the Jacobson's organ forms as an extension of the nasal cavity, but the physical connection between the two is lost as the embryo develops further. The Jacobson's organ is connected directly to the brain by a branch of the olfactory nerve.

All snakes periodically flick out their long, forked tongue, and the frequency of this tongue-darting increases when the snake finds something of interest. The surface of the snake's tongue picks up microscopic scent particles in the air and transfers them to the Jacobson's organ. People used to believe that this transfer occurred when the snake inserted the forked

The snake's long forked tongue picks up chemical clues and transfers them to the Jacobson's organ. This provides the snake with most of its information regarding its surroundings. (Burmese Python)

tips of its tongue into the twin openings in the roof of the mouth. Today, it is believed instead that the tongue transfers scent particles to a fleshy pad in the roof of the mouth, and from there these particles are carried to the Jacobson's organ. The Jacobson's organ and the long, forked tongue are also found among the monitor lizards, another result of the common ancestry of snakes and lizards.

The chemical testing of the Jacobson's organ, which functions like a cross between the senses of taste and smell, provides the snake with most of its information regarding its surroundings. Contrary to what many people believe, a snake cannot sting or bite with its tongue. Also, most snakes do not have any taste buds on the surface of their tongue, and thus probably cannot taste their food. A few taste buds have been found on the tongues of some sea snakes and a few species of thread snakes.

Heat Pits

Several groups of snakes have developed infrared-sensitive pits at the front of the face that can detect the body heat of warm-blooded animals. In boas and pythons, these take the form of a row of pits in the upper lip; in the pit vipers, they consist of two openings on either side of the face. In both cases, the pit is a deep hollow with a thin layer of cells lining the

The heat pits are clearly visible on the lips of this adult Burmese Python. They help the snake locate warm-blooded prey.

inside. This layer is filled with a large number of nerve endings. In some boids, the pits are covered by exterior scales, but are still capable of sensing external heat.

The pits are connected to the snake's brain through a branch of the optic nerve, and it is likely that the information they provide is coupled with the visual information from the eyes to give a "heat image," allowing the snake to "see" varying temperatures much as we see colors. Even in the dimmest light conditions, then, a rattlesnake's warm-blooded prey would shine brightly with infrared wavelengths and would be readily visible to the snake.

These pits are extremely sensitive to heat and can detect changes in temperature as small as one-eighth of a degree Fahrenheit. Snakes that possess these pits feed upon warm-blooded prey such as

rodents or birds, sensing their presence by detecting their body heat. Because the pits are located on both sides of the face, snakes that have them can compare the perceived heat intensity from one side with the other, and thus triangulate the position of the heat source. Pit vipers and boids can locate and strike at prey using their facial pits even if they have been blindfolded.

Among the boids, the most sensitive heat pits are found among the arboreal hunters, such as Green Tree Pythons and Emerald Tree Boas. In boas, the pits are found between the scales of the lips; in pythons, they are found in the middle of each lip scale. A few groups, including the common Boa Constrictor, the sand boas, rosy boas and burrowing pythons, do not have any heat pits. Most

THE SPECIAL PITS OF PIT VIPERS

In the pit vipers, an improvement is made by adding a thin layer of very sensitive skin stretched across the pit about halfway down. In this arrangement, the temperature of the ambient air is recorded in the rear portion of the pit, while the radiant heat from a warm-blooded animal is sensed only at the front of the pit, allowing the viper to differentiate the heat produced by a prey animal from a random warm breeze.

biologists believe this is because those groups diverged from the main ancestral boid line before the heat pits evolved.

Brain

The structure of a snake's brain is somewhat similar to that of a bird, but it is very primitive. The cerebral hemispheres, which in mammals and birds control learning and intelligence, are small and undeveloped and lack the grooves and ridges that characterize the brains of more intelligent animals. Directly behind the cerebral hemispheres is the interbrain, or diencephalon, which processes information about the temperature and external environment. The mid-brain processes the information received from the snake's sensory organs, including the eyes and Jacobson's organ. The cerebellum coordinates many of the muscular movements, although much of the snake's muscular activity is controlled directly by the spinal cord. (Snakes that have been decapitated can still crawl and swim normally for a short time.) At the rear of the brain is the medulla oblongata, which controls the heartbeat, breathing rate and other internal organs.

The medulla connects the brain to the spinal cord, which branches off into a number of nerves to different parts of the body. In some snakes, there are still rudiments of the large nerves that control the

limbs—indications that the ancestors of snakes did indeed once possess legs.

Lungs

The reptilian lung was an evolutionary innovation when it first appeared. Although some amphibians have functional lungs, they depend for the most part on direct diffusion of oxygen and carbon dioxide through their thin, moist skin (some families of salamanders do not possess lungs at all). Terrestrial reptiles, with their dry impermeable skin, were forced to develop another method of respiration.

The lungs of a snake must fit inside a narrow, elongated body, and thus their structure is somewhat different from the lungs of most animals. In most snakes, the right lung is large and extends for almost a third of the body length. The left lung is greatly reduced in size and may even be completely absent in some species. In effect, snakes have only one lung. In many aquatic snakes, the lung may extend back into the body almost to the tail. This extension is called the "saccular lung," and it functions mainly as a method to provide buoyancy, similar to the swim bladder of a fish.

In addition, many snakes have a forward extension of the lung, near the windpipe, which is known as the "tracheal lung." This extension ensures that during feeding, when

the prey animal is pressing against successive portions of the lung and prevents it from expanding, at least one section of the lung will always be available for breathing.

In mammals, the chest cavity is expanded and contracted by the diaphragm muscle to allow breathing. Snakes, like all reptiles, lack a diaphragm, and instead use the muscles in their body wall to pump air in and out of their lungs like a bellows. As ectotherms, snakes do not need large amounts of oxygen and will often go several minutes between breaths. Aquatic snakes can remain underwater for over an hour before they must surface to breathe.

During feeding, when the mouth may be blocked for up to an hour by food, the snake is able to breathe by extending a muscle in its windpipe, called the epiglottis, from the bottom of the mouth, which protrudes from underneath the prey to reach air.

Heart

Like all reptiles (with the exception of the crocodilians), snakes have a primitive three-chambered heart that is not as efficient as the four-chambered hearts found in mammals. In snakes, the blood is pumped to the lungs by one of the two upper chambers, known as atria, and returns to the single lower ventricle, where it mixes with the oxygen-depleted blood returning from the rest of the body. This mixture of oxygen-rich and oxygen-depleted blood is then pumped into the other atrium, where it enters the aortic arches and is distributed throughout the body.

Because of this inefficient method of distributing oxygen, even the most active of snakes tire easily and cannot sustain activity for any length of time without frequent stops to rest.

Another oddity in snakes is the lack of one of the arteries that carry blood to the head and brain: In most snakes, only the left artery is present. Most snakes have a total of nineteen major arteries that branch off from the aortic arches. Each of these goes to a specific body part or organ.

Like all other body functions, the snake's heartbeat is dependent upon the external temperature. Snakes have an area of the heart known as the "pacemaker," which is part of the ventricular wall, that regulates the heart rate according to the temperature. If this pacemaker is warmed, the heart rate increases correspondingly. In cooler temperatures, the heart rate slows, minimizing blood flow and reducing the rate of heat loss. While basking, snakes depend entirely on their bloodstream to carry warmth from the heated areas of their body and distribute it to other areas of the body.

Skin

Snake skin consists of two layers. The inner layer contains the nerve endings and the color pigment cells. There are several different types of pigment cells, known as chromatophores. The black pigment melanin is found in nearly all snakes. The color yellow is contained in cells called xanthophores, while the red pigment is found in erythristophores. A set of cells called iridophores contains small crystals of purine, which refract incoming light and scatter it to produce the color blue (a process known as "Tyndall scattering"). There is no green pigment; green snakes instead have a layer of iridophores and a layer of xanthophores, and the yellow and blue are optically combined to form green. In some snakes, including Rainbow Boas, Reticulated

Pythons and Sunbeam Snakes, a layer of smooth scales refracts light to produce a shimmering iridescent "rainbow" effect.

The outer layer of a snake's skin consists of large oval scales that overlap each other like the shingles on a roof. Unlike fish, which have

A snake's skin is dry and smooth and not at all slimy. It is made of the protein keratin, also found in human fingernails. (Blood Python)

individual scales embedded in the skin, snake scales are composed of thickened and folded areas of the outer skin, and individual scales cannot be removed. The outer skin and scales are made of keratin, the same protein from which human fingernails are made.

Some snakes have a raised ridge running the length of each scale called a "keel." These may improve the snake's traction on slippery surfaces. Snakes may also possess tiny holes in their scales called "apical pits." The function of these pits is not known, but they each contain a series of nerve endings and probably play some sensory role.

The outer layer of a snake's skin is dead and cannot grow. As the snake grows larger, therefore, the old skin becomes tighter and tighter, and the snake must remove it in order to increase its size. This process of shedding the skin is called ecdysis. Shortly before the shed takes place, the snake secretes a fluid between the two layers of skin and grows a new keratin layer underneath the old one. This fluid causes the snake's colors to turn dark and also makes the eyes look blue. The snake will then rub its nose and lips on a rock or other hard surface until the old skin layer is broken, and then crawl completely out of the old skin, which turns inside out and is removed in one long piece.

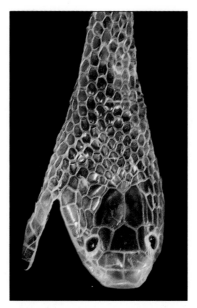

Snakes must periodically shed their skin in order to grow.

Stomach

The snake's stomach is very muscular and elastic, and can expand enormously to contain large prey animals. The digestive juices are powerful and nearly the entire prey animal is digested, including most of the bones and teeth. Because snakes' food requirements are low and their digestive system is very efficient, snakes can go for long periods of time on a single meal.

As in most carnivorous animals, the snake's digestive tract is relatively short and simple, lacking the long coiled intestine necessary to extract energy from low-yield plant foods. Energy from the digested food is stored in a number of fat bodies along the intestines.

The speed at which the food is digested once it reaches the stomach depends upon the surrounding temperature. Higher temperatures cause the digestive enzymes to speed up their action, and a snake that has just fed will usually retreat to a warm hiding place to digest its meal. If the snake is kept too cool, however, the food may actually begin to rot inside the stomach before the digestive enzymes can break it down and the food will be regurgitated. In most of the venomous snakes, the venom begins to break down the body tissues of the prey and begins the digestion process even before the prey animal is swallowed.

Kidneys

Snakes' kidneys are very large in proportion to their body size. These are staggered in the snake's abdominal region, the left kidney behind the right one. The kidneys filter waste products and toxins from the bloodstream and pass them on to the cloaca for elimination.

Whenever proteins are digested by an organism, toxic ammonia products result, and these must be removed from the body. In most animals, these products are converted into water-soluble urea by the kidneys and are dissolved and excreted in the form of liquid urine. This process represents a major loss of body moisture.

Snake kidneys, however, convert their protein wastes into crystals of uric acid, forming a dry white paste that is expelled along with the feces. The water used in this process is reabsorbed by the snake through the walls of the kidney and cloaca. This process allows snakes to be extremely efficient in their use of water.

Cloaca

Unlike mammals, snakes do not have separate reproductive and anal openings. Instead, the digestive and reproductive tracts both empty into a common chamber called the cloaca (this same arrangement is also found in birds—not surprising, as birds are evolutionary descendants of ancient reptiles). Snakes do not have urinary bladders, and all digestive waste products are instead stored in the cloaca until they can be eliminated. The cloaca opens to the outside through a transverse slit just in front of the snake's tail.

In reproduction, snake eggs are stored in the oviduct and are coated with a hard shell just before they enter the cloaca to be laid. In live-bearing species, the embryos are contained in clear fetal sacs, which break open just as the young snake is being expelled from the cloaca.

Some snakes also have a number of special defensive glands which empty into the cloaca. These glands contain a foul-smelling musk that can be ejected whenever the snake is threatened or disturbed.

Hemipenes

Like most reptiles, all snakes practice internal fertilization, in which sperm are introduced directly into the female's cloaca. Instead of a penis, male snakes possess a pair of copulatory organs called hemipenes, which are covered with a particular pattern of spines and knobs. These spines help lock the male into position during breeding. During the mating process, only one of the pair of hemipenes is actually used.

In addition, the projecting spines and knobs are matched by corresponding grooves and pits on the inside of the female's cloaca, in a "lock and key" arrangement, which helps ensure that males mate only with females of their own species.

The sperm runs down a deep groove in the side of the hemipene and is inserted into the female's cloaca. Female snakes possess a sac called the seminal receptacle, which is capable of storing live sperm for several months, allowing females to lay fertile eggs even though they may not have mated that year. Some snakes have laid eggs as long as four years after their last mating.

Size, Life Span and Home Range

The smallest snakes are members of the thread snake and blind snake families, which are seldom more than a foot in length. The smallest known snake is the Reuter's Blind Snake, from Madagascar, which measures less than 5 inches long as an adult. Newborn snakes are less than 2 inches long.

Perhaps no subject is as prone to exaggeration as the size of the largest snakes. The Hollywood movie *Anaconda* is just the most recent of a long string of stories and tales concerning impossibly large snakes. Early travelers to Asia, Africa and Latin America often returned with

During mating, one pair of hemipenes is used. The knobs on the hemipene match the grooves in the female in a "lock and key" arrangement.

The Reticulated Python is the longest snake in the world, measuring up to 33 feet long.

have a girth over twice that of a similar- sized Retic, and snakes measuring 25 feet or more can easily weigh over 400 pounds.

Other very large snakes include the Indian or Burmese Python, which is native to India and southern Asia; the Rock Python, which is found in northern Africa; and the Amethystine Python, a thin-bodied boid from Australia. Each of these snakes can grow over 20 feet long.

Many uninformed people presume that the famous Boa Constrictor is the largest snake in the world, but in reality the boa is, at a mere 10 or 12 feet, a relative midget.

Among the colubrids, the largest snakes are Asian members of the rat snake family. The Keeled Rat Snake (*Elaphe carinatus*) reaches lengths of 10 feet and is the largest of the colubrids. At a verified record of 8.5

stories of snakes 50 or more feet long (one 1948 report from Brazil described an Anaconda 156 feet long). Even today, uninformed persons form mental pictures of constricting snakes "as thick as a telephone pole."

The truth is somewhat less spectacular. The largest snake known to science is no longer alive. *Gigantophis*, a 50-foot boid found in Africa, became extinct at around the same time as the dinosaurs. A full-grown *Gigantophis* was almost twice the size as the largest living pythons and may have weighed as much as 500 pounds.

So what is now the largest living snake? It depends on what you mean by largest. The longest snake in the world is the Reticulated Python, a semiaquatic snake found in southeast Asia. Specimens of this snake have

been reliably measured at 33 feet long. Such a huge snake is exceedingly rare, however—most adult Retics top out at between 20 and 25 feet. The largest snake ever on display in the United States was a female Reticulated Python measuring 28 feet, kept by the Pittsburgh Zoo. Even the largest Retics are rather thin-bodied and slender, however. They rarely weigh more than 250 pounds.

The heaviest and bulkiest snake is the Green Anaconda, which lives in South America. Although many exaggerated claims have been made for this species, the longest snake that has been authenticated was slightly over 30 feet in length. Although the Anaconda doesn't reach the lengths attained by the Reticulated Python, it is much more heavy-bodied than any python. A large Anaconda may

SNAKES ARE NOT LONG-LIVED

One of the most enduring myths of ancient times was the belief that snakes were immortal, a supposition prompted by the observation of snakes shedding their old, faded skins and emerging bright and renewed. In reality, snakes are not particularly long-lived creatures—particularly when compared to some of their reptilian relatives like crocodilians and turtles (a few turtles can top the 100-year mark).

feet, the Indigo Snake is the longest snake in North America. Close behind are the Black Rat Snake, the Bull Snake, the Coachwhip and the Eastern Diamondback Rattlesnake, all of which reach lengths of 8 feet.

The largest of the venomous snakes is the King Cobra, which can reach 18 feet. The Australian Taipan can top the 14-foot mark, while the South American Bushmaster is the largest of the vipers, at a length approaching 12 feet.

In general, the smaller snakes tend to have shorter life spans than the larger ones. The common Eastern Garter Snake has a maximum life span of about nine years, while the Keeled Green Snake lives around eight years. The Northern Copperhead has a estimated life span in the wild of about fourteen years, but specimens kept in zoos, safe from predators, have lived for almost thirty years. Timber Rattlesnakes seem more durable; they have been known to live twenty-five years in the wild and thirty years in zoos.

A Spitting Cobra kept at the San Diego Zoo lived for twenty-nine years. A boa constrictor that was already full-grown when it was obtained by the Philadelphia Zoo lived for forty-one years. The longest known life span for a snake was a Ball Python, also obtained as an adult by the Philadelphia Zoo, that lived an additional forty-seven years, giving it an actual life span of around fifty years.

Studies have shown that most snakes spend their whole lives within a tiny area. Biologists study the distribution and range of snakes by "capture and release" studies, during which a large number of snakes are captured, marked and released where they were found, then recaptured later. Most often, snakes are individually marked by scale-clipping, in which a number of the two rows of scales underneath the tail are cut off at the base in a predetermined pattern. For example, a snake which has the first scale on the left side and the fifth scale on the right side clipped off would be logged as "1L5R," while a snake with the third scale on the left and the second on the right clipped would be logged as "3L2R." Careful record-keeping allows the biologist to gather data concerning the growth rates, range and movements of each individual snake.

A newer method of studying range and movement data consists of surgically inserting a small radio transmitter into the body wall of captured snakes. These devices allow biologists to track snakes for a period of several months using radio receivers, until the batteries wear out. This method has been used to study the habits of rattlesnakes in North America and Fer-de-Lance pit vipers in Central America.

In North America, field studies have shown that snakes do not

SNAKES DON'T NEED TO DEFEND THEIR TURF

Despite the limited area inhabited by each snake, there is no evidence of any territoriality, or any indication that snakes defend their range from others of their own species. It is likely that the high mortality rate among snakes (particularly yearlings) prevents overcrowding and allows each snake to find a range of its own.

tend to move around very much during their lifetime. Once they have dispersed from their hibernation dens in the spring, they tend to stay put. Most snakes tend to stay in a home range of around 25 acres, usually in a spot not very far from where they were born. The vast majority of snakes are recaptured within 30 yards of the spot where they were originally tagged, even after a period of several years. Such studies also demonstrate that individual snakes return to the same hibernation den, which may be several miles away from their normal territory, each winter.

How Smart Are Snakes?

Like all reptiles, snakes possess brains that are similar to those of birds or mammals, but which are much more primitive. The portions of the brain that control sensory information (particularly sight and smell) are very highly developed, but the cerebral hemispheres, the large, wrinkled lobes that make up most of the human and mammalian brain, are largely absent in snakes. Because these are the portions of the brain that control learning and reasoning ability, snakes are not as intelligent as some animals. Although they do have the capacity to feel pain, they are not capable of complicated learning or emotional states.

For the most part, then, snakes are creatures of instinct and habit. However, they are capable of some degree of learning. There is evidence to indicate that the highest mortality among young snakes occurs in their first year of life, when they are inexperienced and haven't yet learned how to efficiently avoid predators and find food. Captive snakes do demonstrate the capacity to learn their daily routine. They may learn to associate their keeper with food, and also quickly learn to differentiate a cage-cleaning shovel from feeding forceps.

There is some controversy over whether snakes can learn to recognize their keepers. One side holds that snakes can indeed differentiate their owner from other humans by scent and learn to tolerate handling by their owners better than by

strangers. Captive rattlesnakes have been seen to rattle when approached by a person they have never seen before, yet remain quiet if their regular keeper approaches.

A contending school of thought, however, argues that the snake is reacting to the body language and mental state of the human rather than recognizing the specific person. People who are used to handling snakes are calm and confident, while other people may be hesitant and nervous—signals that are quickly picked up by the snake. My snakes tend to remain calm and docile when handled by strangers who are experienced snakers, but can be noticeably nervous and exhibit increased tongue-flicking and shyness when handled by friends of mine they have seen before but who do not normally handle snakes.

Animal intelligence is most often tested by means of a maze test, in which subjects are taught to run a simple maze using reward and punishment. Turtles, for example, have been taught to run a simple T maze by using a cold spot or a mild electric shock at one end and a bit of food reward at the other. In these tests, some species of turtle have learned to run the maze as quickly as lab rats can, which is pretty impressive for a reptile. A series of such tests with differing species of snake could help answer many interesting ques-

tions, such as whether a difference in intelligence exists between the passive "sit and wait" ambushers and the active predators, or whether different families of snake exhibit differing abilities to learn and retain information.

Locomotion

A seemingly difficult problem faced by snakes is how to move quickly on a variety of surfaces in order to capture prey and escape predators. These limbless animals have devised several efficient methods of moving about.

The most common method of locomotion is the typical serpentine crawling, in which the body is wiggled from side to side in successive waves. The rear edge of each body wave catches on small, rough irregularities in the ground and propels the body forward. As the snake advances, each successive point along the body catches the same irregularities as the point immediately ahead of it, tracing the same path. Thus, the track left by the snake appears to be a single continuous line, even though the snake is moving by a series of lateral undulations. The more rapidly the snake is able to undulate its body, the faster it is able to move.

When swimming, snakes resort to the same lateral undulations, using the back edge of each body loop to push against the water and propel itself forward. Most snakes can, therefore, swim reasonably well using the same body movements that they use on land. In the sea snakes, which spend all of their time in the water, the body is laterally compressed to form a wider pushing surface, allowing these snakes to undulate their way effortlessly through the water.

Another method of movement is called concertina, and is used by burrowing snakes to crawl through tunnels as well as by arboreal climbing species. With the body compacted into a series of tight loops, pressed against the sides of the burrow or around a tree branch, the head and neck are extended as far as they can reach, and the forward part of the body gains purchase. Then, the rear portion of the body is drawn forward to loop itself behind the head and neck. The head is then extended to begin the process again. The snake thus moves in a series of fits and starts, somewhat like an inchworm.

The corn snake can move quickly using a serpentine motion. (albino Okeetee Corn Snake)

The rat snakes, which are excellent climbers and often ascend into trees in search of bird eggs and nestlings, have two thickened keels running along both edges of their belly, giving them a cross section that is rounded on top and flat on the bottom, like a loaf of bread. These belly edges allow them to gain a better grip on small twigs and rough patches of bark, enabling

Corn snakes have keels on their bellies, which help them to climb.

them to make ascents that would be impossible for other snakes.

While the heavy-bodied boids and vipers can utilize both the lateral undulation and concertina methods of movement, they prefer to use another strategy that minimizes their use of energy. The snake uses special sets of muscles attached to the ribs to lift the large rectangular belly scales off the ground and pull them forward. Once the loose edges of these scales have caught on the irregularities in the ground, the muscles contract and pull the snake forward, using the scales as anchor points. Each point on the body uses the same rough spots on the ground as the one before it, causing the snake to move in a straight line. During this process, the ribs themselves do not move (a number of people mistakenly assume that the snake is "walking on its ribs"), but serve simply as fulcrums for the muscles to pull against. Most snakes resort to this "rectilinear crawling" when they are stalking food, but the heavy snakes always prefer it to other methods of locomotion. If pressed, however, even the largest boids are capable of resorting to the typical serpentine crawling.

If a snake is placed on a smooth surface, such as a piece of glass, it also cannot crawl in any of these manners, because all snakes depend on the ability to push against slight irregularities in the surface. A similar problem is faced by snakes that live in desert areas with loose sand—if the snake attempts to push against the surface, the sand will merely shift and leave the snake stranded. As a result, desert-dwellers have developed an elegant

method of moving over shifting sand by utilizing downward pressure to compact the surface rather than a lateral motion. This method is called sidewinding. To sidewind, the snake throws its head and neck forward and presses them against the sand to gain a purchase. Using this as an anchor point, it then loops the rest of its body forward and sideways to press it against the ground at another point. At the same moment, the head and neck are extended forward again to gain a new anchor point, and the process is repeated. The snake appears to move with a curious sideways rolling motion, at about a 45° angle to the direction it is facing. The tracks left by a sidewinding snake look like a series of short parallel slanted lines in the shape of a thin letter J.

Because desert snakes from several areas of the world, including

The Gaboon Viper, like all heavy-bodied snakes, prefers to move using a rectilinear motion.

SNAKES HAVE NO REVERSE GEAR

It should be noted that snakes cannot crawl backwards using any of these methods of locomotion. If they encounter an obstruction in a tunnel that is too narrow for them to turn their head, they are trapped—they cannot back out. Veterinarians who handle venomous snakes take advantage of this characteristic by using clear plastic tubes to confine hot (venomous) snakes while they are working on them.

the American Sidewinder, the African Horned Viper and the Sand Viper, use this method of locomotion, it is apparent that sidewinding has evolved independently in those groups of snakes that needed it. However, even common snakes such as garters are capable of sidewinding to some extent if they are unable to move in any other way.

Although many snakes will shelter in burrows or holes in the ground, only a very few species are able to actively dig their own burrow. The small family of snakes known as the shield tails have specially modified skulls and neck bones, as well as a compact cone-shaped snout, to allow them to tunnel their way through soil with sideways motions of the neck and head. Other snakes, with their light

SOME SNAKES "FLY"

The most unusual method of snake locomotion has to be that of the tree snakes of Borneo. These arboreal snakes are able to leap from a tree branch, flatten their bodies and pull in their stomachs to form a concave channel that traps air and acts as a parachute, allowing the snake to glide downwards to another tree or to the ground. For this reason, they have also earned the name "Flying Snake."

Desert snakes, such as the American Sidewinder in the foreground of this picture, have evolved a special method of locomotion that allows them to move quickly across the sand's shifting surface.

skull structures, cannot dig their own tunnels and instead usually appropriate an abandoned one (or stay on in a rodent tunnel where they have just fed).

Defense

Like all animals, snakes must survive long enough to reach sexual maturity and reproduce if they are to pass their genes on to the next generation. Because snakes are on the menu of many predators, they have developed a number of defensive strategies, each different but designed with the same goals in mind.

A wide variety of animals include snakes in their diet, including foxes, skunks, raccoons and several birds of prey such as hawks and eagles. (Incidentally, the African Mongoose, famed as a snake killer, in reality tends to specialize in rodents and birds and only occasionally eats snakes.) A few birds, including the African secretary bird and the American roadrunner, specialize in eating snakes. A large percentage of fellow reptiles, such as alligators, crocodiles and monitor lizards, also prey on snakes, and a few species of snakes, including the King Cobra, feed almost exclusively on other serpents. Very young snakes are preyed upon by everything from tarantulas to turtles to large fish. On one occasion, an African bullfrog was found with sixteen baby Spitting Cobras in its stomach.

Studies have shown that the mortality rate of wild snakes is heaviest in their first year of life,

Birds of prey are a snake's deadliest enemy. This African secretary bird is a highly specialized snake eater.

when they are smaller and less experienced. Of a typical litter of twenty or thirty young snakes, only one or two will survive long enough to have young of their own.

One way to avoid predators is to hide from them. All snakes spend most of their time safely hidden within a nook or cranny, such as a burrow or a tree hollow, where they are safe from predators. They particularly dislike being exposed out in the open, as this makes them vulnerable to birds of prey, against which they have virtually no effective defense. For this reason, whenever snakes move, they tend to stick to areas that provide cover. Snakes cannot dig and do not excavate their own burrows. Instead, they will move into an unoccupied den, or they may appropriate a burrow that belonged to the latest meal. Most snakes only rarely venture very far from the safety of their den or burrow.

Some snakes, however, prefer to practice the art of camouflage, allowing them to lie in wait of prey and at the same time avoid attracting the attention of predators. Arboreal snakes are usually green in color, to allow them to blend into the foliage and escape the notice of passing predators. Two species that have adopted this tactic are the Emerald Tree Boa of South America and the Green Tree Python of Southeast Asia. These two snakes are only distantly related, but in response to similar ecological niches they have developed virtually the same characteristics, a phenomenon known as convergent evolution. Some arboreal snakes, including members of the palm viper group, are speckled with brown and white splotches that resemble lichens and moss, increasing the effectiveness of the camouflage. Other tropical tree snakes have long thin bodies which, when the snake is lying in wait, look like a twig or vine.

Ground-dwelling snakes often possess a complicated color scheme that acts to disrupt their outline and camouflage them as they lie in wait among rocks or dry leaves. The corn snake's red, brown and orange color pattern seems gaudy and obvious when seen against a plain background, but, when the snake is coiled up in a patch of dry leaves on its native forest floor, the color patches disperse the snake's outline and make it almost impossible to see. The African Gaboon Viper is colored with small patches of brown, blue, black and tan, which conceals it as it lies in wait on the forest floor.

Some species of snakes, rather than attempting to remain hidden, instead make every effort to advertise their presence. The coral snakes are covered with bright red, yellow and black rings which stand out boldly against a background of dirt or leaves. In nature, brightly colored and contrasting bands are a warning signal, and one need only think of the wasps and bees, with their instantly recognizable black

Snakes do not like being in the open and prefer to stay in safe, enclosed areas like rock piles. (South Pacific Rattlesnake)

and yellow stripes, to realize that such conspicuous animals usually have a weapon at the ready to defend themselves if they have to. The coral snake, an elapid, is dangerously venomous. The highly visible coloration, therefore, is a warning signal to potential predators to stay away.

A few species of nonvenomous snakes, moreover, have also taken advantage of this widely recognized danger signal. Some commonly kept subspecies of the milk and king snakes, which lack any venom apparatus at all, nevertheless are clothed in much the same gaudy black, yellow and red bands as are the lethal coral snakes. In the coral snakes, the red and yellow bands lie next to each other along the body, while in the North American mimics the red and yellow bands are

separated by black, leading to the old mountain adage, "Red touch yellow, kill a fellow. Red touch black, venom lack." However, to a potential predator that suddenly uncovers one of these snakes, both of these patterns signal danger, and the harmless snake thus gains a measure of protection from predators because it so closely resembles the dangerous species.

If detected by a predator, many snakes will make an aggressive display to try to threaten the intruder. One well-known strategy is to pass air rapidly over the epiglottis and produce a loud hissing sound. While nearly all snakes can hiss if alarmed, the various races of the pine snake are probably the best practitioners of this art. When cornered, these snakes rear up threateningly, puff up their necks and

BATESIAN MIMICRY

The Eastern Milk Snake uses a clever defense strategy—its body pattern of brownish red splotches resembles that of the venomous Copperhead. The tactic whereby a harmless animal protects itself by mimicking a dangerous or bad-tasting animal is known to biologists as Batesian mimicry.

expel a long burst of air that sounds like steam escaping from a valve. When combined with their generally rattlesnakelike color pattern, this display is often enough to make all but the most determined predator turn tail. The Burmese Python, when disturbed, also hisses loudly as a warning.

Several other species of snakes use sound to warn away potential predators. The most well known, of course, are the rattlesnakes, which have a number of hard, interlocking pieces of skin at the tips of their tails. When threatened or stressed, many common species of snake will vibrate the tips of their tails rapidly, the result of biochemical changes that produce tremors in the muscles. The rattlesnakes have improved upon this by adding a device that produces a loud buzzing sound, which can be heard several feet away, warning potential intruders to keep their distance. Most biologists believe that the rattle originally appeared

This Pueblan Milk Snake gains protection from its bright color pattern, which somewhat resembles that of the venomous Coral Snake.

as a device to warn large herbivores (bison were once common in the habitats favored by rattlesnakes) that the rattler is in the area, preventing the big animal from accidentally stepping on the snake.

The Saw-Scaled Viper, found in desert areas from North Africa to India, has also developed an auditory warning system using modified scales. Some of the scales on the viper's body are heavily keeled, with a prominent ridge running the length of the scale. These ridges, moreover, are tilted at an oblique angle rather than running parallel to the body, as in most snakes, When alarmed, the Saw-Scaled Viper takes up a characteristic defensive position, with its body drawn into a tight U-shape and several of the body coils lying alongside each other. The snake then rapidly rubs these body coils together, causing the oblique scale ridges to rasp against each other and produce a loud warning signal that sounds somewhat like the sizzling of frying bacon.

Another common defense tactic is to inflate a part of the body in an effort to make the snake look bigger and more threatening. The cobra's "hood" is the best known example of this. Normally, the various species of cobra look like any other ordinary snake. However, the skin at the neck stretches enormously, and the ribs in this area are much longer than normal and are attached to a set of muscles. When

When threatened, some snakes stretch the skin around their neck into the familiar hood, making them appear larger and more intimidating. (Black Mamba)

the cobra is alarmed, the muscles pull the elongated ribs erect, stretching the skin into the familiar "hood" and making the snake look bigger and more imposing. Several other species, including the Boomslang, lack the cobra's elongated ribs, but instead swell their necks with air, puffing them up to make their heads look bigger.

The cobras and Boomslang can back up their intimidation display with lethal venom, but the North American Hognose Snake, which has only a very weak venom, resorts to pure bluff. When threatened, the hognose swells up its throat and gives an impressive hissing display. It then flattens the ribs in its neck to produce a hood just like a cobra's, and makes a number of mock strikes at the intruder—each with mouth closed.

Usually, this display is enough to convince a predator to find easier prey. If the hognose's bluff fails, however, it will abruptly change tactics. Now, instead of trying to appear threatening, the hognose will begin to writhe about as if in pain, and then roll over onto its back, protrude its tongue and go limp in an attempt to appear dead. Because the attack response of many predators is triggered by movement, the hognose's strategy of playing opossum will sometimes save it. The European Grass Snake has also been known to feign death when threatened.

Many snakes have glands on either side of their cloaca that produce a foul-smelling oil or musk that can be expelled when the snake feels threatened. Garter snakes and water snakes in particular often expel the contents of their anal glands when they are afraid, spraying the oily concoction all over their tormentor. This is often enough to convince the predator to hunt elsewhere.

The Water Moccasin of the southeastern United States has a much more direct defensive display. At the slightest disturbance, the snake will open its mouth and gape widely in the direction of the intruder, displaying the white interior of its mouth—a warning

THE BALL DEFENSE

Another, very unusual, defense tactic is utilized by the Ball Python. When threatened, the Ball Python rolls its body into a tight ball with its head tucked inside, surrounded by the heavy coils. Smaller predators find the balled-up snake very difficult to bite or grasp in their jaws. At the same time, the snake's vulnerable head is safely protected from the predator's attempts to bite. In some species, such as the North American Rubber Boa and the African Sand Boa, the balling technique has been further improved. These species possess a rounded, blunt tail, which is protruded from the ball and waved about in the air when the snake is threatened. The predator takes the moving tail to be the head and attacks it, protecting the real head and giving the snake a few precious moments to escape. Some of the sand boas have developed markings on the tip of the tail that resemble a mouth and eyes, to improve the illusion.

The Ball Python got its name from its habit of coiling the body into a ball when it feels threatened, hiding the vulnerable head within its coils.

display that has earned it the name Cottonmouth. The Parrot Snake, from South America, also gapes its jaws when threatened, displaying a bright blue patch of skin that serves as a warning.

If all else fails, snakes will bite in self-defense. The head and neck are most often drawn into an S-shaped curve, and are then suddenly thrust out, mouth open, to strike. The snake will then recoil again should another attack become necessary. Even the large constrictor snakes, which are capable of killing 100-pound leopards, do not usually use their constricting coils to attack potential enemies. The constriction method is usually used only on prey. If threatened by an intruder, the big boids will usually strike with their teeth in the manner typical of all snakes.

Most snakes can strike for a distance about one-third the length of their body. A very few species, including the Jumping Viper, which can propel itself forward at an attacker, and some of the arboreal boids, which can hang on with their tails and extend much of their body for a strike, can reach further than this.

The venomous snakes, although they possess a defensive weapon that can be lethal to any attacker, are usually very reluctant to use it. Venomous saliva originally evolved in snakes as a means of procuring food, not as a defensive weapon, and this is still its primary role today. A snake's venom is its sole means of killing prey, and because meals may be few and far between, the snake needs to have a ready supply of venom at all times to take advantage of any passing prey animal. For this reason, most venomous snakes attempt to warn potential predators away with some sort of threat display, and will strike with their fangs only as a last resort.

Even when forced to strike in self-defense, venomous snakes will take steps to conserve their precious venom. Because the muscles that squeeze the venom glands and force venom through the fangs are under the conscious control of the

If all else fails, a snake will bite in self-defense.

snake, the snake is able to control how much or how little venom it injects with each bite. In about one-third of all defensive bites, the snake will not actually inject any venom at all—a defensive strike known as a dry bite. (In the rear-fanged snakes, however, ejection of venom is not under the voluntary control of the snake—the venom is squeezed out from the Duvernoy's gland whenever pressure is applied to the jawbones.)

Most venomous snakes, therefore, use their fangs only as a defensive weapon of last resort. One group of African cobras, however, has modified its venom apparatus specifically for use as a defensive weapon. These are the Spitting Cobras. In these snakes, the fangs are hollow and connected to venom glands in the cheeks by a short duct, as in other venomous snakes. In the Spitting Cobras, however, the exit hole is not located at the tip of the fang as in other snakes, but is higher up on the front of the fang and faces forward. The exit hole is smaller than normal and also turns sharply upwards.

When the snake is threatened, it rears up and opens its hood in typical cobra fashion. If the attacker persists, however, instead of biting and striking, the Spitting Cobra squeezes an amount of venom from its glands through the hollow fangs, where it emerges as a high-pressure stream of liquid that can spray up to 10 feet away. The upturned exit hole in the fang directs the spray of venom upwards, towards the attacker's face, and the snake makes a conscious effort to aim at the eyes of the intruder. If the venom enters the eyeball, the attacker is temporarily blinded and experiences great pain. The spitting action is purely a defensive weapon, and is not used to obtain prey; during feeding, the Spitting Cobra bites and strikes in the same way as any other venomous snake.

CHAPTER 3

Ecology

All life on earth is ultimately dependent on the energy that travels to the planet in the form of sunlight. While only a tiny fraction of the total radiant energy released by the sun reaches the earth's surface, it is enough to provide energy for

The Copperhead is an ambush hunter that lies in wait on the forest floor for prey. (Southern Copperhead)

the myriad living things that inhabit our planet.

The earth is tilted on its axis as it revolves around the sun, and accordingly, certain areas of the globe are better positioned to capture sunlight and thus are more energy-rich than other areas. Because energy is unevenly distributed over the earth's surface, the biosphere is divided into several distinct climate zones. These climate zones in turn support a characteristic set of plant and animal life that interact with each other to form a unique ecosystem.

Within each of these ecosystems, particular organisms play specific roles, according to the habitat they require, the food they eat and the other environmental needs they must meet. This inter-locking set of requirements is called the animal's niche. In the tropical rain forest ecosystem, for example, one niche may consist of a ground-dwelling snake that lies in ambush for its prey and feeds on diurnal rodents. Another snake's niche may consist of actively hunting for nocturnal mammals in the forest canopy.

A fundamental rule of ecology is that no two species may occupy the same niche within the same geographic area. If this happens, one of the two species will be outcompeted and eliminated. In many instances, the dividing line between niches may be very thin. In the temperate woodlands of the eastern United States, for instance, garter snakes and ribbon snakes both share the same habitat—they prefer areas along the edges of streams within lightly wooded areas. Both are diurnal hunters that actively pursue their prey. The garter snake, however, feeds largely on earthworms and small amphibians, while the ribbon snake concentrates on amphibians and small fish, and only rarely eats earthworms. By thus "dividing up" the available food resources, the two species occupy slightly different ecological niches and avoid competing with each other. In the tropical rain forest ecosystem, both the Emerald Tree Boa and the Green Tree Python occupy the same ecological niches—both are large nocturnal tree climbers that feed largely on arboreal mammals and birds. However, these two species are separated by geography. The Emerald Tree Boa is found only in Latin America, while the Green Tree Python is an Asian snake. Neither species occurs in the same geographic area as the other, allowing them both to exploit the same ecological opportunities without ever competing directly with each other.

Taken as a whole, global ecosystems show a definite pattern depending on the latitude. Near the earth's equator, the sun's rays are more direct and the surface lies at about the same distance from the sun year-round. Towards the poles, the sunlight becomes less intense, and the distance to the sun varies throughout the year.

Tropical Rain Forests

The typical habitat in the equatorial regions is the tropical forest ecosystem, which takes advantage of the high energy input provided by the sun to produce an amazing diversity of life. Tropical rain forests are the most prolific ecosystems on the planet, and may contain as many as half of all living species.

The climate of the tropical forest is characterized by heat and humidity. Temperatures range up to the 90s during the day, dropping to the high 70s at night. Although there are few seasonal changes in temperature, rainfall increases and decreases in a yearly cycle of "dry season" and "rainy season"; however, it showers almost every day in the tropics, producing ambient humidities as high as ninety percent.

Among the animal life, competition for living space and resources is intense, and ecological niches tend to be very narrow and sharply defined. The characteristic distribution of animal and plant life consists of a huge number of different species, each of which is spread thinly throughout the area. A typical area of forest may have several hundred species within it, but may have only one or two individuals of each.

The canopy of leaves and branches overhead filters out much of the sunlight, and the forest floor is often open and rather bare of vegetation, but is richly blanketed

THE NICHE OF THE TROPICAL SNAKES

Snakes fill a wide variety of niches in the tropical forest. The Reticulated Python is a "sit and wait" hunter that makes its living by lying along forest paths to strike at prey animals that happen to pass by. The tree boas are specialized as arboreal hunters, prowling along the canopy for birds, bats and tree mammals. The Anaconda carves out its niche along jungle streams and rivers, where it seizes mammals that have come to the water's edge to drink. The South American Cat-Eyed Snake specializes in a diet that consists almost exclusively of tree frog eggs, which are laid in clumps on leaves overhanging jungle streams.

with a layer of dead and rotting leaves. In clearings and along riverbanks, plants often grow in a thick, impenetrable tangle as they compete for scarce sunlight. Since the growing season lasts all year, tropical plants do not shed their leaves in fall, but replace them year-round as they wear out and fall off.

The warm and humid conditions are ideal for reptiles, allowing them to maintain the preferred body temperature year-round. The warm temperatures and high humidity also make egg-laying easier, and the incredible diversity of life in the tropical forest presents a wide variety of potential food sources. Because of these conditions, tropical areas exhibit an enormous diversity of snake species. Representatives of all but two of the living snake families can be found in the tropics. The boids tend to be the dominant snake family—with a few exceptions, the boids are limited to tropical forest habitats. A large number of vipers and pit vipers also inhabit the tropics.

Grasslands

In areas where the rainfall is lower but the temperatures remain high, the tropical forests give way to grasslands, characterized by open fields dominated by grasses, with a few scattered trees and shrubs. This ecosystem is known under a variety

The North American green snakes are one of the few snake species that has adapted to life in open grassland areas. (Keeled Green Snake)

of names—savannah, prairie, veldt, steppe and pampas—but its ecological traits are consistent from one to the other. The grassland ecosystem is warm and dry. The soil is generally rich and fertile (cultivated grasslands usually make the best farming areas), but the relative lack of rainfall limits the natural vegetation to a few hardy species of grass and some trees and shrubs. Many grasslands are maintained by periodic fires that are sparked in the dry grasses by lightning, burning off any young tree seedlings and enriching the soil for the next generation of grasses.

While the warm, open conditions might seem to be suitable for snakes, relatively few species are found in such areas. The open, featureless ground exposes the snakes to their deadliest enemies—birds of prey. Those species that do inhabit open grasslands are either large snakes with little to fear from predators, such as the Australian Amethystine Python and the African Rock Python, or species that stick to local rock outcroppings for shelter, such as Prairie Rattlesnakes and Bull Snakes. The green snakes of North America, which camouflage themselves in grassy fields, are unusual among snakes in adapting to insect prey, feeding largely on grasshoppers, spiders and hairless caterpillars, which they actively hunt among the grasses.

Deciduous Temperate Forests

The deciduous temperate forests, found largely in North America and Europe, are characterized by a relatively high rainfall coupled with sharply varying seasonal changes in temperature. At these latitudes, the distance to the sun cyclically increases and decreases as the planet moves around its orbit. During the summer, temperatures can range up to the high 80s, while during the winter temperatures drop below freezing. The forest is dominated by deciduous trees that shed their leaves every winter, and the forest floor is carpeted with decaying leaves and herbaceous plants, producing a rich, dark soil that holds moisture well.

Food sources in temperate areas are not as rich as in the tropics,

leaving fewer ecological niches to be filled. The garter snakes are diurnal hunters that actively search for salamanders and earthworms in the rich layer of humus and leaf litter on the forest floor. The Timber Rattlesnake and the European Adder are ambush hunters, concealing themselves in the leaf litter and waiting for prey to pass by. The rat snakes fill many arboreal niches, prowling in trees and shrubs for nestling birds and eggs.

Boreal Forests

At higher latitudes, the deciduous forest gives way to the boreal forest, sometimes known as "taiga," marked by cool weather year-round. Pines and spruces dominate the plant life—they use their evergreen needlelike leaves to conserve water and prevent their branches

TEMPERATE CLIMATES ARE NOT SNAKE FRIENDLY

This environment presents many challenges to reptiles, and, not surprisingly, it has a rather low number of snake species. Unlike the snakes that inhabit the warmer climates, temperate snakes must cease their activity every winter and find a sheltered spot to hibernate. The relatively low temperatures and short growing season also present problems for egg-laying snakes. Many temperate species have solved this dilema by becoming viviparous and bearing live young, allowing the mother to carry her developing embryos with her, ensuring they always have the proper temperature range. Snakes from temperate areas tend to be smaller and darker in color than their tropical cousins, an adaptation that allows them to warm themselves quickly after being chilled all night.

Rat snakes fill the arboreal niche in temperate areas, often ascending into trees to search for bird eggs and nestlings.

from accumulating snow and breaking under the weight. Only a very few snakes are able to survive in these harsh conditions. These include the garter snake and the European Adder, both of which can be found near the Arctic Circle. Snakes in these habitats spend nearly the entire year hibernating in underground dens, emerging only during the brief period in summer when the snow melts and prey becomes available.

A few species of reptile and amphibian have developed specialized protective strategies to help them survive the cold conditions in the boreal forests. The Grey Tree Frog (*Hyla versicolor*), a small species that is found almost up to the Arctic Circle, is able to tolerate being frozen solid throughout the

winter, and thawing and reviving in spring when warm weather returns. In most animals, frozen tissue is destroyed by ice crystals that develop inside the cells, puncturing the cell walls. The tree frog prevents this by producing the chemical glycerol as a cryoprotectant. The glycerol lowers the freezing point of the frog's body fluids and prevents the fluid inside the cell walls from freezing. Although the fluids outside the cell walls freeze solid, the delicate cell membranes are protected and the frog is unharmed when the temperature rises and the ice crystals are melted.

A similar strategy is used by the Red-Sided Garter Snake (*Thamnophis sirtalis parietalis*), which inhabits North America up to the Arctic Circle. Experiments have

shown that the temperature tolerance of Red-Sided Garters varies according to the time of year. In the fall, when the snakes are normally preparing for hibernation, they can tolerate temperatures as low as 22°F for a short time, and can survive temperatures of 27.5°F for up to three hours. Research revealed that, during this time, the snake's body fluids were almost forty percent ice. At exposures to 27.5°F for ten hours, the ice content in the body rose to fifty percent, and only half of the snakes survived. In the mid-winter, however, when the snakes are normally deep in hibernation, they could only survive temperatures as low as 30°F.

The snakes secreted an increased level of glucose in the liver and lactase in the heart (both of these are cryoprotectants), but the main protection seemed to come from high levels of the amino acid taurine. The varying susceptibility to cold suggests that the cryoprotectants evolved as a means of protecting the snake during the period of time just prior to hibernation. In late fall, while the snakes are still out wandering, sudden cold snaps can trap them outside, away from the protection of the hibernation den. In these conditions, the garter can survive short cold spells that would normally kill other reptiles, by preventing the formation of ice crystals inside cell walls. In mid-winter, though, this protective ability is decreased. To survive the winter, then, the snake must have been successful in finding a hibernation den with tolerable temperature levels.

Deserts

The desert ecosystem is marked by hot, dry conditions. About one-third of the earth's surface is covered by desert, including the large Sahara region of Africa, the Gobi Desert in Asia and the several deserts making up the southwestern United States and northern Mexico. Rainfall in these areas is sporadic at best, and plants and animals must engage in a constant struggle to avoid the lethal heat and lack of moisture. Desert animals must also be able to combat cold, for temperatures drop sharply at night. Food sources are rare, and species diversity is usually very low.

Snakes, however, dominate these harsh habitats, and a large number of species are exclusively desert dwellers. Their low need for food and efficiency with water allows them to outcompete mammals and birds in this spartan environment. Although some colubrids, such as the bull and gopher snakes, can adapt to desert areas, and even a handful of boids (the Rosy Boa, the sand boas) can make a living there, it is the vipers and pit vipers that dominate this ecosystem. Most of the American

species of rattlesnake can be found in desert areas, as well as a large number of Asian and African vipers, including the Saw-Scaled Viper and the Palestine Viper. The Horned Viper and the Sidewinder Rattlesnake have adapted almost completely to the open desert, even specializing in the sidewinding method of locomotion to move efficiently in dry loose sand.

Most desert species avoid the heat of the day and the cold of the night by staying in underground burrows or burying themselves in sand, emerging when temperatures are suitable. They get most of the moisture they need from their food.

Snakes have thus evolved to fill nearly every available climate zone and play a very important ecological role in different ecosystems, both as predator and as prey. In most

ecosystems, the largest number of living organisms are plants, which are capable of manufacturing their own food from sunlight and atmospheric materials using the process of photosynthesis. Ecologists thus refer to plants as producers. Because animals cannot photosynthesize and cannot manufacture their own food, their only means to obtain it is to eat either plants or other animals that have eaten plants. This sequence, in which plants make food from sunlight, and herbivores then eat the plants, and are themselves eaten by carnivores, who in turn are preyed upon by larger carnivores, is called the food chain.

In any local ecosystem, there will be a number of food chains that exist side by side. For instance, in an open field ecosystem, there

This king snake is enjoying a mouse.

will be large numbers of grasses, which produce food energy. There may also be a number of small shrubs or saplings, which produce food through photosynthesis and store it in their leaves. The grasses are fed upon by mice, who obtain the food energy they need from the sugars and proteins manufactured by the plants. Likewise, the leaves of the shrubs will be eaten by caterpillars. The mice, meanwhile, in turn are preyed upon by king snakes, who get their food energy from the proteins stored in the mice. Similarly, the caterpillars that feed on the tree leaves will themselves be preyed upon by green snakes. Finally, at the top of each food chain will be hawks, which will prey on both species of snakes.

Each food chain will have links to the others. The hawks will sometimes eat mice, while the mice will sometimes eat the buds of shrubs and trees and the king snakes will sometimes eat the green snakes. This interconnecting network of predator and prey is referred to as the "food web." Because a little food energy is lost at each step in the food chain, the number of producers is always much larger than the number of consumers, and each successive step in the food chain will be less numerous than the one before it. In our example above, there will be many thousands of grass plants in the local ecosystem, while the mice

that feed upon them number only in the hundreds. There may be only several dozen king snakes able to feed off the mice, while at the top of the food chain may be a single breeding pair of hawks. Because the food web is much wider at the bottom than it is at the top, it takes the form of a pyramid. The wide base of the pyramid is formed by the plant producers, and each succeeding layer of consumers narrows until it reaches a point at the top.

The various species of reptiles, including snakes, form important links in these food webs and pyramids, because they form a bridge between the upper and lower levels of the food pyramid. If the hawks were to attempt to live solely by eating mice or caterpillars, they would not be able to obtain enough food energy to survive. Instead, they depend upon the snakes as their food source, which prey upon the herbivores and thus concentrate their food energy. On the other hand, if the snakes did not feed upon the mice and caterpillars, these animals would have no check on their population and would reproduce explosively, overpopulating the ecosystem and draining it of food sources. By serving their dual role as predators and prey, snakes and other reptiles play important parts in maintaining the stability of their local ecosystems.

Unfortunately, many species of reptiles and amphibians are now

HABITAT DESTRUCTION

A far more devastating killer than the pet trade is the loss of habitat and the fragmentation of existing range. Reptile populations require a sizable contiguous area where they can forage for food and water. Housing developments and other construction projects, however, have fragmented most of the original habitats into small "islands" of wildland in a larger sea of cement and concrete. The tiny patches of undisturbed habitat that remain are not big enough to support a breeding population, and as a result population levels of many American reptiles have dropped to dangerously low levels.

becoming rare and are in danger of extinction, due largely to human activities. The Eastern Indigo Snake, for instance, was very popular as a pet, and several hundred were captured every year. Local snake populations cannot make up that kind of loss, and the indigo snakes are now under the protection of Federal laws and international treaties concerning threatened and endangered species.

The steady loss of species, meanwhile, can have profound effects on the entire food web. The food web tends to be somewhat redundant; that is, certain species, if lost, can be readily replaced by other species that can fulfill the same ecological role. However, today humans are drastically reducing such large numbers of species that gaping holes are being ripped into the local food webs, and we simply do not know enough yet about how all of these ecological chains are interconnected to foresee what kind of damage this will do.

It is for this reason that snake keepers must do all they can to protect our natural resources and our natural biodiversity. By helping to educate others about the important ecological roles played by snakes and other reptiles, and by taking steps to protect wild populations of reptiles and amphibians, they are helping to preserve and maintain the vast ecological web that supports all life on this planet—including us.

Guam and the Brown Tree Snake

One cause of ecological destruction is the introduction, either accidentally or deliberately, of nonnative species into ecosystems where they have no natural predators or population checks. Examples include the accidental introduction of zebra mussels into the North American Great Lakes and the deliberate introductions of the

CONTROLLING THE BROWN TREE SNAKE INVASION

One tactic that has been discussed to help control the snake population is the introduction in Guam of a "bounty" to be paid for dead Brown Tree Snakes. A number of researchers are investigating the possibility of launching biological warfare against the invaders, by releasing ophidian paramyxovirus organisms on the island. The virus has a fifty percent lethality rate in infected snakes. Endangered species of birds have been gathered into refuges where they are protected by large snake-proof fences, in an effort to prevent any more extinctions.

Cane Toad and the Prickly Pear Cactus in Australia. Such introduced species can become established and cause extensive damage to local populations.

One of the most recent examples of ecological damage by an introduced species centers around the Brown Tree Snake, a large, rear-fanged species found in New Guinea, Indonesia, and parts of Australia. Sometime in the early 1950s, a number of Brown Tree Snakes were accidentally introduced to the island of Guam, some 800 miles outside the species' normal range. Most likely, the snakes stowed away in the cargo hold of merchant

ships traveling from New Guinea to Guam. Until then, the only species of snake found on Guam was the tiny Brahminy Blind Snake, an inconspicuous burrower.

In the absence of natural predators, the Brown Tree Snake's population exploded, and by 1968 the invader was being found throughout the island. A prolific breeder, the serpent can lay up to two clutches of a dozen eggs per year. Young snakes grow quickly. Measuring $1^1/_2$ feet long at hatching, they can reach a length of up to 3 feet at one year of age. The snakes can reproduce by the time it is three years old, when they reach a length of between 4 and 5 feet. Full-grown snakes can reach a length of 8 feet and weigh around 5 pounds. Today, some areas of Guam contain up to 13,000 snakes per square mile.

As the name suggests, the Brown Tree Snake is an excellent climber, and spends most of its time in trees and shrubs. It also enters houses in search of food and shelter. Although the venom is not particularly powerful and the snake presents little danger to adults, there have been several attacks on infants and small children. One particular problem resulting from the snake's climbing habits is its tendency to climb electric power poles and short out the wires, causing blackouts and damage to electrical equipment.

The preferred food of the Brown Tree Snake consists of lizards, small mammals and birds. In its native habitat, prey species have evolved defenses that prevent them from being hunted too heavily by the snake. On Guam, however, where there are no naturally occurring hunting snakes, the huge bird population has no effective defense against the Brown Tree Snake. As a result, the snakes have virtually wiped out the entire forest bird population on the island. At least twelve species of birds (all of which were unique to Guam) have been completely exterminated by the snake, and other species have been reduced to drastically low levels. In many areas, the snakes have been forced to prey on native lizards, as well as domestic birds, poultry eggs and small pet animals.

Because the snakes are secretive and are active only at night, they are very difficult to find and exterminate. They are also adept at hiding in cargo containers, baggage and even in the wheel wells of parked airplanes. Hitchhiking Brown Tree Snakes have been found on Okinawa, Diego Garcia, Saipan, Tinian, Kwajelien and Rota, and although they have not yet established themselves on any of these islands (with the possible exception of Saipan), the possibility of such an introduction is sufficiently alarming to prompt actions to control the snakes. Government officials in Palau, the Mariana Islands and Micronesia have all adopted aggressive inspection programs to prevent the snakes from being accidentally transported to these islands. In Hawaii, specially trained dogs are used to inspect cargo and airplanes and search for stowaway tree snakes.

CHAPTER 4

Taxonomy and Classification

The science of classifying plants and animals is known as taxonomy. Biologists have classified all living things into a hierarchical system, in which organisms are grouped into categories according to their biological characteristics (their "morphology") and their evolutionary relatedness ("phylogeny"). The basic unit of this classification system is the *species,* which is defined as a population of organisms, the members of which are capable of exchanging genetic material and interbreeding to form fertile offspring. A few species are further broken down into *subspecies,* often referred to as "races." These are distinct populations that vary from each other in noticeable ways, but are still capable of interbreeding with the other populations.

A number of species that are closely related to each other through anatomy and evolutionary descent are grouped together in a *genus* (the plural is *genera*). Organisms that are more distantly related to each other are grouped at successively higher levels. A group of related genera forms a *family,* and a group of related families forms an *order.* The next higher level of classification is the *class,* and groups of related classes form a *phylum* (plural is *phyla*). The largest group of organisms is the *kingdom,* which consists of several related phyla. If necessary, other categories may be added, such as subfamilies and suborders. By convention, family names always end in the Latin letters "-idae" or "-ids," and subfamily names always end in "-inae" or "-ines."

To distinguish a particular species, scientists refer to it by its scientific name, which is made up

The Southern Black Racer pictured here is known scientifically as *Coluber constrictor priapus.*

of its genus and species (and, if necessary, its subspecies). Scientific names are usually written in Latin, and allow scientists from around the world to avoid confusion by assigning a specific name to that organism, regardless of what the varying local names for that animal may be. This Latin name contains the name of the genus, species and subspecies to which that particular animal has been assigned, and it always refers unequivocally to the same animal. The vernacular name black snake, for instance, may refer to anything from the Black Rat Snake to the Black Racer to some varieties of king snake. The scientific name *Elaphe obsoleta obsoleta,* however, refers specifically and unequivocally to the Black Rat Snake, while the Latin name *Coluber constrictor constrictor* always refers

unmistakably to the Black Racer. Scientific names not only distinguish these snakes from each other, but also differentiate races within the same species (such as *Elaphe obsoleta quadrivittata,* the Yellow Rat Snake; or *Elaphe obsoleta lindheimeri,* the Texas Rat Snake).

The taxonomic system therefore allows biologists to classify living things in a way that reflects both their unique characteristics and their shared ancestries. The complete classification for the endangered San Francisco Garter Snake, for instance, is:

Kingdom Animalia Multicellular organisms that lack rigid cell walls and chloroplasts for photosynthesis. Excludes plants and fungus; includes insects, crustaceans, fish, reptiles and mammals.

Phylum Chordata Animals that possess a spinal cord protected by a bony vertebral column. Excludes crustaceans and insects; includes fish, reptiles, amphibians, birds and mammals.

Class Reptilia Ectothermic vertebrates that can lay shelled amniote eggs on dry land. Excludes fish, amphibians, birds and mammals; includes snakes, lizards, turtles, crocodilians, the wormlike amphisbaenians and the unique Tuatara.

Order Squamata Shell-less reptiles with scaly skin and a set of particular skull characteristics. Excludes turtles, crocodilians, amphisbaenians and the Tuatara; includes the snakes and lizards.

Suborder Serpentes Scaled reptiles with limbless elongated bodies, no eyelids and no external ears. Excludes the lizards; includes the snakes.

Family Colubridae Snakes that lack any trace of a pelvic girdle, have only one functional lung and share a number of traits in the skull structure. Excludes the blind and thread snakes, the pipe snakes and wart snakes, the boas and pythons, the cobras and sea snakes and all of the vipers and pit vipers; includes the rat snakes, king snakes, garter snakes, racer snakes, water snakes and many others.

Genus *Thamnophis* A group of snakes that share a semiaquatic habitat and a number of skeletal and scale characteristics. Includes the garter and ribbon snakes; excludes all other colubrids.

Species *Thamnophis sirtalis* One of the several populations of garter snakes ranging throughout the United States that can exchange genetic material. Characterized by a number of bright stripes running along the length of the body. Excludes the ribbon snakes, the Checkered Garter Snake, the Plains Garter Snake and several others; includes the Eastern Garter Snake, the Florida Garter Snake, the San Francisco Garter Snake and several others. All of these varieties of *T. sirtalis* are members of the same species and are capable of interbreeding with each other.

Subspecies *Thamnophis sirtalis tetrataenia* San Francisco Garter Snake. The particular variant of the *T. sirtalis* species, characterized by its distinctive red markings, and confined to a limited habitat in California.

The evolutionary history of the San Francisco Garter Snake is thus reflected in its classification. The San Francisco Garter Snake shares a common ancestry with the other varieties of *Thamnophis sirtalis*, and these garter snakes in turn share a common ancestry with the other species of garter snakes and with ribbon snakes. Both the garter and ribbon snakes share ancestry with the other colubrids, which in turn developed from a common ancestry with the boids, elapids, viperids and other snakes. All snakes share an evolutionary tie with the lizards, and all scaled ectotherms are related to the other reptiles. The reptiles in turn share an evolutionary heritage with vertebrates, such as birds and mammals, and with animals, such as crustaceans and insects.

In general, the scientific name for a species is assigned by the

The Green Tree Python, scientifically known as *Morelia viridis*.

biologist who first describes it, and once assigned, it is not changed or altered. However, as our knowledge of snake taxonomy increases, it sometimes becomes necessary to adjust a particular snake's classification in order to more accurately reflect its evolutionary history and morphological similarity. In particular, the science of molecular biology has provided new tools for herpetologists. Techniques such as genetic sequencing and DNA-DNA hybridization now allow us to directly measure the "genetic distance" between various snakes, giving us a much better idea of how closely related they actually are.

The Bull Snake was once considered to be a subspecies of the Pine Snake, but will soon be classified as a separate species.

Thus, a number of snakes have recently been reclassified and given new scientific names that better reflect this new knowledge. The Green Tree Python of Australasia, for instance, was long classified in its own separate genus, as *Chondropython viridis*. Today, however, we know that it is very close, genetically, to the other Australasian

pythons of the genus *Morelia,* and the Green Tree Python has therefore been renamed *Morelia viridis.* Currently, taxonomists are making plans to divide the existing species *Pituophis melanoleuca,* by moving the Bull Snake into a separate species (*Pituophis sayikeru*). Although it is currently classified as a subspecies of the Pine Snake, the

Bull Snake exhibits several biochemical differences and breeding practices that warrant placing it in its own species. Finally, genetic analysis has confirmed that all of the fourteen or so previously named subspecies of the Asian Cobra (*Naja naja*) are actually separate and distinct species. (This discovery is significant to medical authorities as well as herpetologists, since many of these species have different venoms, and an antivenin prepared for one species may not be effective against bites from another.)

Leptotyphlopids

There are about eighty species of thread snakes, which are found in hot dry areas of Africa, Asia and

Using molecular studies, it has been found that the Green Tree Python is closely related to the Australasian pythons.

THE FAMILIES OF SNAKES

There are around twenty-five recognized families of snakes (some taxonomists, known as "lumpers," argue in favor of combining several of these families into a smaller number of groups, while other scientists, the "splitters," argue in favor of dividing snakes into even more families). About half of these families have become extinct. Many of the remaining families, such as the leptotyphlopid "thread snakes," the typhlopid "blind snakes," and the uropeltid "shield-tailed snakes," are very rare and are poorly known. Some other families, including the elapids, hydrophiids and viperids, consist solely of venomous species, some of which are maintained in zoos and public collections, but which should never be kept at home by private keepers. Only two families, the colubrids and the boids, have members that are commonly kept by private snake keepers.

Latin America. All of the species except one belong to the genus *Leptotyphlops*—the sole member of the second genus, *Rhinoleptus koniagui*, from Africa, is distinguished from the others by some scale differences on the head. A few species of thread snake—including the Texas Blind Snake and the Western Blind Snake—can be found in the southern parts of the United States.

These small snakes, about $1^1/_2$ feet long, are highly specialized burrowers, and resemble large earthworms in appearance. The head is the same diameter as the neck, and the whole body is round and thin. The scales are thick and very smooth, giving the reptile a slimy appearance.

The thread snakes are extremely primitive and lack many of the characteristics found in the more common snakes. Like the boids, the thread snakes have the remnants of a pelvic girdle and vestigial rear limbs, in the form of small clawlike protrusions near the cloaca. Unlike the boids, though, the leptotyphlopids have only one functional lung.

The leptotyphlopid skull is compact and heavy, with extremely short jaws. The eyes are small and covered with scales. Most of the teeth are gone, and the jawbones lack the flexible ligaments that allow other snakes to extend their gape for swallowing large prey. Unlike other snakes, thread snakes have a coronoid bone in their skull, a trait that they share with lizards.

Not much is known about the lifestyle of these serpents. They are secretive burrowers and spend their whole lives underground. Since their jaws are small and cannot open widely, they are limited to small invertebrate prey. Most species feed on termites and other insects. The snakes grasp the insects on the soft abdomen and use their short jaws to suck out the body contents before releasing the empty chitinous shell.

Typhlopids

The blind snakes are another group of small primitive burrowing snakes. There are about 180 species in this family, of which the best-known is the Brahminy Blind Snake, which is unusual among snakes in its parthenogenic reproduction strategy. The Brahminy is the only member of this family to be found in the United States; although it is native to Southeast Asia, it has been widely introduced to nonnative areas. Its habit of hiding in the soil of flowerpots has earned it the name Flowerpot Snake. At slightly over 5 inches in length, the Brahminy Blind Snake is one of the smallest snakes in the world.

In size, the typhlopids range from the Peter's Blind Snake (*Typhlops dinga*) from Africa, which reaches 3 feet in length, to the tiny Reuter's Blind Snake (*Typhlops reuteri*) from Madagascar, which measures less than 5 inches as an adult.

The blind snakes actually do have eyes, but they are small and covered with translucent scales. Although they closely resemble the thread snakes in appearance, the blind snakes differ in lacking vestigial rear limbs (though they do have the remnants of a pelvic girdle), and also have a looser skull structure with more mobile bones than the leptotyphlopids. The typhlopids bear teeth on their upper jaw and not on the lower; the leptotyphlopids have teeth on the lower jaw but not the upper. Nevertheless, the blind and thread snakes are so similar to each other that they are grouped together in the infra-order scolecophidia.

The two recognized genera in this family are differentiated by the structure of the male hemipenes, which are solid in the genus *Ramphotyphlops* and tubular in *Typhlops*. A third genus, *Rhinotyphlops*, is proposed by some taxonomists—it differs from the *Typhlops* in scalation.

Very little is known of the biology of these secretive snakes. The primary food consists of ants, termites and other insects.

Anomalepids

This is a primitive group of snakes, consisting of four genera and about twenty species. All of them are found in Latin America. Although they are closely related to the blind and thread snakes, the anomalepids lack any trace of pelvic girdles and are thus more advanced in an evolutionary sense than the other burrowing snakes. Almost nothing is known of their lifestyle or natural history.

Uropeltids

This group of primitive subterranean snakes, known as the shield-tail snakes and the pipe snakes, contains about fifty species. The shield-tail snakes, which make up the subfamily Uropeltinae, are found solely on the Indian subcontinent. Like the other burrowers, the skull is compact and solid, and the eyes are small and buried under translucent body scales.

The characteristic feature of the shield-tails is the large circular patch of thickened skin at the end of the blunted tail. Presumably this is used to plug up the entrance of the snake's burrow to protect it from predators. Shield-tails also have an unusual structure to their neck vertebrae, allowing them to burrow by thrusting their pointed snout into the dirt and using exaggerated neck movements to widen the tunnel.

The shield-tails vary in length from 1 to 3 feet. They feed largely on earthworms. They are unusual among the primitive snakes in giving birth to live young instead of laying eggs.

The pipe snakes, in the subfamily Cylindropheinae, are a small primitiive family consisting of less than a dozen species. Most are found in Southeast Asia. They were formerly classified in the aniliid family, but have now been placed in the uropeltids.

The skull is somewhat loosely structured and the mouth is large, but the gape is still severely limited. Pipe snakes differ from the thread and blind snakes in possessing large well-developed eyes that are protected by a brille or eyecap. Although they spend most of their time underground, hunting for other snakes and caecilians, they are not as specialized for a subterranean life as the typhlopids and leptotyphlopids. They may represent a transition between the more primitive burrowers and the boids.

None of the Uropeltids are commonly kept in captivity, and almost nothing is known about their natural history.

ANILIIDS

The aniliids are a primitive family that used to contain a number of species known as pipe snakes. The pipe snakes have since been moved to the uropeltid family, and the aniliids now consist of just a single species, the False Coral Snake (*Anilius scytale*), from Latin America. This snake has black and red bands on its back to mimic the venomous coral snakes.

The aniliids have a fossil record extending back to the Cretaceous period, and may be considered a transition from early snakes to the boids.

Acrochordids

The acrochordids or wart snakes, have only one genus, with three species. All of these are found in Southeast Asia and Australasia. The Elephant's Trunk Snake or Javan Wart Snake (*Acrochordus javanicus*) is, at a length of 8 feet, much larger than its cousins the Indian Wart Snake or File Snake (*A. granulatus*) and the Arafura Wart Snake (*A. arafurae*). All three species are exclusively aquatic and feed almost solely on fish.

Although they are similar in appearance to the boids, wart snakes lack many of the primitive features found in boas and pythons. The acrochordids lack any trace of a pelvic girdle and also have only one functional lung. They are adapted to an aquatic life, and possess valves in the nose to close the nostrils when underwater. The Indian Wart Snake inhabits both fresh and saltwater, while the other two are exclusively freshwater snakes.

Although none of the wart snakes are commonly kept in captivity, the Elephant's Trunk Snake is important in the international reptile trade. Unlike most snakes, the acrochordids do not have overlapping scales on their skin. Instead, they are covered with small round granular scales, like warts. When crushed and tanned, their skin makes excellent leather, which is sold under the name "karong."

Large numbers of karong products are exported each year.

Xenopeltids

This family of snakes contains only one species, the Sunbeam Snake, which is native to southeast Asia. This 3-foot snake is similar in appearance to a small boid, and like the boids it possesses two functional lungs. Unlike the boas and pythons, the Sunbeam Snake lacks a pelvic girdle and cloacal spurs.

The common name comes from the brilliant iridescence of its smoothly polished scales, which refract sunlight into a rainbow of shimmering colors as it moves. Like some colubrids, the Sunbeam Snake vibrates the tip of its tail rapidly when it is annoyed, which can produce a buzzing or rattling sound in dry leaves.

Although the Sunbeam Snake appears occasionally on dealer lists, not much is known about its lifestyle in the wild. Although it is capable of burrowing, the Sunbeam Snake spends most of its time prowling the forest litter looking for small mammals, frogs and smaller snakes.

Boids

The boid family, which includes all of the ninety-five or so living species of boas and pythons, is widely represented in the herpetoculture trade and contains some of the best

LOXOCEMIDS

Loxocemids are a single-species family, containing the Mexican Burrowing Snake (*Loxocemus bicolor*). This is a semiburrowing species that is active only at night, and little is known of its habits or natural history. It lays eggs and preys on eggs and small vertebrates.

The Burrowing Snake possesses a rudimentary pelvic girdle and was at one time classified along with the pythons. It has since been moved to a separate family of its own. Its evolutionary relationship to the other snake families is completely unknown.

known and widely kept species of snakes. For the most part, boas are found in North and Latin America, while the pythons are found in Africa, Asia and Australia.

Biologically, the boids are among the most primitive of the living snakes. All boids retain the vestigial bones of their pelvic girdles, all that is left of the rear legs of their lizard ancestors. In the males, the single remaining rear toe is enlarged to form a claw or spur, which is used during the mating process to stimulate the female.

Boids also differ from the more advanced snakes by retaining a left lung that, although quite a bit smaller than the right, remains fully functional. The boids also have heavier skulls and less moveable bones than their more

The boid family, which contains the boas and pythons, is the most primitive of the living snakes. (Annulated Boa)

advanced cousins. It is generally believed that the boids are similar to the ancestral *Dinilysia* in their structure and habits.

The boid family been divided into several subfamilies, many of which have members that are widely available in the pet trade and are kept by many herpers. The "true boas" are placed in the subfamily Boinae, which contains the familiar Boa Constrictor (which includes several subspecies scattered throughout Latin America) as well as the Madagascar Ground Boa and the Dumeril's Ground Boa. The Emerald Tree Boa and the Amazon Tree Boa, both arboreal snakes from Latin America, are also members of the Boinae. Another large group is the *Epicrates* genus, which contains all of the

various races and subspecies of the Rainbow Boa. Finally, the Anaconda and its smaller cousin the Yellow Anaconda, are members of the Boinae family, and are sometimes known as the "Water Boa."

The subfamily Erycinae or "dwarf boas," while not true boas, nevertheless contain a number of popular species which are included in the boid family. Among the most commonly available are the Rosy Boa, which occurs in four or five subspecies in western North America, and the various species of sand boas, which are found in Africa and southwest Asia.

The pythons, which contain some of the most popular and widely bred snakes, are currently classified in the subfamily Pythoninae. A number of taxono-

mists have argued that they should be placed in their own family, the Pythonidae. In any case, this subfamily contains such well-known and popular species as the Burmese Python (a subspecies of the Indian Python), the Royal or Ball Python, the Reticulated Python, the Blood Python, the Green Tree Python and the Carpet Python.

Bolyeriids

This small group was once classed with the boids, but has now been given family status of its own. Its members differ from the boids by lacking any pelvic girdle and by possessing only one functional lung. The bolyeriids contain only two genera, each with a single species. Both are found only on Round Island, a tiny speck of land (less than one square mile) off the coast of Madagascar. The Round Island Burrowing Boa (*Bolyeria multicarinata*) and the Round Island Boa (*Casarea dussumieri*) are both severely endangered and are protected under Appendix I of the CITES treaty, an international treaty that regulates trade in endangered and threatened species.

In the nineteenth century, merchant seamen introduced rabbits and goats to the island, and these efficient browsers removed most of the shrubbery and ground cover. As a result, populations of both snakes plummeted. In the mid-1970s, efforts were made to eradicate the introduced browsers and save the snakes. For the Burrowing Boa, it may have already been too late—no living *B. multicarinata* has been seen on the island since 1975. The species is probably extinct.

Fewer than seventy-five Round Island Boas live on the island, making it one of the rarest snakes on earth. It feeds on the single species of gecko and single species of skink found on the island. The Round Island Boa is the subject of an intensive captive breeding effort to repopulate the island. It is an egg-layer, which differentiates it from the true boas.

Tropidopheids

This Latin American and Caribbean group of snakes, numbering about twenty species grouped in four genera, was once classified with the boids. The snakes in this family differ from the boids in possessing large tracheal lungs and, in some cases, in lacking a pelvic girdle.

Known as wood snakes or West Indian boas, the tropidopheids are a little-known group of reptiles that are not often kept in captivity. Most are between 1 and 3 feet in length. Most are terrestrial in habits, but a few are arboreal and several species are semiburrowers. They feed on small rodents and lizards, which they kill by constriction.

One genus of West Indian boas, *Trachyboa*, is known as the "Eyelash Boa" because of the projecting scales above the eyes. Another group of these snakes, the *Tropidophis* genus, has an unusual defense mechanism—when threatened, it may force a stream of blood from its eyes and mouth, reminiscent of certain horned lizards.

Colubrids

The colubrid family contains many well-known and widely kept varieties of snake, classified into a number of subfamilies. It is by far the largest and most diverse of the

snake families—of the 2,700 species of living snakes, about 2,000 are colubrids. The colubrids are a "taxonomic garbage can," and many members have been placed there simply because they don't seem to fit anywhere else. As our knowledge of the taxonomy and evolutionary history of snakes increases, the large colubrid family is likely to be divided into several smaller groups.

From the herper's point of view, probably the most important of the many genera which make up the colubrid family are the *Elaphe*, commonly known as rat snakes. There are about thirty species of rat snakes scattered around North America, Europe and Asia. Several of these are widely bred for the pet trade, including the Yellow Rat Snake, the Black Rat Snake and the Red Rat Snake (more commonly referred to as the corn snake), all native to North America; the European Four-Lined Snake and the Asian Mandarin Rat Snake. The corn snake in particular has been captive-bred in a wide variety of color variations or "morphs," and is probably the most widely kept snake on earth.

Another popular genus of colubrids is the *Lampropeltis* genus, which includes the closely related king and milk snakes. These are found only in North and South America. Although only eight species have been confirmed, there

The Yellow Rat Snake is a typical colubrid.

are over two dozen subspecies and races of king and milk snakes. The most popular in the pet trade are the Chain or Eastern King Snake, the Florida or Speckled King Snake, the California King Snake, the Sinaloan Milk Snake and the Honduran Milk Snake.

The genus *Pituophis* has three recognized species ranging throughout North America and Mexico, but all three of the most commonly available snakes from this genus, the Pine Snake, Bullsnake and Gopher Snake, are races of the species *P. melanoleuca* (which, as was noted earlier, is in the process of being broken into several separate species).

The water snakes of the American genus *Nerodia* and the European genus *Natrix* do not make particularly good captives, but are nevertheless widely available. On the other hand, the ribbon and garter snakes, genus *Thamnophis,* make excellent pets, particularly for beginners, and are widely bred for the pet trade. Both the water and garter snakes are classified in the subfamily natricinae. The European and North American water snakes were once placed in the same genus, *Natrix,* but were divided into two groups, since the European water snakes lay eggs and the North American species bear live young.

A few subfamilies of the colubrid family are opisthoglyphs, and possess modified rear fangs for injecting venom. In most species the venom is not dangerous to humans; however, a number of opisthoglyphs, such as the African Boomslang and the Twig Snake, have been known to cause human deaths. A number of rear-fanged colubrids are available on dealers' lists, including the harmless Hognose Snake and the potentially more dangerous Mangrove Snake.

Elapids

The elapid family contains about 170 living species, including the well-known cobras as well as the closely related kraits, mambas and coral snakes. All of the members of this family are venomous, and many species, including the cobras and kraits, have caused human fatalities. None of these snakes should ever be kept by any private collector. Sometimes elapids that have had their venom glands surgically removed are available.

The cobras, genus *Naja,* are probably the best-known of the elapids. About thirty species of cobra can be found ranging throughout Africa and Asia, along with a large number of subspecies. The most common in captivity is the Asian Cobra, from southern Asia, and the Egyptian Cobra, from northern Africa. The King Cobra, also a common captive, is classified by itself in a separate genus.

The coral snake, of the genus *Micrurus,* is the only elapid found in North America. About fifty species of coral snake are found throughout Latin America (only two species reach the southern half of the United States).

There are twelve species of kraits found throughout southern Asia. Most are nocturnal hunters that feed almost exclusively on other snakes. Although the venom is powerful, they are not usually aggressive and bites are relatively rare.

The mambas (genus *Dendroaspis*) are fast, active elapids from Africa. Although they feed largely on lizards and birds, their venom is extremely powerful and the snakes themselves are aggressive and strike vigorously when disturbed. They are difficult to handle safely and are widely feared in their native habitat.

Two of the most dangerous snakes in the world are elapids from Australia, the Tiger Snake and the Small-Scaled or Inland Taipan. Although neither is particularly rare, they are found only in isolated and remote areas, and thus do not present a very great danger. Their venom is among the most potent on earth, however, and until recently there was no antivenin available for these species.

The Australian Copperhead is not a pit viper like its American namesake, but is an elapid. Another odd Australian snake is the Death Adder, which closely parallels the structure of the vipers—it has a short, stocky body, a wide triangular head and even has hinged fangs in its mouth.

Because of Australia's tight export regulations, it is not common to see these species in captivity.

Although the elapids are a relatively small group of snakes, in Australia they are the dominant family, and Australia has the unusual distinction of having more species of venomous native snakes than nonvenomous snakes. This once led biologists to conclude that the tectonic plate containing the Australian landmass probably broke away from the mainland after the elapids had evolved but before the vipers had appeared, isolating the continent and allowing the elapids to flourish in the absence of any competition from the newer viperids. Today, however, we know that the viperids are much older than had previously been believed, and it remains a mystery why Australia lacks vipers.

Hydrophiids

The fifty or so species of sea snake are among the most highly specialized of the living reptiles. If the theories that claim that snakes developed in the sea from marine varanoid lizards are correct, then the hydrophiids have reversed the evolutionary step taken by their distant ancestors, and have returned to the sea from the land.

The sea snakes are so closely related to the cobras and kraits that some taxonomists prefer to place them as a subfamily of the elapid family. They have the same short fixed fangs as their elapid relatives, but their bodies have been adapted to a marine existence. Most species have tails that are laterally compressed, which helps them swim. A valve in the nose allows the snake to close its nostrils when submerged, and a special gland on the head excretes excess salt from the body. They can remain submerged for over an hour before surfacing to breathe. Some sea snakes have a special light-sensitive detector on their tail, which tells them when a portion of their body is protruding from a burrow or shelter.

There are two subfamilies of sea snake. The three genera making up the laticaudines, known as the "sea kraits," are the most primitive of the hydrophiids, and still retain many of the features of their terrestrial cousins. They spend much of their time on land and can often be found sunning themselves on shore. They still retain the wide belly scales found on terrestrial snakes, and are capable of moving quickly on land. Unlike most sea snakes, the sea kraits also must leave the water and lay eggs on shore.

The majority of the sea snakes belong to the five genera making up the subfamily Hydrophiinea. These snakes are completely adapted

for life in the sea and never leave the water. The wide belly scales necessary for terrestrial locomotion are gone, and the snake's body is uniformly covered with small scales that help reduce drag. Most important, the hydrophiines are capable of giving live birth in the water, eliminating the need to come ashore to lay eggs. Since the young snakes are exceptionally large when born (almost half the size of the mother), the litters are seldom larger than five or six young at a time.

One of the more widely studied of the sea snakes is the Yellow-Bellied Sea Snake (*Pelamis platurus*), which ranges further from the shore than any other sea snake and can often be found in the open sea. The Lake Taal Snake (*Hydrophis semperi*) is unique among sea snakes in adapting to a freshwater life, and is only found in Lake Taal in the Philippines. In a previous geological period, this lake once had an outlet to the sea that has since disappeared, trapping the snake inside. Other species include the Beaked Sea Snake (*Enhydrina schistosa*), the Black-Banded Sea Krait (*Laticauda laticauda*) and the Small-Headed Sea Snake (*Microcephalophis gracilis*).

Atractaspidids

The mole vipers or burrowing asps have at various times been classified with the viperids and with the colubrids. Most taxonomists now classify them in their own separate family.

There are eight genera with fifty-five species, all of them venomous. Some genera have foldable fangs at the front of the mouth, while others have rear fangs like the colubrids. Only one species, the Natal Black Snake (*Macrelaps microlepidotus*), is potentially dangerous to humans. Most lay eggs, but a few species bear live young. Most feed on lizards and small rodents. One genus, *Apparallactus,* with eleven species, consists solely of specialized centipede-eaters. None of the mole vipers are widely kept as captives.

It is likely that this taxonomic family contains a number of different evolutionary lineages, and that many of these species will need to be reclassified as our knowledge increases.

Viperids

The viper family has a large number of members, about 180 species altogether. Only about fifty of these, however, are "true vipers," which lack facial heat pits. On the whole, vipers are short, heavy-bodied snakes with broad heads, and are usually lethargic and nonaggressive unless disturbed. All of the vipers are venomous, and some have potent venom and have caused a large number of human deaths.

Although no true vipers are found in North or South America, they are widespread and common throughout Asia, Africa and Europe. The widest-ranging snake in the world, the European Adder—found from the British Islands to the eastern areas of Russia and Siberia—is a member of the viper family. Other members of the *Vipera* genus are the European Asp, the Sand Viper and Russell's Viper. Russell's Viper, which is found in several subspecies from India to Indonesia, is a large snake with powerful venom. In many areas, it is responsible for more human deaths than any other snake.

Vipers of the genus *Bitis* are hardy animals and are often seen in captivity. These include the Gaboon Viper and the Puff Adder. These are large, heavy-bodied snakes that can measure up to 8 feet long. The

The Gaboon Viper is a true viper and lacks facial pits.

Gaboon Viper has the longest fangs of any venomous snake, measuring over 2 inches. Some *Bitis* species, such as the Gaboon Viper, are lethargic and are not apt to bite unless severely threatened. Others, like the Puff Adder, defend themselves aggressively at the slightest provocation. Although they are common in zoos, these

This Rhinocerus Viper (*Bitis nasicornis*) is a member of the viper family.

species are extremely dangerous and should not be kept in any private collection.

Other true vipers that are often seen in zoos and public collections are the Desert Horned Viper, Russell's Viper and the European Asp.

Some of the most dangerous of the vipers belong to the genus *Echis*, including the Saw-Scaled Viper. The genus *Cerastes* contains the Horned Viper, which parallels the American Sidewinder Rattlesnake—right down to the horns over the eyes and the sidewinding method of locomotion.

None of these venomous snakes should ever be kept by a private collector. Although specimens that have been surgically devenomed are occasionally available, they do not do well after such surgery and usually die within a few months.

Pit Vipers

The pit vipers, known scientifically as the crotalines, are actually a subfamily of the viperids. There are about 150 species of pit viper, which makes this group the largest of the viper subfamilies. (Some taxonomists have argued in favor of separating the pit vipers into their own family, the crotalids.) They are distinguished from the true vipers by the presence of heat-sensitive pits on either side of the face. The familiar rattlesnakes are pit vipers, as are the North American copperheads and all

of the Latin American vipers. With the exception of the coral snakes, which are elapids, the pit vipers are the only venomous snakes found in North America. Pit vipers are also common in southern Asia.

The rattlesnakes are widely kept in captivity by zoos and educational institutes. There are two genera of rattlesnakes. The *Crotalus* genus is characterized by numerous small scales covering the top of the head. The *Sistrurus* genus possesses large head shields, like those of colubrids. The most commonly kept *Crotalus* species are the Western Diamondback, the Eastern Diamondback, the Timber Rattler and the various subspecies of the Prairie Rattler.

The genus *Agkistrodon* is very similar to the rattlesnakes, but lacks the tail rattle. The North American Copperhead (*Agkistrodon contortrix*) is rather common and is seen in some zoos. The Cottonmouth or Water Moccasin is also from this

genus. Other *agkistrodon* species are found in Asia.

Other widely available pit vipers include several of the arboreal snakes, from the genera *Trimeresurus* and *Bothriechis*. The *Trimeresurus* genus includes about thirty species, ranging from southern Asia to Japan. Most are arboreal. The *Bothriechis* genus, known as the palm vipers, contains seven species, all from Central and Latin America. The best known of the palm vipers is the Eyelash Viper, which is found in several color morphs, but is easily recognized by the distinctive scales projecting above the eyes. The palm vipers are arboreal snakes that feed on birds and small mammals.

All of the pit vipers are venomous, and none should ever be kept by any private collector. Devenomed pit vipers are sometimes available, but they cannot tolerate the operation well and usually die within a short time.

Philipenes hatchlings (*Trimeresurus mcgregori*).

Snakes in Captivity

CHAPTER 5

A Snake for You

In general, a snake suitable for captivity should possess a number of particular characteristics. It should be docile and tame and easy to handle. It should have a diet that can be easily provided, and it should be tolerant of a wide range of environmental factors. Since most snakes have life spans of almost twenty years (and some snakes can live as long as forty years), it is important to choose a snake that you can afford to care for over a period of several decades.

Choosing a Snake

Several captive-bred species have become well-established in the pet trade and make excellent choices, particularly for those new to the hobby. These include the following:

Corn Snake
(Elaphe guttata)

Corn snakes, which are native to the southeastern United States, are probably the most widely bred snake on earth and are an excellent addition to any snake collection. They are sometimes sold under the name Red Rat Snake, and are available in a wide range of strikingly beautiful color patterns. Naturally colored corn snakes are reddish brown with a pattern of large darker splotches along the back and attractive red and black checkers along the belly. Other color patterns include the Snow Corn, which is pale in color with darker blotches, and the Okeetee or Orange Corn, with the same basic pattern as the natural snake but with much brighter orange colors. Albino corn snakes are also readily available. New morphs of this serpent appear regularly.

The Yellow Rat Snake is an attractive species that does well in captivity.

Corn snakes reach a maximum length of around 5 feet and are very docile. They are reliable feeders, and can tolerate a wide range of environmental conditions. In captivity, they can live for over twenty years. The name comes from the rectangular pattern on the belly, which resembles the Indian corn.

King Snake
(Lampropeltis getula)

There are several different races of the king snake available in the pet trade, all of them attractively patterned. The most commonly available are the Common or Chain King Snake, which is glossy black with a network of thin yellow or white stripes; the Florida or Speckled King Snake, which is black or dark blue with numerous tiny white or yellow spots; and the California King Snake, which is black or dark blue with wide white or yellow crossbands. All of these varieties are subspecies and can interbreed with each other.

In the wild, they eat a variety of prey, including birds, lizards and small mammals. Captives will usually feed on mice. The king snake

The Eastern King, or "Chain" Snake, is docile and easy to care for in captivity.

A wild Bull Snake will often hiss and strike at its keeper, but will rarely try to bite.

Pine Snake and Bull Snake (Pituophis melanoleuca)

The Pine Snake and the Bull Snake are geographical groups of the same species (although there is a move among herpetologists to reclassify them as separate species). The Pine Snake is found in the temperate forests of the southeastern United States, while the Bull Snake is adapted for the arid semideserts of the American West. They are very similar in their care requirements, with the Bull Snake requiring somewhat higher temperatures and drier conditions than its eastern cousin.

Wild-caught individuals tend to be defensive and nervous and will often hiss and strike at their keepers, but the strikes are usually made with the mouth closed, and it is rare for a Bull or Pine Snake to actually attempt to bite. In captivity, they become tame very quickly and soon settle into hardy and active pets.

is, however, a confirmed snake-eater, and earned its name because it is capable of overpowering and eating nearly any other snake, including the venomous rattlesnakes. King snakes must therefore be kept individually in separate cages. Even siblings from the same litter will eat each other.

conditions, and are tough and resilient snakes that can take a fair amount of abuse and still thrive. They also do not get very big—usually less than 3 feet—and tame quickly. And, because they breed readily in captivity, they are widely available and are very inexpensive. They are an excellent choice for a first snake.

Garter Snake (Thamnophis sirtalis) *and* Ribbon Snake (Thamnophis sauritus)

These two very common North American snakes range from northern Mexico all the way to Canada near the Arctic Circle. Not surprisingly, they are very tolerant of a wide range of environmental

The garter snake is undemanding and makes a good first snake. (Checkered Garter Snake)

Ball Python
(Python regius)

The Ball Python, known in Europe as the Royal Python, is extremely popular in the pet trade, and several tens of thousands of them are sold each year. These West African snakes are very attractively patterned, with large black or chocolate brown markings on a tan or light brown background. In captivity, they can live as long as thirty years.

Although the Ball Python is extremely heavy-bodied and weighs a lot for its size, it is one of the smallest of the boid family, and rarely exceeds 4$^1/_2$ feet in length. They are not aggressive and seldom try to bite. When frightened, they may coil their bodies into a tight ball and tuck their heads inside. In captivity, they soon lose their fear of humans and give up this trick.

Because of their manageable size and their docile temperaments, they make very good pets, provided that suitable conditions can be maintained. Like all boids, Ball Pythons need high temperatures and high humidity to thrive, and are susceptible to a variety of health problems if these conditions are not maintained. They can also be problem feeders, and are prone to suddenly stop eating for distressingly long periods of time, for no apparent reason. This problem is much more apparent in wild-caught individuals. Individuals that

have been bred in captivity are much easier to care for than those taken from the wild.

Red Tailed Boa
(Boa Constrictor)

Despite what you may hear, Boa Constrictors are not the longest of the snakes; in fact, they do not even rank in the top five. An average boa will reach a length of around 10 feet. They have been known to live in captivity for over forty years.

Boas are tough and undemanding snakes that can be cared for easily. They are also available in a wide range of morphs and races, which vary greatly in size and temperament. Captive-bred specimens are to be preferred, because wild-caught snakes often carry a heavy parasite load and are more difficult

to handle. In the wild, Boa Constrictors are legally protected throughout much of their range.

A large number of snake species are available through dealers and breeders which, though not suitable for beginning snake keepers, may be kept by more experienced hobbyists.

Reticulated Python
(Python reticulatus)

The Reticulated Python is the longest snake in the world, and can reach lengths of up to 33 feet. Although individual snakes may be calm and docile, most are temperamental, unpredictable and irritable (the best description I ever heard of the Retic's disposition is "like the Grinch with a bad case of hemorrhoids"). This is the only snake in the world that is reliably confirmed

Its brilliant colors and bright sheen make the Brazilian Rainbow Boa a much sought after snake.

to have killed and eaten human beings, and over the years several zookeepers have been killed by large Retics in their collections.

They are not a snake for an inexperienced herper and should be treated with respect for their size and power. Although they are kept by serious amateur herpers, Reticulated Pythons are best suited for large public collections, where the snake's space and food requirements can be easily met. Great care and caution must be used whenever you are handling a Retic.

Burmese Python
(Python molurus bivittatus)

These snakes are extremely common in the pet trade and are, unfortunately, very popular among beginning herpers. Their appeal is increased by the fact that they have been bred in several quite attractive color patterns, including albinos.

An albino Burmese Python, one of the many variations or "morphs" available from breeders.

And, because they breed readily in captivity, they are relatively inexpensive to obtain.

Although not as large as the Retic, a full-grown Burm can still reach 15 to 20 feet in length and weigh around 60 to 100 pounds, reaching an age of over twenty years. They are large and very powerful animals that must be treated with respect.

Burmese Pythons are normally docile and calm and do not usually resent handling. They are, however, voracious feeders. Problems usually result when the snake mistakes its handler for a food item and attacks. Over the years, a number of amateur snake keepers have been killed by Burmese Pythons ranging in length from 8 to 13 feet.

Green Snakes
(Opheodrys species)

These beautiful snakes, with their long, slender bodies (up to 4 feet) and their attractive lemon-lime color scheme, are very common in the pet trade. Unfortunately, however, they are only rarely bred in captivity, and nearly all of the individuals in the pet trade are wild-caught.

Green snakes are also extremely delicate, and even experienced snake keepers can have enormous difficulty in keeping them alive for more than a few months. Part of the problem lies in their specialized food requirements. Unlike most snakes, green snakes are entirely insectivorous, and will usually eat only soft-bodied, hairless caterpillars. They also do not tolerate moisture very well and must be kept in warm and dry conditions.

Hognosed Snakes
(Heterodon species)

Hognosed snakes measure less than 4 feet long and can tolerate a wide range of environmental conditions. Although they are not difficult to care for and make interesting captives, their very specialized food preference may present some problems. Although the Western species may feed on mice, most hognosed snakes will not eat any food other than toads. Providing sufficient

NEVER HANDLE A CONSTRICTOR ALONE

As with all large constrictors, Burmese Pythons should never be handled alone, and safe handling usually requires a minimum of one person for every 5 feet of snake. If properly treated, Burms can make good companions. They are not, however, suited for beginning snake keepers.

food for a hognose can be a daunting and frustrating task.

Hognose snakes also have enlarged rear fangs and a mild paralytic venom for subduing their prey. Although the venom is not dangerous to humans, this snake may nevertheless be classified in some jurisdictions as a venomous species.

Water Snakes
(Nerodia *species*)

Water snakes, though not difficult to care for, are nasty and aggressive captives. Although some individual snakes can be tamed enough to handle, most will turn on their keeper with unbelievable ferocity, biting repeatedly and emptying the contents of their anal glands while struggling to escape.

On occasion, the European water snakes (*natrix* species) also show up on dealers' lists. They differ from their American cousins by laying eggs instead of giving live birth.

"PRACTICE" WITH AN AGGRESSIVE, NONVENOMOUS SNAKE

Whenever someone asks me about keeping a venomous snake, I always respond by telling the potential keeper to first obtain a large, aggressive snake such as a water snake or Coachwhip—something really mean and nasty—and keep it for a year. Feed it, change its water and clean its cage regularly. Every time the snake gets one of its teeth in you, write yourself a note saying "I could be dead right now, and if I survive I'll owe the hospital $30,000-plus," and tape it to your snake cage. After a year, decide if you really want to keep a dangerously venomous snake.

Venomous Snakes

Although it should go without saying that keeping venomous snakes is very dangerous, both to oneself and to others, a number of venomous species, including such lethal serpents as cobras, vipers and rattlesnakes, are available from breeders and snake dealers. Although most experienced snake keepers (including myself) would recommend that no one ever keep a dangerously venomous snake in a private home or apartment, the

fact remains that experienced amateurs have successfully maintained rear-fanged colubrids, elapids and viperids. If properly housed and handled by properly trained and experienced keepers, raising venomous snakes can be not much more dangerous than keeping some of the larger species of constrictors.

This does not mean that inexperienced snake keepers (or even experienced ones) should rush right out and buy that rattlesnake or cobra. Keeping venomous snakes requires absolute concentration and attention that cannot waver for even an instant. Experienced herpetologists and zookeepers, with years of practice, are bitten by venomous snakes every year, and very few people can go more than a few years actively handling venomous snakes without being bitten at least once. No one is immune to the single momentary lapse that leads to disaster. In fact, over half of all the snakebites reported in the

Although Eyelash Vipers are attractive and wisely bred in captivity, no venomous snake should be kept by a private collector.

LEGAL RESTRICTIONS

Although some municipalities and local governments have ordinances banning the possession of venomous snakes, for the most part there are few legal restrictions on the practice. One exception is the state of Florida, which has a licensing system for venomous species that could serve as a model for the rest of the country. It is illegal to buy, possess or exhibit any venomous snake in Florida without a Venomous Reptile Permit. Permits can only be obtained by people who have spent a minimum of 1,000 hours caring for venomous snakes under the guidance of an experienced snake keeper, and who can meet the stringent housing and security requirements. In addition, venomous snake keepers are required to demonstrate that the nearest hospital always has on hand a supply of antivenin for treating snakebite. It is better if the keeper himself maintains a supply of antivenin in his residence, bringing it along to the hospital if it becomes necessary.

United States are the result either of heroics in trying to capture or kill a snake found in the wild, or of accidents while handling a captive snake.

If you absolutely must have a venomous snake and have the proper training and experience to handle one, it is best to start with those species that do not have very powerful venom and that normally do not threaten human life. These would include the Copperhead, the Mangrove Snake, the European Adder and the Eyelash Viper. Although bites from these serpents cause tremendous pain and tissue damage, they are not usually lethal.

Is there a way to keep these species of snake without all of these necessary legal and safety precautions? In many areas, "devenomed" or "venomoid" snakes are available.

These are venomous species such as cobras, vipers and rattlesnakes, that have been surgically altered by a veterinarian, sometimes by removing the venom sacs completely by using a laser, but more often by making a small slit in the side of the snake's cheek and severing the duct leading from the snake's venom sac to the fang. This has the effect of rendering the snake incapable of injecting its venom.

Since the venom is a part of the snake's digestive process, this process of devenoming can have a serious impact on the snake's health. In general, vipers and pit vipers, which depend on their hemotoxic venom to break down body tissues for digestion, do not tolerate the operation very well, and most devenomed viperids will stubbornly refuse to eat and will die within months. In general, viperids are more prone to stress than other snakes and do not tolerate captivity well—a condition that would only be aggravated by the stress of an operation. Although some viperids can be successfully devenomed, usually long-term captives that have already become accustomed to eating pre-killed food, most cannot. The elapids, however, with their neurotoxic venom, seem better able to withstand the operation, and devenomed cobras have been kept successfully in captivity for several years. The operation, again, is usually most successful in long-term captives that are already regularly feeding on pre-killed prey.

These "devenomed" snakes are not able to inject any venom and thus do not present any danger of poisoning. However, although the venom ducts have been cut, the snake still possesses a full complement of fangs (the fangs cannot be permanently removed, since, like all of the snake's teeth, they are constantly replaced during life). This means that, even though it may not be able to inject any venom, it can still bite and strike with its fangs, and such a bite can be extremely painful. It should also be pointed out that, in a very few documented instances, snakes that had been devenomed were able to recover their capacity to inject venom, either by regenerating a portion of their venom gland or

Although devenomed snakes, such as this Eastern Diamondback Rattler, are available from dealers, they do not do well in captivity.

because they possessed more than one duct. For this reason, even devenomed snakes should be treated with respect and handled at all times as if they were "hot."

It should also be noted that, in some jurisdictions that have outlawed keeping venomous snakes, the fact that the snake is devenomed may not change its legal status.

My own opinion is that the only justification for surgically altering a venomous snake is when the animal is to be used for educational purposes (lectures and talks), where safety considerations and insurance problems make using "hot" snakes impractical or undesirable. No snake should ever be surgically altered just to make a "pet" out of it. It is also my firm opinion that no one should ever keep a venomous snake in a private home or apartment.

Nevertheless, a number of venomous species are available to amateur collectors. Many of these are also available as "devenomed." The most commonly kept include the following.

Cobra
(Naja *species*)

This is probably the most instantly recognizable snake in the world—the spreading hood and upright stance are familiar to everyone. There are several species of cobra found throughout Africa and Asia. The most common in captivity are the Egyptian Cobra and the Asian Cobra. Although most adapt well to captivity and are not difficult to keep, they are fast and agile snakes that are extremely difficult to handle safely. Snake tongs and "catch boxes" are necessary for such routine tasks as cage cleaning. Devenomed cobras are widely available, and they tolerate the operation better than most snakes.

After a period of time in captivity, cobras adapt to the human presence and no longer "hood."

Eastern Diamondback Rattlesnake
(Crotalus adamanteus)

The largest venomous snake in North America, and one of the largest in the world, the Eastern Diamondback Rattler can reach lengths of 8 feet. Although the venom is not particularly powerful, the large venom glands produce copious amounts of it, making the bite dangerous (Eastern Diamondbacks cause more human deaths each year than any other North American snake). They do well in captivity, feeding on rabbits and other large rodents. The somewhat smaller Western Diamondback Rattler (*Crotalus atrox*) is also widely bred and kept in captivity.

Gaboon Viper
(Bitis gabonicus)

Another large viper, the Gaboon Viper is native to forested areas in sub-Saharan Africa. It is a strikingly beautiful snake, covered in an intricate pattern of brown, blue, tan and red patches. Although the venom is powerful and the snake is extremely dangerous, it is a lethargic animal that rarely strikes unless provoked. The closely related Puff Adder (*Bitis arietans*) is also widely available. It is more active than the Gaboon Viper and therefore more dangerous. Both species breed readily in captivity.

Eyelash Viper (Bothriechis shlegelii)

This small arboreal pit viper, recognizable by the projecting hornlike scales above each eye, is native to Central America. It is found in several distinct color phases, including pink, green with brown splotches and bright orange or yellow. Although the Eyelash Viper can be aggressive and nervous, its venom is not very powerful and its bite, though painful, is not usually fatal. It has been bred in captivity and often appears on dealer lists.

Copperhead (Agkistrodon contortrix)

A small pit viper measuring about 3 feet, the Copperhead is found in several distinct races throughout the eastern half of North America. A quite attractive snake, the Copperhead is tan or orangish brown in color with large triangular

chestnut or brown patches along the sides, which meet at the spine to form a large hourglass pattern. The venom is weak and the snake cannot inject much of it, and this, combined with its relative docility, makes the Copperhead a relatively safe species to keep. It does, however, have a reputation for being a very finicky eater in captivity. It feeds on small rodents, frogs and even large insects such as cicadas or grasshoppers.

Pygmy Rattlesnake (Sistrurus *species*)

These snakes vary in adult size from just over 1 foot to around 3 feet. The smaller species has tiny rattles that sound more like an insect than a snake. They can be quite pugnacious to handle, and the venom is, drop for drop, much more potent than that of their larger cousins. However, the pygmy rattlers are so tiny that they cannot inject large amounts of venom.

They are not known to have caused any human fatalities.

Obtaining a Snake

It used to be that the very best way to obtain a wide variety of snake species was to go into the bush and catch them yourself. In the interests of conservation, however, wild-caught snakes should be avoided, as the pet trade has been a major factor in the depletion of many snake populations. Wild-caught snakes also tend to be heavily parasitized, and many have great difficulty adjusting to captivity.

Fortunately, a growing number of species are now being captive bred and farm-raised by professional and amateur breeders. These captive-bred animals are healthier and have better dispositions than wild-caught snakes. Before you buy any snake, please check and make sure that it was captive-bred and not taken from the wild.

Before you buy any snake, make sure it was captive-bred here in the United States. (Grey-Banded King Snake hatching)

One of the best ways to obtain a snake is through a local breeder or collector. Most snake breeders are very conscientious about their animals and take extraordinary care in keeping and caring for them. (Snakes only breed under optimal conditions, and if the breeder is giving them substandard care, he would have no litters of young snakes to sell.) And, because the breeder has a wealth of experience in keeping and raising this species, he will be able to answer any questions that you have and pass on useful information and tips on caring for your particular breed of snake.

The biggest problem in dealing with a local breeder, however, is to find one. Unless you live in a large city, there are unlikely to be any snake breeders near you. Even if there were, few local snake breeders advertise, and the only way to find them is through word of mouth. Members of your local herpetological society should be able to point you to any reputable breeders in your area.

Another potential problem is variety. It takes a lot of space and money to breed snakes on any appreciable scale, and most private breeders therefore tend to specialize in one or at most a small number of species. The most popular snakes for small-scale breeding seem to be corn snakes, milk snakes and Burmese Pythons. You

may not be fortunate enough to find a person who breeds the species that you are looking for.

For some of the more exotic snakes, the only source of that species may be a mail-order dealer. A few of these dealers offer only snakes that they themselves have captive-bred. The larger dealers will also offer imported wild-caught snakes. Most are very conscientious in their care of the animals, because they depend greatly on repeat business, and those outfits that sell sickly or ill-treated animals usually do not stay in business for very long. If you buy a snake by mail order, be sure to select a reputable dealer who has been in business for some time and has a good reputation among experienced herpers.

Most dealers will send you a price list of available species upon request. Some of the larger mail-order dealers will also have Web pages on the Internet, where you can see prices and sometimes photos of available snakes. Because snakes may be sold under several different names in the pet trade, most dealer lists will give the scientific names as well, and this is the name that you should rely on when ordering, to ensure that you get the exact species you want. The better snake dealers will be happy to send you a photograph of a particular snake if you request it, so you can judge it for color, pattern and condition.

In general, you can expect to get a good price for a snake from a dealer. On top of this price, however, you will need to pay the shipping costs. It is illegal to send snakes through the mail, so most dealers ship their snakes using air freight, and this costs between $35 and $45. In cool weather, you will want to have your snakes shipped by "Delta Dash," which places the packages in the cabin rather than the unheated cargo hold. This costs quite a bit more than regular air freight, but is absolutely necessary for the health of the snakes.

Often (especially if the weather is cool), you will also have to pay a "box charge" of $10 to $15 to cover the expenses of boxes, bags, heaters and shipping materials. Finally, many dealers have a

Snakes must be carefully packaged to be shipped by air from a breeder or dealer.

CALL IN YOUR ORDER

The best way to place an order with a dealer is by telephone. The dealer will need to know what species you want and what airport you would like them shipped to (for an extra charge, you can sometimes have the airport itself deliver the package right to your door). After you have confirmed that the dealer has the species you want in stock and has not sold it since the price list was printed, you will need to send a money order or check for the total amount, or place the order on your credit card. As soon as payment has been received, the dealer will package your snakes and book them on a flight to the airport you have specified. Once the snakes are ready to be shipped, he will call you and give you the flight number, the arrival time and the airbill number of your package.

"minimum order" requirement for anything they ship out, which can range from $50 to over $100.

Once all of these additional costs are factored in, the price you pay may end up being very close to what you would pay in a pet store. One option to explore if you want to reduce this cost is a local "snake buyer's club," in which a number of people get together and order a number of snakes that they then have shipped out as one order. Because the shipping charge is per box, not per snake, this practice will lower the shipping cost per person and allow everybody to obtain the specimens they want at a lower cost than if they sent in their order individually. Your local herpetological society can probably help you set this up.

At the appointed time, call the air freight center at your local airport and make sure the flight has arrived on time. Your package may not actually be unloaded from the plane for an hour or more after the arrival time, so make sure the freight office knows that the package contains livestock (it should be clearly marked "Live Harmless Reptiles") and ask them to make sure they keep the package in a warm place until you get there.

At the air freight terminal, you must provide the clerk with your airbill number (and your money— most dealers ship their snakes "collect"), and he will retrieve your package. Unfortunately, nearly every air carrier will require you to pay in full and sign a release stating that the package arrived in suitable condition *before* they will allow you to open the box. Any reputable dealer, however, will guarantee live arrival of your snake at the airport. Once you get your package, you should immediately open it, with a shipping clerk present, to verify the condition of your snake. If there is a problem, you must contact the dealer at the earliest opportunity (within twenty-four hours).

Most snake keepers, especially beginners buy their animals from a local pet shop. Generally, pet shop prices may be higher than the prices charged by other sources, and of course, your selection will be limited to the species that the pet shop has available. However, some stores will be able to special-order a particular species for you. Moreover, you will be able to handle and examine any snake you may be interested in before you buy it.

Some pet shops specialize in exotic animals, and if you can find one in your area, that would probably be a good place to start your search. Because snake-keeping is unlike caring for other pet shop animals, you will want to take advantage of a knowledgeable staff.

Like any kind of retailer, from grocery stores to car dealers, pet shops vary in the way they maintain their stock. Some stores will have more spacious and well-maintained housing for their snakes than others. You will probably want to shop at as many stores as possible before you buy your snake. Your local herp society can be a good source of information as to the stores in your area with the best reputation. Naturally, you will want to purchase your snake from

ATTEND A HERP SHOW

An excellent source for a snake is one of the various "herp shows," which have sprung up all over the country. These are rather like large flea markets, where dealers and breeders from all over the country set up tables to sell herps of all sorts, as well as books and equipment. Many of these shows sell captive-bred reptiles exclusively, and the variety of different species and morphs available is stunning.

From a financial point of view, herp shows are a good deal, as you get to pay breeder prices without the shipping costs. You also have the advantage of being able to examine the snake for potential health problems, and to select an individual snake for a particular color pattern or sex. However, herp shows are generally limited to large cities, and unless a show is held near you (or unless you are willing to travel), you'll be out of luck.

a store with large, spotless housing conditions, in which the animals have a fair amount of room to move around. Because you will have a chance to examine the snakes up close, look for the snakes that seem the most alert, active and healthy. Snakes that are well-maintained from the start will make the best pets—they will be unstressed and will best adjust to captivity in your home. They are also more likely to remain in good health.

If you find a snake that you want to purchase at a pet store, you should take advantage of the opportunity to give the animal a thorough examination. The process of shipping and marketing reptiles is very stressful for the animals, and choosing a healthy snake at the start will help you to avoid problems later.

Always handle a snake before you buy it. This not only allows

you to judge how tame the snake is and how well it tolerates handling, but it also gives you the opportunity to closely examine it for any potential health problems. If you see small moving dark dots between the scales, particularly around the eyes and lips, reject the snake. These are mites, and they are highly contagious. If you bring home a snake with mites, you are likely to infect other snakes in your collection.

If the snake is audibly wheezing while it breathes, if it is breathing with its mouth open or if you see a fluid bubbling or dripping from the nose, it may have a respiratory infection, which is potentially life-threatening.

Carefully open the jaws and examine the inside of the mouth and throat. A healthy snake's mouth should be smooth and free of any foreign matter. If you see any red inflamed areas, an excess of

watery fluid or gray, cheesy matter, it is a sign that the snake is ill.

Snakes are remarkably muscular for their size, and a healthy animal will look and feel "solid." If the outline of the snake's backbone is visible, or if there are longitudinal folds or creases in the skin, it means that the snake hasn't been eating, which may be a sign of further trouble. Make sure that the snake you want has been eating regularly and willingly. It may not be a bad idea to ask that the pet shop staff feed the snake in front of you before you buy it.

Quarantine

It is always a good idea to quarantine any new snake that you bring home, particularly if you already have other snakes or reptiles. Quarantining is simply the process of isolating any new snake for a period of time so that any potential health problems can be seen and treated before the rest of your collection is exposed. Once a disease or parasite has been introduced into a large collection, it is very difficult to contain and control. Even if this will be your first snake, you should not skip the quarantine—it is necessary in order to watch for signs of any impending illness.

The quarantine tank should be designed for spartan functionality rather than attractiveness. A 10- or 20-gallon aquarium (depending on the size of the snake) with a locking screen lid, a newspaper substrate, a cardboard hide box, a water dish and a heating lamp will do. The quarantine tank should be in an entirely separate room from the rest of your collection. Whenever you service your snake cages, for feeding, cleaning and so on, you should always service the quarantine tank last, to prevent carrying pathogens or parasites from one cage to the next. It may also be helpful to keep the temperature in the quarantine tank a few degrees higher than normal.

Keep a close eye on your new snake for a period of at least thirty or sixty days, watching for signs of any potential health problems. You should also examine the snake's feces whenever they appear. A healthy snake's feces will appear somewhat similar to a large bird dropping. Over half of the feces might consist of a dry chalklike powder—these are uric acid crystals and they are perfectly normal. If the feces are loose or watery, if they begin to develop a greenish color or if the feces begin to take on a strong unpleasant odor, this may indicate the beginning of intestinal troubles. Also, if the feces contain a number of thin objects that look like pieces of thread, these are worms, and they will need to be eliminated by a vet.

If, at the end of the quarantine period, your snake is still healthy and feeding regularly, you can move it into its regular cage. After removing the snake, the entire quarantine cage and all of its contents should be emptied and cleaned with disinfectant (do *not* use any cleanser containing pine oil or pine tar—they are very toxic to snakes), followed by a thorough rinsing with a large amount of water. After replacing the hide box and the newspaper flooring, the quarantine tank is ready for the next new arrival.

At this point, we must introduce an unpleasant topic. It remains a fact that a large number of people buy a snake on impulse and, after they have had it for a while, lose interest in it. Most people who buy a young boa or python keep it for a year or two, until it gets too big to safely handle alone, and then attempt to sell it or give it away. Or perhaps you must relocate and your new home does not allow you to keep your snake. For all of these reasons, we must examine the options you have when, for whatever reason, you can no longer keep your snake.

One option that you can rule out right away is donating your snake to the local zoo, unless it is a very small zoo with a limited collection. Most of the larger zoos have strict policies against accepting any snakes from private owners, unless the snake is in exceptional health and is of a particularly rare species. Many people also have the mistaken idea that the larger a particular snake is, the more valuable it is, and the more anxious zoos would be to have it. The simple fact, however, is that no zoo is likely to take your unwanted snake. Boas and pythons breed so readily in

The quarantine tank need not be elaborate: The basics will do. (Amazon Tree Boa)

captivity that most zoos already have all they can handle.

Another option that should be ruled out (but, unfortunately, very many times is not) is releasing your snake to the wild. If your snake is a tropical species and you live in a temperate or subtropical area, the first snap of cold weather will kill it. On the other hand, if your snake is able to tolerate the local climate but is not a native species, it may not be able to find a suitable food source in the wild, and may not be able to compete for resources against the local populations of native reptiles. Conversely, and more dangerously, it may be able to compete too well, and may be able to establish a breeding population that will crowd out the local species.

In addition, by releasing a captive snake into the wild, even a native species, you may not only be endangering the life of that particular snake, but possibly the lives of every other snake in the area. Breeders, pet stores and herpers with large collections usually have

GIVE YOUR SNAKE TO A HERPETOLOGICAL SOCIETY

If you must give up your snake, one good place to go is your local herpetological society. Many of the larger herp societies have "adoption" programs that can place unwanted reptiles with new owners. The advantage to this will be that herp societies will only adopt out an animal to someone who can demonstrate that he or she is able to care for it properly. (Incidentally, herp adoption societies are good places to obtain reptiles, although the selection of species is usually limited to Burmese Pythons, Boa Constrictors and iguanas.)

a wide variety of snakes from different parts of the world. Because of this, captive reptiles are often exposed to foreign disease organisms that they would not normally encounter in the wild, and to which they have not developed any natural immunity. In many cases, these diseases will prove fatal. Some

infected snakes, however, will survive and harbor the alien germs inside their bodies. If these snakes are then released into the wild, they can become carriers that spread the foreign disease to other snakes they encounter, possibly touching off an epidemic that will decimate the local reptile populations.

Therefore, no one should *ever* abandon any pet snake into the wild. Not only is this thoughtless and dangerous, but in many jurisdictions, introducing nonnative wildlife is illegal and will be treated as a criminal offense. In fact, because of the danger of spreading disease and parasites, in some states it is illegal to release *any* captive animal, native or not, into the wild.

The final option, and the one that most people will turn to first, is to place an ad in the newspaper and sell your snake to someone else. If you choose to do this, be selective about who you sell the snake to—do not sell your snake to anybody who is not capable of providing proper care for it.

CHAPTER 6

Housing Your Snake

For the vast majority of snakes, the most practical and least expensive accommodation is an ordinary tropical fish aquarium. Any pet shop will have a number of different aquariums in several different shapes and sizes, and at very inexpensive prices.

Snake cages must be equipped with a hide box, heat source, water dish and suitable substrate.

Tank Size

The size of the tank you will need depends on the size of your snake. Most snakes are not very active, and spend most of their time curled up in a corner or inside their hide box. Therefore, a pet snake can get by with a surprisingly small cage. Small snakes, such as garters or green snakes, will have plenty of room in a standard 10-gallon aquarium. Medium sized snakes, such as corns, kings or young boids, can get by with a 10-gallon, but would do much better in a 20-gallon tank. Active snakes such as Racers or Bull Snakes will require the larger size tank. Larger boids will need at least a 55-gallon tank, but eventually they will outgrow even that, and will require a custom-built cage. As a general rule of thumb, a snake's

When it grows, this Florida King Snake hatchling will fare best in a 20-gallon tank.

YOUR TANK SHOULD GROW WITH YOUR SNAKE

Snakes, like all reptiles, grow continuously through life. Keeping your snake in a smaller tank will not, despite what is widely believed, limit its growth—it will only ensure that it becomes crowded and unhealthy. For this reason, it is important to have a cage that provides sufficient space for the snake. This should be done by continuously upgrading the size of the cage as the snake grows. Since snakes like to feel closed in and secure, placing a small or neonatal snake in a very large tank may actually stress it and cause health problems.

cage should be about two-thirds as long as the snake, and about half as wide as the snake's length.

Tank Shape

The shape of the tank is just as important as the size. For snakes that spend most of their time on the ground and do not climb very much, the tank does not need to be tall, but should have as much surface area at the bottom as possible. If your snake is a climber or arboreal tree-dweller, the tank should have as much vertical space as possible, to allow sufficient tree branches to be added for climbing.

Escape-Proof

No matter what size or shape tank you select, you will also need a securely locking lid. The plastic "hoods" with fluorescent lighting available for tropical fish aquariums are not suitable for keeping snakes because they offer an easy avenue of escape. Fortunately, many reptile supply houses sell pre-manufactured screened lids of the correct dimensions needed to fit the standard aquarium sizes. Unfortunately, there are no locking screen lids commercially available for the popular tall "hexagon" style aquariums, which would otherwise make very good cages for arboreal snakes.

Some very good accommodations for small- and medium- sized snakes can be made from the plastic

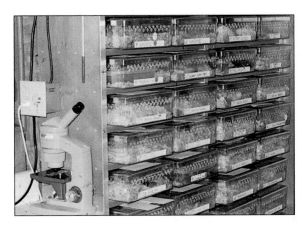

Modified plastic sweater boxes can make good homes for small snakes and hatchlings.

boxes sold in department stores for storing sweaters and other clothing. These are made from one piece of clear or translucent plastic, and have matching lids that snap into place. They come in a variety of sizes—from small boxes suitable for newborn snakes to large tubs that can house full-grown colubrids. A number of these boxes can be

Commercial cages with securely locking doors make good homes for captive snakes. ("Calico" Burmese Python)

neatly stacked atop each other in order to save space.

Some modifications need to be made to transform a sweater box into a suitable snake cage. A large number of airholes need to be added along the top and bottom on all four sides of the box to provide ventilation. The lid can also be perforated with air holes, but this is of no use if you intend to stack the finished boxes atop one another. These holes should be less than $1/4$ inch to prevent possible escapes. Snakes that prefer dry conditions should be given a large number of airholes, while humidity-loving snakes can be given fewer. Airholes can be produced using an electric drill, or by carefully heating a nail or screwdriver and melting a hole through the plastic (this process produces toxic fumes, and should be done in a well-ventilated area).

The lids on these boxes are, of course, not intended for keeping animals securely inside, and they are rather loose-fitting, providing an easy means of escape. Many snake keepers use heavy rubber bands to lock the lids into place. Because I keep a number of different reptiles and stack the boxes atop each other, my solution has been to place several boxes containing non-escape-prone species, such as frogs or salamanders, atop those containing active snakes.

Several herpetological supply companies sell specially made snake cages, consisting of a single piece of molded plastic or fiberglass and fitted with securely locking sliding-glass doors. These are intended for housing venomous snakes in the laboratory, and are usually fitted with a padlock. They are advertised as being "escape-proof," and if properly used they are. They are usually available in a variety of sizes.

Such specialized snake cages are rather expensive, but are absolutely necessary for those hobbyists who keep venomous snakes. They

Large collections can be kept in stackable cages that slide on rails.

should be securely locked at all times, and should be kept in an escape-proof room that is also locked all the time.

A number of reptile suppliers also have large racks, containing a number of separate cages, available for hobbyists. Each compartment consists of a plastic tub that slides into a rail, with the floor of the rack above it serving as the lid.

These arrangements are desirable for keeping a number of different species in a limited area of space. These racks usually have provisions for connecting electric basking lamps and heat tapes.

THE ESCAPE-PROOF ROOM

An escape-proof room is really a must for the owner of a venomous snake. If possible, the door to this room should have a window to allow a view of the cage without opening the door. The cages of all venomous snakes should be clearly labeled with a warning placard containing the species name, the name and address of the keeper and written directions for obtaining a supply of antivenin for that species.

Escape-proof plastic cages are commercially available in a variety of sizes. Although intended for keeping venomous snakes, they are suitable for any species.

Building Your Own

If you are at all handy with a hammer and screwdriver, building your own snake cage is not difficult. Basically, you will be building a large box with a glass front and a hinged lid.

Make the cage as big as practical. For most boids, the minimum size cage should be 6 feet long by 3 feet wide by 3 feet high. This can comfortably house a 10-foot snake, and can even hold a pair of such snakes (though it would be just a bit cramped). A bigger cage is more appropriate for a large snake. About a third of this area will be occupied by a water pan.

The sides and back of the cage can be made from quarter-inch plywood (if desired, wood with a better appearance, such as maple or other hardwood, can be used, but

this will increase the price substantially). The bottom of the tank must be very sturdy, and should be at least half-inch plywood to prevent it from sagging and bending under the weight of its occupants. The bottom of the cage should be elevated an inch or so above the surface upon which it sits, particularly if you will want to use an undertank heater or heat tape. This means that the cage will need legs of some sort. The best way to do this is to use three pieces of wood, 1 inch wide and 1 inch tall, that are as long as the completed cage will be wide. These should be fastened crosswise on the bottom of the cage, one at each end and one in the middle (to prevent the floor from sagging). If your cage is very long, you may need to use two crosspieces in the middle instead of one.

The back, sides and bottom of the cage should be cut to size and assembled first. Once this framework is done, you will need to fit a glass front to the cage. Some snake keepers use Plexiglas in their tanks. It is cheaper as well as easier to work with, but glass (particularly tempered glass) is much stronger and will stand up better to the pushing and shoving that your boid is likely to give it. It is also far less likely to become scratched or marred.

The best way to insert the glass is to build a frame consisting of three thin pieces of wood arranged to form a gutter, or slot. Insert the edges of the glass into this, and then screw them all together tightly so the glass is sandwiched into place. This arrangement prevents the edges of the glass from getting chipped and exposing your snake to sharp surfaces. It also prevents the snake from wedging its nose between the glass and the frame and possibly escaping.

The top of the cage is hinged so it can open and close to remove the snake and perform tasks such as feeding, cleaning and so on. The cage lid should consist of strong heavy screening that has been attached to a wooden frame that fits the cage snugly. The screening should be attached to the inside of the frame so the snake cannot push it outwards. It must be fastened very securely, or it will give way to

A large, homemade wooden cage is a necessity for such large snakes as boas or pythons.

Because snakes are escape artists, any cage must have a securely locking lid.

the snake's incessant pushing and prodding. The lid is attached by means of strong hinges at the back.

Such large homemade cages are particularly suitable for very large colubrids or smaller boid species. Homemade cages are not suitable for keeping any venomous species.

LOCK YOUR CAGE!

Some provision must be made for locking the cage. The best way is to arrange two eyehooks and eye-screws at both front corners of the tank, which can latch securely to prevent the lid from being lifted until they are undone. For added safety, these eyehooks should be of the type that have the little spring-loaded locks, which prevent them from falling out.

If, moreover, you have a large species such as a Boa Constrictor or a Burmese Python, even this cage will become too cramped in a few years. At that point, the best solution is to convert an entire room or a walk-in closet into a snake "cage."

A Snake Room

A suitable snake room must be chosen carefully. The room must be completely "snake-proofed." Breakable objects must be removed, as should any other possible sources of injury. Any potential escape routes such as heating ducts or window screens must be securely closed. The door to the room should be kept locked at all times, since a large boid may be strong enough to force it open and escape.

Cleanup and maintenance is much easier in the snake room if there is no carpeting, just a bare linoleum or hardwood floor. Also, heating the room becomes much easier if there are a number of large windows, preferably facing south to catch all of the sun's rays.

The same environmental needs must be met in the snake room as in an individual cage, i.e., the snake must be provided with heat, humidity and secure hiding places.

For a large boid, the entire snake room should be heated to around 85°F. In cooler weather, this may need to be accomplished with the

MAKE YOUR ROOM A BASKING HAVEN

The sunlight shining through the windows will also produce hot spots on the floor for basking (it is helpful to place a flat pile of rocks at these locations, where they will be warmed by the sun and help retain heat at night). Some provision must also be made for basking if there is no sun on any particular day, and this is best accomplished by focusing a large incandescent spotlight on a spot on the floor. This bulb should also be covered with a screen mesh so the snake cannot touch it. The temperature underneath any bask-ing spots should be around 100°F.

help of a small electric space heater, which should be placed in one corner of the room and screened off so the snake cannot physically touch it. If the windows in the room face south, sunlight will shine through nearly all day long and push the temperature into the mid 80s. This should produce a cycle of 85°F during the day, dropping to the high 70s at night.

All snakes require access to water, and boids in particular need large water pans in which they can submerge themselves completely and soak. The best way to provide this in a snake room is with a large kiddy swimming pool, the kind that is molded from a single piece of plastic. These are leakproof, unbreakable and are available in a variety of sizes and shapes. Placed in a corner of the snake room and surrounded by several piles of rocks, they provide soaking spots and a steady supply of drinking water. Large boids do not require hide boxes, but will curl themselves up in a favorite spot (usually near the basking spots) and stay there for days at a time.

Substrate

There are a wide variety of materials that can be used as the substrate for a snake cage. Each has its advantages and disadvantages, and each has its advocates and detractors among long-time snake keepers.

Newspaper is one of the best substrates for a snake's cage.

The most functional and least expensive lining is ordinary newspaper. This can be cut to size and placed in the cage, three or four layers thick, and can be quickly and easily cleaned when necessary simply by removing the old layers, throwing them away and replacing them with fresh sheets. Because newspaper is fairly absorbent and snake droppings do not contain much moisture, it is unlikely that there will be any problem with wastes soaking through to the cage floor. A newspaper substrate also makes it easy to spot ticks, mites and other parasites, as well as changes in the snake's feces. For this reason, all quarantine tanks should use newspaper as a substrate.

The disadvantage to a cage lined with newspaper, of course, is that it looks ugly and unnatural. If you don't mind the rather "sterile" appearance of such a cage, then newspaper substrate is plentiful, easily obtained and costs next to nothing.

Shredded tree bark, aspen wood chips (*not* wood shavings), cocoa bean shells and ground-up corn cobs are all commercially available for use as cage substrates, and all work well. If, however, you will be feeding your snake slimy prey such as frogs or worms, these substrates should be avoided, since pieces of material may stick to the prey and be swallowed by the snake, where they can cause serious problems.

SUBSTRATES TO AVOID

Substrates to definitely avoid are pine or cedar shavings, such as those used to keep mice or hamsters. The small particles of dust that are produced by these shavings are very irritating to a snake's lungs and mouth, and the volatile oils that are present (particularly in cedar) can be very toxic to snakes.

Tanks that contain a layer of soil with live plants as a substrate should also be avoided. They are difficult to clean and maintain, and the snakes will be continually digging up the soil and messing everything up. Some desert snakes, however, such as sand boas, can have a substrate consisting of several inches of clean sand.

This Everglades Rat Snake is being kept on a substrate of aspen wood chips.

Another disadvantage is that most of these substrate materials tend to get moldy and begin to rot if they get wet, either from the snake's droppings or from water splashed from the snake's dish.

Although ordinary aquarium gravel is a workable substrate, it does present the danger that it can be swallowed by the snake and pass on to the intestines, where it can cause severe blockages. Also, gravel is not very absorbent and will be difficult to keep clean unless it is either replaced often or is periodically removed, rinsed and dried.

Another popular substrate for captive snakes is a sheet of green artificial plastic material, known as "Astroturf," which lines the bottom of the cage like a carpet. This material comes in single sheets which are pre-sized to fit inside most standard aquariums.

Although Astroturf is attractive, relatively inexpensive and easy to use, it does present a problem. Being plastic, it is not absorbent and will quickly become messy with feces and spilled water, and so must be cleaned frequently. This entails dismantling all of the cage furnishings and removing the liner.

Hide Box

Because snakes are prey animals as well as predators, in the wild they spend most of their time safely hidden in a burrow or tree hollow. Captive snakes still have this instinctive fear of predators, and will need to feel physically secure and safe before they will become active. Snakes that are physically afraid quickly become stressed and will cower in a corner, refuse to eat and deteriorate until they die.

Captive snakes can be provided with a feeling of security by allowing them to use a "hide box." This is simply any sort of dark closed-in retreat where the snake can curl up and feel protected. Commercial hide boxes are available, molded from plastic, which look like natural rocks. A usable hide box can also be constructed inside the tank by using flat rocks to make a cave or shelter. Hollow logs or wooden boxes can also be used. An ordinary shoe box with a small hole cut in one side can serve as a temporary retreat.

To feel secure, the snake will prefer a small closed-in area, where it can coil up with its body touching all sides of the box. The hide

This Arizona Mountain King Snake is entering its hidebox. Most snakes need an enclosed area where they can feel secure.

box therefore need not be very large—a box measuring just 8 by 10 by 3 inches is big enough for a typical 5- or 6-foot snake. The entrance hole should be just wide enough for the snake to squeeze through.

If possible, the cage should have two hide boxes, one at the warm end and one at the cool end.

Heat

Because snakes cannot produce their own body heat, they must be provided with sufficient outside heat sources to maintain their body temperatures. Temperature control is therefore a crucial factor in successfully keeping snakes in captivity. Nearly every potential health problem snakes face can be directly traced to how well their temperature requirements are being met, and more captive snakes are killed by being kept at a too low temperature than by any other cause.

The best snake setups will provide a range of different temperatures, or a "temperature gradient," within the cage, allowing the snake to select the temperature that it wants by moving from warmer to cooler areas as needed.

A snake's cage should never be placed in direct sunlight in order to warm it. The infrared radiation will pass through the glass and be trapped inside, quickly raising the temperature to lethal levels.

COMMERCIAL HOT ROCKS ARE A POOR CHOICE

The electric "hot rocks" or "sizzle stones," which are often sold in pet stores, should not be used in any snake's cage. The cheaper ones usually do not have any means of controlling the heat output and thus no way to regulate the temperature. They are prone to malfunctions and will often overheat until they melt their wiring, presenting serious risk of burns to the snake. Because snakes have few nerve endings in their bellies, they will often sit unknowingly on an overheated hot rock, completely unaware that their skin is being severely burned.

Another problem is that sizzle stones do not warm the surrounding air very much and only heat one small spot in the tank. They do not provide a usable temperature gradient and do not allow the snake to effectively thermoregulate.

One of the best ways to provide a temperature gradient is through the use of artificial basking lights. For some reptiles, such as lizards, special full-spectrum lamps, like Vita-Lite, which duplicate natural sunlight, are necessary. Lizards use the ultraviolet wavelengths found in natural sunlight to manufacture vitamin D3, which is essential for proper bone development, in their skin. Without full-spectrum lighting, lizards will suffer from nutritional deficiencies and die.

Snakes, however, do not need any exposure to natural sunlight or ultraviolet wavelengths, and they do not require full-spectrum lighting in their cages. The best way to set up a snake's basking spot is to mount an ordinary incandescent light bulb with a reflector on the outside of the cage, at one corner of the screen lid. A flat pile of rocks or a heavy tree branch should be arranged directly below the bask-

ing spot. The basking light thus produces a localized "hot spot" for basking while leaving the far end of the tank relatively unheated. The temperature directly under the basking light should be in the range 95° to 100°F, while the temperature at the far end should be around 75° to 80°F to produce a suitable temperature gradient.

A very useful arrangement is to connect the basking light to an electrical timer to turn it on and off automatically. Although snakes do not have a pineal eye on the top of their head like lizards, they do have circadian rhythms and use light cues and changing photoperiods to regulate such processes as hibernation and breeding. For this reason all snakes should be provided with a natural light cycle. Most tropical snakes prefer a twelve-hour on, twelve-hour off light schedule, which mimics the length of the tropical day. Temperate snakes will

An incandescent floodlight can provide a safe basking spot for your snake.

One disadvantage of the sweater box cage is that it is impossible to set up a ceramic heater or basking light inside the cage. These accommodations must therefore use another type of heat source. Also, a few snakes do best if, in addition to a radiant heat source from above, they have an artificially warmed substrate to produce "belly heat," which aids in digestion. One solution to this problem is the undertank heater, which is constructed like a tiny heating pad or electric blanket. This is placed underneath a portion of the snake cage, where its heat diffuses through the floor of the tank and substrate to produce a hot spot. The heat tape is similar to the undertank heater, but takes the form of a wide electric ribbon, which fastens to the bottom of the tank. Some

also do well with a tropical light schedule; however, if it is intended to breed the snake, it is best to mimic the natural length of the day, making the photoperiod shorter in winter and longer in summer.

Recently, a new heating device has been introduced to snake hobbyists that has replaced incandescent basking lights in many collections. This is the ceramic heating element, which uses a mushroom-shaped heat emitter and a socket, that looks somewhat like a light bulb. These

ceramic heaters produce only heat, with no light. They can be connected to small thermostats for very precise heat control—which unfortunately also makes them much more expensive than ordinary basking lights. If a ceramic element is used to provide a temperature gradient, a source of light must be added to produce a photoperiod.

MONITOR THE CAGE TEMPERATURE

Every snake cage needs at least one thermometer to allow the temperature to be monitored. The stick-on thermometers used in tropical fish tanks work well and are inexpensive. Some snake keepers like to have two thermometers, one at the warm end and one at the cool end of the tank.

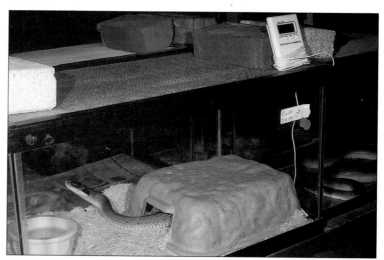

Make sure that a thermometer is always available to keep an eye on the temperature in your snake's cage.

brands of electric heat tape, however, will eventually crack and burn. They need to be checked often and replaced if necessary.

Cage Furniture

Climbing branches should be provided for all species that are arboreal or that like to occasionally climb. These must be strong and sturdy enough to support the weight of the snake without breaking, and long enough to provide ample climbing space. A number of plastic tree branches—some of them electrically heated—are for sale from dealers and distributors, but these should be avoided. Real tree branches are safe (with the exception of pine, spruce and other resinous trees), provided they are properly disinfected.

Boa Constrictors are largely arboreal and should be given heavy tree branches for climbing.

Clean tree branches thoroughly. (*Dryophis nasuta*)

A small flat pile of rocks at the bottom of the cage will help retain heat from the basking light, and also provide the snake with a rough surface upon which to shed its skin. Rocks, tree branches, bark and other such things must be carefully cleaned and disinfected before they are placed in the cage, as they may harbor parasites such as mites and ticks. To disinfect them, soak them overnight in a three percent solution of sodium hypochlorite (ordinary laundry bleach). Afterwards, thoroughly wash them in a large amount of water to rinse away any trace of the disinfectant.

Humidity

For most snakes, the humidity level that is found in the average home (about fifty-five percent) will be acceptable, and no other changes need be made. One of the most common problems in captive boids, however, is incomplete shedding of the skin, which is nearly always caused by a humidity level that is too low. One sure sign that the humidity level is too low is the appearance of "dents" or "dimples" in the clear scale covering the snake's eyes. Ball Pythons and Rainbow Boas in particular require quite high humidity levels.

High humidity should *not* be maintained by closing off the screen lid, as this will cut off the circulation of air within the tank. Because carbon dioxide is heavier than air, it tends to settle at the bottom inch or two of the tank, right where the snake lives. In a well-maintained tank, the heat

Pythons and boas need high humidity and will often soak in their water pan.

produced by the basking site causes stale air to become warmed and rise, where it exits from the screen lid. Meanwhile, fresh air enters to replace it. Thus, a circular current of air is maintained which constantly refreshes the tank. Sealing off the top of the tank to keep the humidity in, however, prevents this air cycle, and can cause health problems for the snake.

The best way to maintain high humidity is to place a large water pan (or even several pans if necessary) inside the tank. Species that require high humidity should also be sprayed daily with a plant mister, using ordinary warm tap water. Another technique which works well is the "moss box." This can be produced quickly by inverting a closed, lidded plastic box, with a hole cut into one end as an entrance, which has been packed with damp moss or a damp towel. The snake will use this as a hide box. The moss box can produce local humidity levels as high as ninety percent, and virtually guarantees a complete shed. The moss or towel will have to be dampened again periodically as it dries out.

CHAPTER 7

Handling Your Snake

All snake keepers must learn how to properly handle snakes because it will be necessary to do so in order to perform tasks such as cleaning the cage and visiting the vet. Most colubrids do not present any special difficulties in handling,

Most snakes don't object to being handled, as long as things don't get too rough.

as long as the snake has been tamed and is accustomed to people.

Handling a big boid, however, is a job that should not be attempted by any solitary person. A 15-foot python can easily weigh over 75 pounds, and if a snake that size becomes aggressive, there is not much you will be able to do to stop it by yourself.

Every time a snake attack occurs, the consequences for herpetoculturalists are severe. The fear and misunderstanding that surrounds reptiles (and their keepers) is increased, authorities become more likely to pass uninformed laws in an attempt to "do something about the problem," and the efforts of responsible herpers to educate the public about these animals are undermined and crippled.

The problem of fatalities and attacks by captive snakes is very small, but is growing steadily. Between the years 1978 and 1988, according to the American Federation of Herpetoculturalists, there were four reported instances of amateur keepers killed by their snakes, and only one of these involved a Burmese Python (the others involved Reticulated Pythons). A check of the *New York Times* index between 1970 and 1992 turned up only one report of a fatality involving a captive python. In the five years since then, however, at least two deaths and a number of attacks have been reported, nearly all involving Burmese Pythons. This appears to be a direct result of the growing popularity of captive Burms. Inexperienced snake keepers and large, potentially aggressive constrictors make a particularly dangerous combination. The sad fact that many thousands of hatch-

ling Burmese Pythons have been purchased in the pet trade—most of them by people who are inexperienced and unprepared to deal with them once they reach a large size—means that the number of incidents involving these snakes will only increase in the future. Everyone who has or who is considering obtaining one of the large constrictors, therefore, must be aware of all the safety precautions that are necessary to keep these snakes, and must practice all of these safeguards until they become second nature.

Constricting Snakes

Only five species of constricting snakes get large enough to pose a serious threat to human life. These are the Reticulated Python, the Amethystine Python, the Green Anaconda, the Indian Python (the Burmese Python is a subspecies of

---

CAUTION *IS* REQUIRED

In 1996, a 19-year-old man was killed in New York City while preparing to feed his 13-foot Burmese Python. In January 1994, a 6-foot python escaped from its owner in Santa Rosa, California, by crawling down the toilet, causing a panic among residents in the apartment building. In July 1993, a 15-year-old boy in Commerce City, Colorado, was attacked and killed by an 11-foot Burmese Python. In June 1991, a 9-year-old boy in Long Beach, California, was bitten on the foot and coiled by a 12-foot pet python. In August 1984, a large python escaped its cage in Solvay, New York, causing a panic for nine days before it was found in the ceiling. In November 1980, a 7-month old girl in Dallas was killed when the family's 8-foot python escaped from its cage and crawled into the crib, smothering the infant.

the Indian) and the African Rock Python. Only two of these, the Burmese and the Reticulated, are commonly found in the pet trade. The Reticulated Python can reach a maximum length of over 30 feet; the Burmese Python can reach lengths of up to 20 feet. The common Boa Constrictor has never been demonstrated to have killed a human being, but it can reach adult lengths near 10 feet and can sometimes be difficult and unsafe to handle. For purposes of this discussion, then, any constricting snake that reaches an adult size of 8 feet or more should be considered potentially dangerous.

Because Burmese Pythons are tough and undemanding snakes, and are reliable feeders, they are sometimes recommended as "good snakes for beginners." The fact is, however, that they are large and powerful animals that grow quickly, reaching a potentially-dangerous size of 8 to 10 feet and a weight of 50 pounds within two years. Some people have attempted to control the snake's growth by feeding it only a limited amount of food—a practice that is harmful to the health of the animal, and also produces a snake that is always hungry and sometimes aggressive. Despite what you may hear, Burms are not suitable for beginners, and should not be kept until you have a few years of snake-keeping experience to your credit.

KEEP YOUR HOUSEGUESTS AND YOUR FAMILY SAFE

Under absolutely no circumstances should a large constrictor ever be allowed to free roam in a room that is occupied by humans. Even though a snake may have been around humans since its birth, it is still a wild animal, with all its natural behaviors and instincts intact. If, for whatever reason, the snake suddenly feels threatened, or if it momentarily confuses its keepers with food, it can attack suddenly and unpredictably.

The first priority in keeping large constrictors is to make sure they are under strict control at all times. Housing for a big boid is a much more complicated affair than it is for a corn or king snake; it is more akin to the requirements for keeping a venomous snake. The enclosure for a boa or python must be spacious and extraordinarily strong. Large snakes are immensely powerful and can push their way out of all but the strongest cages. The cage should be locked at all times and, if possible, should itself be within an escape-proof room that is also locked. Very large snakes can be kept in a room of their own, or a walk-in closet that has been converted into a snake cage. These must be kept securely locked at all times. Be aware that boas and pythons can push their way through windows or screens.

A number of rules must be followed in order to safely handle large constrictor snakes. While most boas and pythons are not usually aggressive, they are potentially lethal animals whose power and strength must be respected. No one should ever attempt to handle a large snake (8 feet or more) by himself. This includes even such routine tasks as changing the water or cleaning the cage. A rough guide recommended by most experienced snake keepers is to have one handler for every 5 feet of snake (every 3 feet is suggested for nervous or aggressive species such as Reticulated Pythons or Anacondas).

When handling a large constrictor, never allow any of the coils to

Do not allow constrictors to wrap themselves around your neck or shoulders.

wrap around your torso or your neck. Boas and pythons are extremely powerful animals, and can cause problems for you even if they are not attempting to constrict, simply by hanging on. If startled or frightened, the snake's reaction will be to tighten its grip—which can present immediate and serious problems if the snake has you coiled in a vulnerable spot.

Feeding time is an especially dangerous moment to be near a large constrictor snake. Although Burmese Pythons are not aggressive animals, they are very eager feeders, and will often strike and constrict potential prey that is obviously too big for them to swallow. Because they have poor vision, snakes distinguish prey almost entirely by scent, and can easily confuse prey and keeper. As far as the snake is concerned, if you are moving and have the odor of food on or near you, you are probably food. The feeding response is largely reflexive, and the snake, if it thinks you are a potential meal, will instinctively constrict and kill you before realizing that you are too big to swallow. By the time the snake realizes its error, it will be too late for you. Nearly all fatal accidents involving large constrictors are the result of unsafe feeding procedures, known to experienced snakers as "Stupid Feeding Errors" (SFEs).

For this reason, great care should be taken to avoid confusing the snake during feeding time. Do not ever approach a large constrictor after having handled any potential prey animal (live or dead) or if any potential prey animal is in the area. Potential prey animals that may trigger a feeding response include virtually any warm-blooded creature, such as dogs, cats, rodents, birds and rabbits. In general, live prey animals should be avoided, and large snakes should be fed pre-killed prey exclusively. Dead prey animals intended as food should never be handled with the bare hands. Instead, keepers should use tongs or long-handled forceps to offer prey animals from a safe distance. It is a good idea to wash your hands thoroughly with soap before handling a large constrictor, to remove any trace of prey scent, and to never attempt to handle a large snake that is in a feeding mood.

Some experienced snake keepers suggest a routine of moving your snake to a different cage for feeding, under the belief that if the snake is always fed in the same cage in which it lives, it will learn to associate the opening of the cage door with food, and may go into "hunting mode" whenever the cage is opened, striking at the keeper by mistake. In my experience, however, this has never been a problem. Because the cage door must be opened regularly for such nonfeed-

START SNAKE-KEEPING WITH A YOUNG SNAKE

Potentially dangerous species of snakes should be obtained when they are still very young. This allows the keeper and the snake to learn each other's habits and idiosyncrasies. At this stage, the keeper can learn to handle the snake and avoid Stupid Feeding Errors while risking nothing more serious than a few bites and puncture wounds. Snakes that are regularly and properly handled when young are less apt to be nervous and defensive when older.

ing tasks as cleaning and watering, most snakes will not come to associate cage-opening with feeding. In addition, the "feed in another cage" strategy is not workable for very large constrictors, who should not be handled more than necessary and definitely not when they are hungry. Mistaken attacks on the part of the snake can usually be avoided if you use long-handled tongs for feeding and do not allow prey scent to get on you or your clothing.

Even if you do not intend to feed the snake, you should carefully watch its body language if you must go near it. If the snake begins to approach you stealthily, with tongue flickering and its eyes riveted on you, it is looking for prey and may be potentially aggressive. If, on the other hand, it draws back and pulls its neck in an S-shape, while hissing or breathing heavily, it is afraid and may strike at you in self-defense. Most large snakes will only use their coils to constrict a potential food item—in self-defense, they will strike with the teeth in the manner typical of all snakes. A bite from a large boid is an intensely painful affair, however, and is nothing to trifle with. Moreover, once the snake has struck, it may be enticed into a feeding response and begin to throw coils around you, especially if you begin to struggle.

Highly publicized attacks by large snakes usually lead to a flood of local regulations and ordinances that restrict ownership of these animals. Many municipalities have already banned possession of any snake larger than 8 or 10 feet. A few have banned ownership of any boa or python species, no matter what adult size it reaches. My former home, the city of Allentown, Pennsylvania, outlaws the possession of any "constricting snake"— which makes even such harmless colubrids as king snakes and corn snakes technically illegal. The problem of attacks by captive snakes should, however, be kept in perspective. Of the tens of thousands of large constrictors maintained in captivity, only a handful have ever attacked their owners. A much higher number of people are killed by Rottweilers every year than have ever been killed by large pet snakes. While most large constrictors are not usually aggressive, they are potentially lethal animals whose power and strength must be respected, and they must be handled cautiously and carefully. Even a single unthinking error can lead to tragedy. This is doubly true of venomous or "hot" snakes, which are often aggressive in their defensive efforts and can kill with a single bite.

Venomous Snakes

Nobody should ever attempt to handle any venomous snake without extensive training with an experienced snake keeper. To safely handle venomous snakes, you will need a tempered steel snake hook, which can be purchased from a number of suppliers and dealers. These work best for slow, heavy-bodied snakes such as vipers and rattlers. For active and fast snakes such as cobras, the snake hook must be rejected in favor of "tongs" or "grab sticks," which are long-handled devices that enable the user to squeeze a hand grip and close a pair of jaws around the snake. Another useful device is the "catch box," an escape-proof enclosure with a doorway that can be opened and closed from outside the main tank. Once the venomous snake has entered the catch box, it can be closed and safely lifted out

RULES FOR CONSTRICTING SNAKE OWNERS

In short, a number of simple but vital rules can be laid out for keeping a large boa or python:

1. Never handle a large snake alone.

2. Never allow the scent of a prey animal to get on or near you when handling a large snake.

3. Never allow a large snake to free roam in a room occupied by humans.

4. Always keep your large snake in a securely locked escape-proof enclosure, accessible only by you.

If these rules are not followed, the results can be tragic. In the New York case cited earlier, for example, several of the basic safety rules were broken, and the keeper paid for his mistake with his life. According to published reports, the 19-year-old snake keeper took his 13-foot Burmese Python across the street to buy a live chicken for feeding. When he returned to his apartment, he put the snake on the floor in the hallway, opened the door, and took the box containing the chicken into the room. As he stepped back outside, the snake, seeing the movement and catching the scent of live prey, apparently mistook its owner for a chicken and struck at him, constricting and killing him. Alone, the victim was unable to escape the snake's coils.

to allow the keeper to perform routine cage maintenance. These safety precautions should always be used even if your snake has been surgically devenomed.

Surprisingly enough, statistics demonstrate that the majority of people who are bitten by a venomous snake are intoxicated at the time. Intoxicated snake handlers are inclined to take risks and commit stupid errors that they would never do while sober. It should go without saying that potentially dangerous snakes should *never* be handled after one has consumed any amount of alcoholic beverage.

Extreme caution is the rule for handling a viper. (White-Lipped Tree Viper)

Traditional Captive Snakes

The colubrids and the smaller boids do not present the safety dangers that large constrictors or hot snakes do. If your snake is captive-bred and has been handled properly by the breeder and dealer,

When picking up a snake, always support the body weight with one hand and control the head with the other.

it is probably already at least somewhat tamed, does not view humans as potential threats and will seldom attempt to bite. Sometimes, however, commercial breeders and dealers do not have the time to properly handle every snake, and your snake, particularly if it is young, may not yet be accustomed to regular handling. If this is the case, you will have to take on the

task of taming the snake yourself.

The only way to accustom a snake to handling is to handle it. Most often, the toughest part of handling a snake is getting it out of the cage. The cage, and particularly the hide box, is where your snake feels safe and secure, and by reaching in, you are intruding into its territory and acting in a threatening manner towards it. Naturally, unless it has already learned that humans are not a threat, it will react defensively.

When approaching a snake that has not yet been tamed, you must move calmly and deliberately. Quick motions and sudden grabs are the actions of a predator, and if you approach a snake in that manner, you are very likely to be bitten. Move slowly and allow the snake to see your intentions.

Reach into the tank and gently grasp the snake by the neck, just behind the jaws. This allows you to control the head and prevent the snake from biting. You will be much more successful at this if you approach the snake from as low as possible. Most predators of snakes, such as hawks, attack from above, and the sight of a looming shape coming down at it may be enough to provoke defensive behaviors in the snake. (For this reason, snake cages that open from the front, allowing you to reach in along the floor, may be preferable to cages that open at the top.)

To lift the snake out, gently reach under its body with the other hand. You should not be lifting the snake out by its head; this can cause it to thrash around and severely injure itself. When the snake is properly held, the grip on the head should be just tight enough to prevent the snake from turning and biting, while your other hand supports most of the snake's weight.

At this point, the snake may begin writhing vigorously, and may expel the contents of its anal glands. This is a normal defensive reaction and is to be expected. The important thing to keep in mind is, no matter how messy and unpleasant the snake may become, *do not* put it down yet. If you hurriedly put the snake back into its cage every time it sprays you, it will

WHEN YOU MUST TAKE YOUR SNAKE OUT OF THE HOUSE

On occasion, it may become necessary to transport a snake over some distance, if, for example, you are using the snake for an educational lecture or if it needs to see a vet.

The very best way to transport a snake any distance is to bag it securely. Special purpose snake bags can be ordered from many reptile supply houses, but they can be quickly and effectively improvised using an ordinary pillow case, the larger the better. The proper use of a snake bag is simplicity itself. Simply lower the snake into the bag, twist the top half of the bag tightly and tie a loose overhand knot. Take special care that your snake is not trying to climb out of the top of the bag when you tie it, or you will

wring its neck quite effectively. If you hold the bag above the knot and keep it away from your legs and body, you can safely carry any snake.

Don't worry about the snake smothering. The weave in most cloth pillowcases is not airtight, and your snake will receive plenty of air inside the bag. It is also best to use dark cloth for the snake bag, as this keeps it dark inside the bag, which will help to calm the snake.

When transporting a snake bag, be careful that nobody steps or sits on it. And if you are going by car, make sure that the air temperature inside the car during the trip is high enough for your snake.

quickly learn that this trick will get you to leave it alone. Instead, gently restrain the snake's head with one hand while supporting its weight with the other, and allow the snake to wrap its tail around your arm or wrist. After a few minutes, no matter how agitated the snake is, it will tire and calm down. Once it is lying still, it is time to put it back.

If you continue to handle the snake for about 15 or 20 minutes every day, it will soon learn that you are not a threat, and will lose some of its defensiveness. Within a

A snake bag can be used to securely transport even aggressive snakes.

short time, the snake will become accustomed to being handled, and you will be able to release its head and allow it to go where it wants. Keep in mind that even tame snakes do not like being touched on the face or head.

In general, snakes are shy and nonaggressive creatures that tame quickly and easily. Nevertheless, like any other animal, snakes will defend themselves if they feel threatened, and it is not impossible that you will be bitten at least once if you keep snakes for any length of time.

Just prior to shedding, the snake's eyes will become cloudy and bluish. It should not be handled during this time. (Eastern Diamondback Rattlesnake)

Avoiding Bites

Usually, when a snake bites in self-defense, it will immediately release you and recoil for another strike. Sometimes, however, the snake's backwards-pointing teeth can become so deeply embedded that the snake cannot easily get them out. If this happens, do *not* try to pull or pry the snake off, or you will be

The Green Tree Python has long teeth and should be handled with care.

sorry. Instead, you should grasp the snake firmly behind the jaws and push his head *forward,* towards the nose, to disengage the teeth. After this, you may have to gently pry the snake's nose to get him to release you. If the snake has mistaken you for food, it may be quite reluctant to let go until it realizes its mistake. If necessary, a quick dunking in

some ice cold water will convince the snake to find easier prey.

Once you have the snake off you, wash the wound with some soap and water and then forget about it. Because many snakes, including water snakes and garters, have mild anticoagulants in their saliva, the wound might bleed freely for several minutes, However, unless you have been bitten by a big boid (they can cause severe lacerations that may even require stitches), there is not much to worry about.

Being bitten by a venomous species is, of course, another matter entirely. If you have been envenomated by a viper or elapid, you will need antivenin treatments right away. Keepers who maintain venomous species should always have ready access to a supply of antivenin and a plan for getting both themselves and the antivenin to the nearest hospital in case they are bitten. There is a popular saying among snake keepers: "The best equipment for treating a venomous snakebite is a set of car keys." Commercial "venom extractors" are also available, which, if used within minutes of the bite, can remove a significant portion of the venom through the puncture wounds made by the fangs.

Venomous snakes should never be handled alone, even during routine tasks such as changing the water in the cage. You will need someone to contain the snake and render aid if an accident occurs. It should go without saying that no venomous snake should ever be taken out in public except to preannounced, properly planned shows or talks.

We now come to the question of taking your nonvenomous snake out in public—a matter of some controversy among amateur snake keepers. Although herpers view their animals as interesting and fascinating creatures, most other people do not. Few animals on earth cause as much sheer irrational terror in so many people as do snakes. While ophidiophobia, or fear of snakes, may seem silly to you, it certainly is not silly to people who suffer from it. There are several good reasons why no snake keeper should ever take any snake to parks or other public areas. People do have the right to walk down the street or in the park without being suddenly confronted with a large terrifying animal (whether or not such terror is justified is quite beside the point). While you may feel as if you are doing a good deed

by "educating people," you should remember that it is up to other people, not you, to decide when and where (or even if) they want to confront their fear of snakes. The only place that people should see snakes is at preannounced talks or shows, where they are given advance warning and where those who prefer not to see them have the opportunity to leave or turn away.

Sometimes, unthinking snake owners have ended up causing enormous problems for all of their local fellow snake hobbyists. All it takes is one person to react negatively to the snake, and local officials may be induced to do something about the "danger"—usually by passing local ordinances regulating or banning the possession of snakes. Such a scenario is even more likely if, for whatever reason and under whatever circumstances, your snake should happen to bite someone. Incidents involving large snakes will almost certainly make newspaper headlines throughout the area (and are often picked up by the wire services and sent nationwide). The unfavorable publicity caused by irresponsible people does nothing to help the hobby of snake-keeping.

In nearly every state, snakes will be considered under the same liability laws as those that pertain to dogs. This means that the owner will be legally liable for any and all actions taken by the snake—

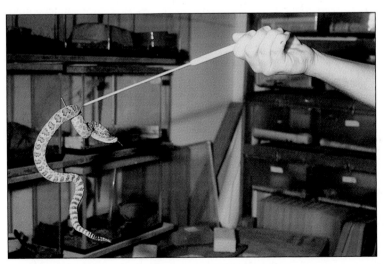

A snake hook should be used to handle venomous or aggressive snakes.

including liability for any damages. If a child approaches your snake while you have it out in public and is bitten, you may be liable for all the medical expenses. You may also be liable for punitive damages, pain and suffering, or emotional distress to the victim. In a case that quickly became famous among snake keepers, a python owner was sued and found liable for damages because, while he was carrying the snake around in a public place, a person with acute fear of snakes saw it, became extremely distressed and had a heart attack.

In addition to the problems it can cause you, taking your snake for a walk may also endanger the health of the snake. Unlike mammals, snakes cannot sweat to cool themselves off, and high temperatures and direct sunlight can quickly cause overheating, which can lead to permanent brain damage or death.

Thus, the considered opinion of most experienced snake keepers is— don't take your snake out in public.

CHAPTER 8

Feeding Your Snake

Although snakes as a group will prey on a large variety of food animals, ranging from rodents to birds to frogs to other snakes, nearly all captive snakes will live happily on a diet of whole mice. Whole mice, including the viscera and stomach contents, are a nutritionally complete diet for all snakes that will eat them. No other vitamin supplements or dietary additions are needed. Some snakes will accept other readily-available foods, such as earthworms or fish, and these are also acceptable diets if they consist of fresh, whole animals, with bones and viscera included.

The large boids present some feeding problems that other species do not. A big boa or python requires food of at least rat size, and may even need larger prey such as rabbits or chickens.

In warm-blooded animals such as humans, approximately three-fourths of the food we eat goes directly toward producing metabolic body heat. Snakes, however, as we have seen, are ectotherms and do not produce their own body heat. They therefore do not need to devote large amounts of food to maintaining their metabolism, and a typical snake can get by on less than one-fifth the amount of food

Because snakes have low metabolic rates, they do not need to eat as often as warm-blooded animals. (Blackhead Python eating a rat)

that would be required by a similarly sized mammal. Also, a snake's digestive system is much more efficient than a mammal's, ensuring that the snake gets more food value per unit of food that it eats.

For these reasons, snakes do not require a large amount of food to be kept healthy. Most medium-sized rodent-eaters, such as corn

A healthy snake needs only one good meal every two weeks. (ribbon snake eating a Cuban Tree Frog)

snakes and king snakes, will grow steadily on a diet of one properly sized mouse every two weeks. (A "properly sized" food animal is one that is slightly larger than the widest girth of the snake.) Larger snakes may require larger food animals, such as rats, and large boids may need to be fed chickens or rabbits, but they are also capable of thriving on one meal every two or three weeks. Snakes that consume cold-blooded prey, such as fish or earthworms, may need to be fed a bit more often, once every six or seven days. And any snake, if fed an exceptionally large meal, may be able to go for a month or two before it needs to eat again.

In most circumstances, snakes can fast for incredibly long times. If you are going on vacation and

LIVE PREY IS NOT NECESSARY

There is a common misperception among people, even among many snake hobbyists, that snakes must have live prey. This is not usually true. Although your snake may prefer to eat live prey, this is not at all necessary. In fact, it is best *not* to feed your captive snakes live prey at all.

need to leave your snake behind for a month or so, it will be fine so long as you feed it a good meal before you leave. In fact, some snakes have gone as long as a year without eating any food whatsoever, but such extended fasts are very stressful for the snake. Although keeping your snake well-fed is an important part of maintaining its health, there is no harm in occasionally skipping one or two regular feedings.

Snakes in the wild will eat live prey, but they do not need to. Some snakes, such as garter snakes, water snakes and green snakes, eat prey animals such as fish, earthworms, insects or frogs, which are defenseless and cannot cause any damage to the snake. In these cases, the snakes do not even bother to kill their prey before they eat it; they simply seize it in their jaws and proceed to swallow it alive. Rodent-eaters, however, are dealing with prey that is potentially lethal, and they must kill their food before they can swallow it.

Constricting Snakes

Most snakes kept as pets are constrictors. In this method of killing prey, the snake will seize the animal in its jaws and very quickly wrap its body into a series of coils that envelop the prey, squeezing it with powerful muscles. Contrary to what many people believe, a constricting snake does not crush its prey to death, or even break any of the prey animal's bones; rather, the snake will tighten its coils every time the prey animal exhales, which squeezes the prey's chest tighter and tighter until it can no longer inhale and smothers (the constricting action also compresses the heart and interferes with the flow of blood through the body).

Once the prey animal is dead, the snake will use its tongue to examine it until it finds the head, and will then proceed to swallow the prey nose-first.

Venomous Snakes

Venomous snakes are not constrictors, but depend solely on their venom to subdue and kill prey. Venomous snakes that feed on harmless food, such as lizards or birds, usually strike and hang on until the prey is unconscious. Rodent-eaters cannot take the risk of being severely bitten, and thus are more likely to strike and release the prey. In a few minutes, after the venom has taken effect, the snake will track it by scent until it finds the dead body, which will then be swallowed. (Devenomed snakes must, of course, be fed pre-killed

A venomous snake can kill its prey with venom alone. (Ceylon Tree Viper)

prey exclusively, because they have no method of killing live food.)

There are several reasons why it is best for the hobbyist to feed all of his captives pre-killed prey exclusively, but the most important is for the safety of the snake. If, for whatever reason, the snake decides that it does not want to eat a live food animal, the prey animal is very capable of turning on the snake and killing it. Even if the snake is willing to feed, it will occasionally make slight mistakes in its attack—it may grab the rodent by the wrong end, or it may miss in its initial strike, and even a slight opening is enough for the mouse to counterattack. Live mice will fight for their lives when they are seized, and will bite, kick and scratch for as long as they can.

Even venomous snakes can usually be taught to accept pre-killed prey. However, because the venom acts to break down the tissues of the prey, aiding in digestion,

pre-killed prey for venomous species should be specially treated. Such food should be frozen and thawed a number of times, causing ice crystals to appear in the prey animal's tissues and breaking open the cell walls, allowing the snake to digest it more effectively.

Pre-killed Food

In most cases, feeding pre-killed food to a snake is a simple matter of dropping a dead mouse or other rodent into the cage and waiting until nature takes its course. When feeding a snake, however, particularly an aggressive snake or one that may be potentially dangerous, such as a large constrictor, there are several rules and precautions which must be kept in mind.

Dead prey animals should never be handled with the bare hands. Snakes hunt almost entirely by scent, and if the scent of a prey animal is in the air or on the keeper's

Always use forceps to present pre-killed prey to a snake.

THAW YOUR FROZEN MICE

If you are using frozen mice, be certain that the mouse is thawed thoroughly. If the center of the mouse is still frozen when the snake swallows it, it can produce severe intestinal distress that might even kill the snake. A good way to thaw a frozen mouse is to place it in a Ziplock plastic bag, and then place this in a pan of hot water for about fifteen minutes. Most snakes will prefer to eat in the dark, just after nightfall, and many snakes will drag their prey into their hide box before swallowing it. Some individuals will prefer to leave their prey sit for a few hours before they will eat it. A few snakes may prefer to constrict the dead prey first (apparently to make sure it is dead). Others will simply grab it and start swallowing.

hands, the snake may attack and bite the keeper by mistake.

Some snakes, however, may prefer their prey to be moving before they will take it, and this can be accomplished with a pair of long-handled tongs or forceps. Hold the mouse by the tail with your tongs and dangle it gently a few inches from the snake's face. After a few exploratory tongue flicks, your snake will seize the food and go through the motions of constricting it. If your snake seems reluctant to feed, lightly touching the food item to

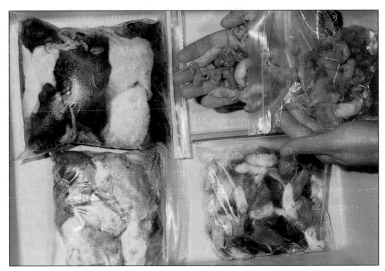

Pre-killed frozen and thawed rodents make a good staple food for most snakes. Be sure the rodents are completely thawed before feeding.

are usually enough to trigger the feeding response even in stubborn snakes. Eventually, the snake will come to accept pre-killed prey without any problem.

An unfortunate lesson from my own snake experiences may help to drive home and emphasize the point about feeding live prey animals. When I first began keeping snakes, I had a beautiful, young, 5-foot Reticulated Python who, unlike most members of her species, was calm and tractable and easy to handle. One day, I opened her cage and plopped a nice, fat, live hamster inside to feed her, as I had done routinely at least several dozen times before. The python promptly seized the hamster by the side of its body, but failed to get a good grip and hesitated for barely a moment. Whereupon, in an instant, the hamster, with its last bit of energy before it went into shock, turned and bit the snake squarely in the skull. Within seconds, both were dead. Ever since,

the snake's nose may be enough to trigger the feeding response. If your snake repeatedly strikes at the mouse and then quickly withdraws, it means he is not hungry. Try again in a day or so.

In very rare instances, you may obtain a snake that refuses to eat pre-killed food. This is unusual with captive-bred specimens, as most breeders prefer to feed pre-killed food to their snakes. It is more likely that a snake that refuses pre-killed food is wild-caught. In any case, the snake can almost always be trained to eventually accept dead food animals. One way to do this is to feed a live animal and, immediately afterwards, while the snake is still in an eating mood, place a pre-killed prey animal near its jaws until it seizes it

and begins swallowing. Next, use the "jiggling on a forceps" method to make the snake think the prey is live. In order to make pre-killed, nonmoving food more appealing, one good trick is to peel a bit of skin from the top of the rodent's nose, allowing a bit of blood and fluid to leak out. These body fluids are a powerful lure for snakes and

Most breeders start their captive-bred snakes off with pre-killed food. This young snake is getting a "pinkie" or baby mouse.

all of my snakes get pre-killed prey exclusively. Please learn from my mistake, and do not ever feed your snakes live prey animals.

If you are nevertheless going to feed live prey animals to your snakes, you have two basic choices for obtaining your food—you can either buy live animals from a pet store or you can raise your own.

Raising and breeding small mammals such as mice, rats or rabbits is beyond the scope of this book; there are numerous books available that explain the process. However, my experience is that raising one's own snake food is a time-consuming, smelly and tedious task that is best avoided. If you absolutely must feed your snakes live food (and remember, my firm advice is that you do *not*), the easiest way to do this is to drive to the pet store and pick up a mouse, rat or rabbit whenever your snake is hungry. Your live rodent will have a higher food value for the snake if you feed it several meals before using it as food.

Feeding your pet snake pre-killed food exclusively is not only much safer for the snake but is much easier logistically for the keeper (and is less expensive, as well). A number of reptile supply houses sell frozen mice, rabbits and other snake food in bulk and usually at less than half the price that live prey animals would cost in a pet store. Or if you have mice in

your basement and set out traps for them, consider this a blessing in disguise. When removed from the trap and frozen hard for a few weeks, those household pests can become your snake's next meal.

Besides price, pre-killed frozen snake food has a number of other advantages for the hobbyist. The freezing process will have killed most of the internal and external parasites that may be present in the food animal, thus reducing the possibility of exposing your snake to mites or worms. Frozen food can also be easily and conveniently stored until needed. The snake keeper can buy several months' supply of mice at one time and stack them neatly in the freezer until he needs them. Also, if a snake is not hungry and refuses to eat a live rodent, the keeper is faced with the task of keeping the food animal somewhere until the snake is ready for it. A frozen and thawed mouse, however, can simply be popped into the refrigerator for a few days until it is needed.

If pre-killed frozen rodents are not available, you will have no choice but to buy a live food animal and pre-kill it before presenting it to the snake. Although it is a morbid and unpleasant topic, we need to discuss the best way to humanely kill a food animal before it can be fed to your snake.

The most popular way of dispatching a rodent is to place it on a

table or other hard surface, and lay a pencil across the back of its neck, near the base of the skull. Press gently but firmly and pin the rodent's head to the table (this won't cause any pain, but the rodent will not like it nevertheless). Then, in one swift motion, pull the rodent's tail sharply and firmly. This has the effect of quickly pushing the skull off the end of the vertebrae, dislocating the spine and causing an instant painless death. This is nearly the unanimous choice of experienced snake keepers.

Having said that, I must now confess that I've never been able to get the knack of this trick and have botched it nearly every time I've tried it. Therefore, in order to cause as little suffering as possible, I have adopted a method that, while it sounds awful, produces a quick and painless death and is, at least for me, virtually foolproof. My method

EUTHANIZING YOUR SNAKE'S FOOD

Some snake keepers like to euthanize food animals by placing them in a sealed jar and filling it with carbon dioxide fumes from a pressurized canister. While this method takes several minutes, it is painless for the animal and is harmless to the snake that eats it. It does, however, require specialized equipment that may be somewhat expensive to obtain.

After a large meal, your snake will have a noticeable bulge where the stomach and skin have expanded to hold the prey.

consists of placing the rodent in a plastic or cloth bag, grasping it by the top and whirling it in a circle once or twice to build up some momentum, and them bringing it down quickly and firmly on a table-top. The rodent is quite literally dead before it knows what hit him.

On to a more pleasant topic. All snakes, even those from the most arid of desert regions, need access to clean drinking water at all times. Snakes drink by submerging their snouts in the water and then using pumping motions in the throat to suck in water. Because most snakes are active at night, you are unlikely to see your snake actually drinking, but it will be taking a nip now and again whenever it needs to—particularly after eating.

Incidentally, it is a good idea not to handle a snake that has just eaten or taken a drink, as the pressure of your hands on the snake's stomach may be enough to cause it to vomit.

Because the water dish is also necessary to keep an acceptable humidity level, and because snakes will often want to soak themselves just before a shed, the water pan in a snake's cage should be large enough for the snake to submerge itself completely. Commercially available water dishes, which are molded out of plastic and made to look like natural rocks, are acceptable. In a pinch, however, any large flat dish that cannot be tipped over will do.

Reproduction and Breeding

One of the most concrete contributions that snake keepers can make to reptile conservation is a vigorous and steady program of captive breeding.

There are two different but important possible goals for a captive breeding program. The first is captive breeding of endangered and threatened reptiles for the ultimate purpose of reintroducing them back into the wild. Because this sort of program is usually reserved as a last-ditch, desperate measure, captive breeding for re-release requires an enormous amount of money, time, energy and know-how (for example, there are some quite serious genetic difficulties that must be overcome in such programs). Such an intensive program is usually beyond the abilities of nonprofit herp societies and serious hobbyists.

The second goal of captive breeding, however, is very much within the scope of the amateur breeder and local herpetological societies. One of the chief threats

HOW TO SEX YOUR SNAKE

In general, female snakes are larger and heavier than their male counterparts. The tails of male and female snakes also differ enough to be noticeable in most cases. In males, the hemipenes are stored inside the base of the tail, which causes the area behind the cloaca to swell out noticeably. In females, which do not have hemipenes, the base of the tail narrows sharply at the cloaca and tapers smoothly to the tip. In male pythons and boas, the claws on either side of the cloaca are much larger than in females. In most species of snake, the male has a relatively longer tail than the female.

With some snakes, it may be possible to sex the snake by "popping." In this method, gentle pressure is applied at the base of the tail, causing the hemipenes in the male to evert from their protective sheath.

The best method of sexing a snake is through probing. Most reptile shops and dealers have commercially available "sexing probes," usually made from stainless steel. Because improper probing can cause serious damage and may even render a snake incapable of breeding, it is best done only by veterinarians or experienced herpers.

The probe should be lubricated with water or petroleum jelly before being carefully inserted into the cloaca with a slight twisting motion. In female snakes, the probe will enter the body only to a depth of three or four caudal scales. In males, the probe will enter the inverted hemipenis, and may be inserted to a depth of up to a dozen scales.

Although the Dumeril's Boa is endangered in the wild, it breeds readily in captivity.

facing many wild populations of snakes, both within the United States and abroad, is overcollection for the pet trade. Several million live reptiles are imported into the U.S. each year, nearly all of them wild-caught, and most of them as pets, and few wild populations can withstand that sort of drain for very long. Other species, such as the Dumeril's Boa from Madagascar, are being threatened by loss of habitat.

One partial solution to this problem is to encourage captive breeding of these species, so they can be made available to hobbyists and collectors without the necessity of taking any more animals from the wild. For this reason, responsible captive breeding of many of these species is to be actively encouraged and supported.

In most snakes, it is the body size rather than age that determines its ability to breed and produce viable young. Most species can begin breeding once they have reached approximately one-half of their adult size, usually at an age of two or three years. The first two or three broods are likely to be small, with full breeding potential becoming established only one year or so after sexual maturity is reached.

Breeding and Habitat

Most snakes will breed every year, usually in the spring after emerging from hibernation. Snakes must be well-fed and in good health in order to breed successfully. In very cool areas, where the habitat allows the snake to be active for only short periods per year, there may not be enough time to find sufficient food to build up the necessary fat reserves for producing young. These snakes therefore tend to store food energy and only breed every other year. Many boas and pythons, which are inactive during

Jungle Carpet Python hatchling.

their unusually long gestation periods, may also need a full year between breedings to build up sufficient food reserves. Snakes from warm tropical areas, however, often produce more than one brood of young per year if the conditions are good.

Snakes from temperate regions must retreat to underground chambers during the winter, when temperatures become too low for sustained activity. During this period, the snake's metabolism and bodily functions slow down greatly, rising or falling slightly according to the external temperature. On mild winter days, some snakes may even emerge briefly and become active. Technically, such a process is called "brumation," which is different from true "hibernation" (in which the body functions stay dormant no matter what the

HOW TO HIBERNATE YOUR SNAKE

To prepare a snake for hibernation, gradually reduce the temperature in the cage by a few degrees per day until it is about 50° to 60°F (the precise temperature depends on the particular species of snake and its habitat). At this point, the snake will be torpid and unmoving. Gently place the snake in a hide box that has been packed with slightly damp moss or towels and place it in a basement, porch or other area with a suitably low temperature. Leave the snake there for a period of at least ten weeks, checking in every few days to make sure that everything is all right.

At the end of the hibernation period, reverse this process by raising the temperature in the tank until it reaches normal levels. If all goes well, your snake should be ready to breed within a few days of reaching optimum temperature.

temperature). This period of dormancy is also necessary, however, for the male to produce viable sperm, and temperate snakes that are not allowed to enter a "cooldown" period before breeding will not be able to produce young.

Spring-breeders produce their young in the summer, when the temperatures are warm enough to incubate the eggs and enough food is available for the young. Some species, such as the hognose snakes, mate in autumn before entering hibernation and then store the sperm until the following spring when they produce eggs. The Trans Pecos Rat Snake departs from the general pattern by mating in the summer and laying eggs in autumn—this practice protects the eggs from the hot dry summer conditions found in its native habitat.

Breeding Behaviors

During breeding season, the female lays a scent trail using her cloacal glands, which males are able to accurately track using their Jacobson's organs. Males seem to be particularly attracted to a breeding female just after she has shed her skin, when her scent is the strongest. Most male snakes will refuse food during the breeding season, and devote nearly all of their energies toward finding a mate.

An elaborate breeding ritual occurs once the male finds the female. The male snake approaches the female from behind, usually rubbing his chin along her body. In the boas and pythons, the males use their rear claws to scratch the female and stimulate her. These tactile sensations seem to help trigger the breeding response. When experimenters have placed rubber sleeves over a portion of the female's body, the male's breeding response ended when he reached the sleeve and could no longer touch the female's skin.

If the female is receptive, she opens her cloaca as the male rests alongside and extends one of his hemipenes. The hemipenis is inserted into the cloaca, and a series of knobs and spines lock it into place while sperm is pumped along a shallow groove by rhythmic contractions. The pair of snakes may remain locked together for several hours and sometimes for a full day.

On occasions when several males have found a single female, a ritualistic form of combat may take place before breeding. The sparring males will intertwine around each other, lifting the front of their bodies and facing each other. Each male tries to gain a position from which he can throw the other and press his opponent's head to the ground in a position of submission. Such ritualistic combat

dances have been observed in a wide variety of snakes, including adders, mambas, bull snakes and several species of rattlesnakes.

The Common Garter Snake practices "mass breeding," in which huge numbers of snakes begin breeding in a large disorganized group shortly after emerging from hibernation. Since several dozen males may be pursuing each female, garter snakes have evolved an interesting mechanism to ensure that the strongest male increases his chances of fertilizing the female's eggs and thus passing his own genes on to the next generation. The first male to successfully catch and mate with the female, after inserting sperm into her cloaca, then inserts a fluid that quickly hardens to form a waxy "plug," blocking the entrance to the female's oviduct and preventing sperm from any other males from reaching the eggs.

Reproductive Strategies

There are three distinct reproductive strategies found in snakes. The first, and rarest, is known as "parthenogenesis." In this strategy, the eggs do not need to be fertilized, but instead develop on their own into viable adults. The Brahminy Blind Snake, also called the "Flowerpot Snake," is a relatively common burrower found throughout the Caribbean. The species is parthenogenic and does not need to mate for breeding. As a result, all of the Brahminy Blind Snakes ever found have been female—no males have ever been described for this species.

A large number of snakes, about one-fourth of known species, do not lay eggs but instead give birth to fully formed young, a process which is known technically as "viviparity." The various members of the boa family are all viviparous, as are a large number of vipers and pit vipers. Viviparity is found most commonly in snakes from cooler temperate areas or high altitudes, where it presents several advantages over egg-laying. By retaining the eggs within her body as they develop, the female snake is able to carry them with her to search for higher temperatures, leading to better incubation and a shorter development time. Most live-bearers drop their young after about four to six months, depending on the external temperature. Viviparous snakes, however, must invest a much larger amount of energy per each developing young than other snakes, and live-bearers tend to have smaller litters than egg-layers.

While inside the female's body, the developing eggs in viviparous species receive oxygen from the female's bloodstream using small capillaries in the lining of the oviduct for gas exchange. In some species, including the European Adder and the Common Garter Snakes, this exchange forms a primitive placenta, similar to that found in mammals, in which the developing embryos are able to exchange water and some nutrients with the mother's bloodstream.

The young are born within thin, clear membranes, which burst open immediately, allowing the newborn snake to emerge. Once born, the young snakes do not require or receive any parental care at all, and are capable of surviving on their own.

"Oviparous" snakes, like most reptiles, lay shelled eggs, which incubate and hatch to produce young. The structure of the amniote egg allowed early reptiles to invade the land and establish themselves in ecological niches that were unavailable to their amphibian ancestors. The shell of a snake egg is pliable and leathery, and is formed in the oviduct by the mother's body after the egg is fertilized. As it develops, the snake embryo produces three distinct membranes inside the shell. The amnion surrounds the embryo and bathes it with fluid. The allantois contains an air bubble for storage of carbon dioxide wastes. The yolk provides fat and food resources for the developing embryo. All of these structures are surrounded by the chorion, which allows air and water to flow through the shell. In the later stages of development, the snake embryo extracts calcium from the egg shell to make bone.

Oviparous snakes cannot carry their eggs for a full term inside their bodies as viviparous snakes

Blair's King Snake laying eggs.

can. However, the eggs laid by oviparous species are vulnerable to predators and changes in environmental conditions after they are laid. Most egg-layers, therefore, practice a sort of compromise, in which the eggs are initially carried in the mother's body for a time and then laid after they reach a viable stage. Female Bull Snakes, for instance, carry their eggs for about forty days before laying them in a suitable spot. The eggs then hatch and produce young about eight weeks later. The European Grass Snake, which lives in a cooler environment, lays sixty to seventy days after mating, with the eggs requiring another forty-five to fifty-five days of incubation before hatching. Pythons, which have large embryos, may carry their eggs for as long as three and one-half months before laying them.

The shells of snake eggs are permeable and allow water and air to pass through freely. Thus, snake eggs

FEW SNAKES ATTEND TO THEIR EGGS

Most snakes do not give any sort of parental care to their eggs—they simply lay them in a suitable spot and leave them to their own devices. A few species, however, are more protective. Most female pythons will curl protectively around their brood of eggs, guarding them against intruders. In the Indian Python, muscular contractions in the female's body can raise the temperature of the eggs several degrees higher than the surrounding environment, incubating them more effectively. Parental care is most highly developed in some of the cobras, which construct a "nest" out of dead vegetation. The nest contains two hollow chambers; the eggs are deposited in the lower chamber and the cobras curl protectively in the upper chamber. Both male and female cobras guard the nest—the only snakes to show monogamy and parental care by both parents.

must be laid in areas that are warm and damp. Most snakes are opportunistic layers and will deposit a clutch of eggs in any well-protected and hidden spot that presents itself. Many species seek out natural piles of decaying vegetation to lay their eggs. This makeshift nest hides and protects the eggs, and the heat released by decaying compost incubates them and minimizes the development time.

When their development is complete, the baby snakes use a temporary "egg tooth" on the tip of their jaw to slice open the leathery shell. Most hatchlings will remain curled up in their eggshells for one or two days before finally emerging.

Incubating Eggs

Incubating snake eggs in captivity requires great care and patience. The eggs should be removed from the snake's cage as soon as they are laid. Signs of an impending clutch include the "pre-laying shed," which usually occurs about a week before laying. The female will also stop eating several weeks before giving birth, because the developing eggs take up a lot of room inside her body.

Before moving any of the eggs, however, use a felt marker to put an X on the uppermost surface of

A Red Milk Snake laying eggs.

each egg. Because turning the egg upside down or sideways can kill the embryo, great care must be taken to ensure that the egg stays in the same orientation it had when it was laid. If the eggshells are stuck together, no attempt should be made to separate them.

The eggs should be placed in a substrate made up of 2 to 4 inches of vermiculite, mixed with an equal amount by weight of distilled water. A plastic sweater box makes a good incubation chamber. The eggs should be half-buried in the substrate, making sure that they do not touch each other. The eggs will absorb water and swell noticeably as they develop. The substrate must be kept damp.

Most colubrid eggs should be incubated at about 82°F, while most pythons should be incubated

A Black Pine Snake hatching.

at around 87°F. The eggs should be inspected daily for signs of mold, and any infertile or dead eggs should be removed. They will hatch within two to three months.

Live-bearers such as Boa Constrictors will usually expel all of the urates they have stored in their cloaca just before giving birth. This will look like a waxy mass. The young are born one at a time. Each litter usually contains a number of infertile eggs, called "slugs," and a number of dead or deformed young. Many times, the female will eat these. Once they emerge from their clear birth sacs, the young can be removed to cages of their own.

Hatchlings and neonates are able to live off their remaining yolk reserves for about a week after emerging. About ten days after birth, they will shed their skin and then be ready to feed. They should be raised on pre-killed prey of appropriate size.

Genetic Mutations

Increasingly, more and more of the snakes that are being captive bred are genetic mutations, which produce oddly colored snakes and new color patterns that may be highly prized by serious snake collectors. These varying color patterns are referred to as "morphs." Some of

A substrate of damp vermiculite works well for incubating snake eggs. (Burmese Python hatching)

Albino snakes can command high prices in the pet trade and are produced by many breeders. This is a baby albino California King Snake.

these forms occur naturally. The Common Corn Snake, for example, is available in a large number of morphs, in addition to its normal coloring. The Okeetee Corn Snake is found in Florida, and has sharply defined borders and exceptionally bright oranges and reds in its color pattern. In addition to the normal Reticulated Python, there is also a "striped morph" and a "calico" version.

Some morphs are the result of genetic mutations that occur during captive breeding. Among the various types of corn snake that have been artificially selected and bred are the "Butter Corn," the "Caramel Corn" and the "Snow Corn." Some of these varieties look so different from the "normal" form that it is difficult to tell that they are the same species.

Snakes that are born without the melanin pigment lack black colors in their pattern, and are referred to as "amelanistic." A number of snakes are born with more melanin than normal, and have their color patterns obscured or obliterated by the black pigment. They are said to be "melanistic." Snakes that lack yellow pigment but still have red or black are called "axanthic," while those that lack red are "anerythristic." "Leucistic" snakes are white except for the eyes, which are black. All of these are usually (incorrectly) referred to as "albinos." A true albino lacks any pigment at all, and is pure white except for the pink eyes.

Not all of the offspring of these mutant snakes will show the same color pattern as their parents. The snake's genetic material is contained in the chromosomes, which are paired in the nucleus of the animal's cells. Each pair of chromosomes works together to express its genetic instructions. These instructions are found in genes. Each genetic trait has a pair of genes, one on each of the paired chromosomes, which controls it (the genetic makeup of a particular animal is known as its "genotype"). Although there may be a large number of possible genes that could control a particular genetic trait, only two will be found in any given individual—one from the

This Western Diamondback Rattlesnake is a true albino.

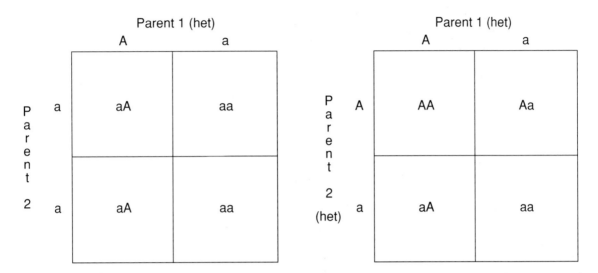

animal's father and one from its mother. Each of these possible genes is referred to as an "allele." For purposes of captive breeding, it is usually assumed that only two alleles are significant, and these are usually referred to as "A" and "a."

Some alleles are dominant—that is, they will be expressed even if only one gene of the pair consists of that allele. Other alleles are recessive—they are not expressed at all if a dominant gene is present, and can only be expressed if both of the genes controlling a particular trait are recessive. By convention, dominant alleles are referred to by a capital letter, and recessive genes are denoted by a lowercase letter.

When both alleles in a given gene pair are the same, either AA or aa, they are said to be "homozygous." If different alleles are present in a gene pair, such as Aa, they

are said to be "heterozygous" (often referred to simply as "het"). Nearly all genetic morphs in snakes are the result of recessive genes, which can only be expressed when the homozygous aa condition is present.

Using some simple mathematics, it is possible to predict what the offspring of a pair of snakes will look like, provided that enough information about the genetics of the parents is available.

Because the gene for amelanism is recessive, we can conclude that any amelanistic snake we want to breed must be homozygous for that recessive gene—it must have the genotype aa. When we breed two amelanistic snakes, therefore, both parents have the aa genotype, and no matter which allele they inherit from their parents, all of the offspring will also have the aa genotype. Thus, all of the offspring

of two amelanistic snakes will also be amelanistic.

Because amelanistic snakes are more expensive than "ordinary" snakes, however, most breeders do not use pure strains of parents to produce them. Instead, at least one of the parents is het for the desired trait, and has the genotype Aa. Since the "A" gene is dominant, this snake will have a normal appearance, even though it carries the gene for amelanism. When we breed a normal het to an amelanistic, there are four possible combinations for all of these alleles.

We can see that two of the four possible combinations produce young that are heterozygous (Aa or aA). These het individuals will have normal coloring but will carry the gene for amelanism. The other two possible combinations produce homozygous young with the aa genotype—and thus the recessive gene will be expressed and the animal will be amelanistic in appearance. Thus, we can conclude that roughly half of the young from this breeding will be amelanistic, and the other half will be normal in appearance but het for amelanism.

By breeding two het parents (both Aa genotypes), the possible combinations will be AA, aA, Aa and aa.

Thus, one-fourth of these young will be homozygous for normal coloring and will not carry the gene for amelanism at all. Half of the young will be normal in appearance but will be het for amelanism, while one-fourth of the young will carry two recessives and thus will exhibit amelanism.

So far, we have only considered one pair of alleles that control just one genetic trait. In reality, most of the interesting snake morphs are the result of the interplay of several pairs of genes, each of which has its own dominant and recessive allele. For instance, if the "A" gene controls the production of the melanin pigment and the "B" gene controls the production of the red pigment, then any particular snake can be homozygous for both traits (genotype AABB or aabb—a

condition referred to as "double homozygous"), heterozygous for both traits (genotype AaBb—referred to as "double het"), or het for one trait and homozygous for the other (genotype AABb, or AaBB—referred to as "single het").

The interplay of these gene pairs has a great effect on the appearance of the young snakes. If we breed a pair of normal-appearing double het snakes (the genotype would then be AaBb for both snakes), there are sixteen possible genotypes for the young: AAbb, AaBb, AABb, Aabb, AaBb, aaBB, AaBB, aaBb, AABb, AaBB, AABB, AaBb, Aabb, aaBb, AaBb, and aabb.

Of these sixteen possibilities, one, the AABB, will be normal in appearance and will not carry any recessive genes. Another one, the AAbb, will be normal for melanin production but will express the homozygous recessive gene for defective red pigment and will thus be anerythristic. Four of the young snakes will be double het, or AaBb—they will appear as normal snakes but will carry the recessive genes for both amelanism and anerythrism. Two of the young will have the AABb genotype, and will look normal but will be het for anerythrism. Two more young will be Aabb, and will appear anery-

thristic (they will not appear amelanistic but will be het for this trait). One young snake will be aaBB, and will appear amelanistic and will carry the recessive gene for anerythrism. Two young will be AaBB, and will appear normal but will be het for amelanism. Two others will be aaBb, and will appear amelanistic but will have normal red pigment (though they carry the recessive gene for anerythrism). One of the young snakes will be aabb, and will express both amelanism and anerythrism. A snake that is homozygous for all recessive traits is a true albino.

In reality, of course, the true situation is even more complex. Some traits such as amelanism have more than one gene that controls the final appearance (there are, for example, two different strains of albino Boa Constrictors that have mutations in different genes and cannot be bred to produce homozygous recessives). On top of this, there is a number of "regulatory genes" that can malfunction to produce new and interesting morphs and color patterns. And as a final complication, some interesting color patterns are not genetic at all but are the result of environmental factors that were present when the egg was being incubated.

CHAPTER 10

Health Care

In general, snakes are quite hardy animals and, provided they are being kept in proper conditions, they are unlikely to ever present you with urgent medical problems. However, captive snakes are subject to a number of ailments, several of which can be life-threatening if not promptly identified and treated.

Finding a good veterinarian for your snake may be one of the most difficult tasks that you are likely to face. Only a few vets have had any training in the unique medical requirements of reptiles and amphibians. As a result, most veterinarians will flatly refuse to examine your snake.

Anorexia

Anorexia is the medical term for refusing to eat—perhaps the single most common problem encountered by snake keepers.

There may in fact be nothing wrong with your snake. Snakes normally go "off feed" for a period of several weeks prior to a shed. Males often refuse to eat during the breeding season, and females refuse food just prior to laying eggs or giving birth. Snakes from temperate regions will often go all winter without eating anything, even if

HOW TO LOCATE A VET

To find a suitable veterinarian for your snake, the first choice is to approach your local herpetological society for help. Another, if you have a local wildlife rehabilitation center or zoo nearby, is to ask for their help—they might be able to point you to a good herp vet. The final option is to call any veterinarian in the phone book and ask if he can give you a recommendation for a good reptile veterinarian. Keep in mind, however, that unless you live in or near a large urban area, you are unlikely to find a vet that has had thorough training in reptile care.

If your snake is maintained under proper conditions, it is unlikely that it will ever need more than an annual checkup from the vet. However, problems can arise, and the snake hobbyist should be able to recognize the onset of a condition, address a minor problem, and determine when he needs to get the snake to a vet.

they are kept warm and not hibernated. Some species, such as Ball Pythons, are famous for going off feed for months at a time, for no apparent reason, and then just as suddenly begin eating again. These fasts are not a problem as long as the snake is still active and is not visibly losing weight. Continue to offer food occasionally, and the snake will eat when it is hungry again.

Under other circumstances, refusal to eat is nearly always the

result of some environmental problem. If your snake consistently refuses to eat, the first thing to check is the temperature in its cage. Probably three-fourths of anorexia cases are produced by temperatures that are too cool. The temperature in your snake's cage should be in the low 80s during the day, dropping to the mid-70s at night.

You should also ensure that your snake has a hide box available; most snakes will not eat if they feel threatened or exposed to predators.

If your snake has a hide box, has suitable temperatures, has not shed its skin and still has not eaten for more than six weeks, you should begin to suspect a medical problem. Refusal to eat is a ymptom of a number of health ailments, including mouth rot and intestinal infections. You will have to get your snake to a vet for a checkup.

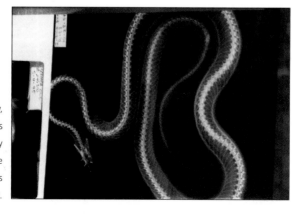

Snakes are hardy, healthy animals and do not usually present severe health problems (X-ray of a snake).

Most health problems are the direct result of improper environmental conditions, such as the undersized, damp and dirty housing shown here.

The best way to prevent burns and wounds is through proper housing. Aggressive snakes that are likely to bite one another should be housed separately. Hot rocks or sizzle stones should not be used, and basking lights must be carefully arranged so that the snake cannot reach them or physically touch them. One of the most common causes of wounded snakes is the practice of feeding live prey animals as food. All snakes should therefore be fed pre-killed prey exclusively.

Wounds

Wounds are most commonly seen in snakes that are housed with aggressive cagemates, or that are being fed live food. Another common cause of wounds is rubbing the nose against the screen top in an attempt to escape, which may rub the scales raw and lead to infection. Snakes that are improperly housed can also suffer burns, either from inadvertent contact with a basking light or from a malfunctioning hot rock or sizzle stone.

Smaller wounds and burns can be treated at home by applying an antibiotic ointment, such as Neosporin, which is available at any drugstore, onto the injury. Snakes have a remarkable natural ability to heal wounds, and, so long as the area is kept clean and

is disinfected with antibiotic, it should heal without further attention. If the wound is large or gaping, however, the services of a vet may be needed to stitch it closed.

Respiratory Infections

Respiratory infections are probably the most common cause of death among captive snakes. Infected snakes will begin having noticeable

MOUTH ROT

Mouth rot, which is known under the technical name of infectious necrotic stomatitis, is a severe condition that is usually the result of an injury to the mouth, teeth or gums. Once the lining of the mouth has been broken by some minor injury, bacteria can invade the wound and multiply, where they produce a corrosive toxin that eats away the surrounding tissues. This produces a swollen red area inside the mouth that will continuously slough off dead tissues as well as a cheesy gray pus. The first sign is usually a

refusal to eat, and examination of the inside of the mouth will reveal the tell-tale lesions and encrustation of dead tissue. If untreated, mouth rot will destroy the lining of the mouth and cause death.

You will need a vet to address this problem. The vet will swab the infected areas with a disinfectant like hydrogen peroxide, and will also administer vitamin shots and antibiotics to help the snake fight off the infection. The sooner the condition is discovered, the better the chance of complete recovery.

difficulty in breathing, and may sneeze or make audible wheezing or bubbling sounds with each breath. Often, the snake will breathe with its mouth held open. Fluid may leak or bubble from the nose. The snake may stop eating. If untreated, upper respiratory infections can spread to the lungs, where they will produce pneumonia, which is difficult to treat and will probably be fatal. Upper respiratory infections are highly contagious, and can sweep quickly through an entire reptile collection, infecting nearly everybody.

This problem is the result of a bacterial infection, but it is nearly always brought on by keeping the snake at a temperature that is too low, leaving the snake's immune system too weak to fight off the invading bacteria. Tropical snakes are vulnerable to respiratory infections if they are chilled for even a short period of time. If it is caught early enough, the infection can usually be cured by improving the snake's conditions and raising the temperature to an acceptably high level (it may indeed help to keep the temperature a bit higher than normal until the infection clears up). Be sure to quarantine the snake until it is well.

If the condition doesn't clear up within one or two weeks, however, or if it is advanced enough that the snake breathes with its mouth open and is refusing to eat, you will need the help of a veterinarian. The vet will prescribe an injectable antibiotic such as tetracycline or baytril, and this will need to be injected every day for a period of several weeks. The vet will show you how to administer the injections, and will supply you with the necessary drugs and syringes. Keep a close eye on the rest of your collection during this time.

After you have cleared the infection up, you will have to correct the environmental conditions that brought it on, or you will be doing the same thing again within a few weeks. The best preventive for respiratory infections is to maintain the proper temperature range, and to carefully quarantine all incoming animals before any other snakes are exposed to them.

Intestinal Infections

The symptoms of an intestinal infection will be obvious and unmistakable. The snake will develop a severe case of diarrhea, and will void watery, slimy feces that will have a powerful odor, and may turn a greenish color. If it eats at all, it may shortly afterwards vomit its meal. The culprit is a form of amoebae that attacks the intestinal linings. This is a serious disease that can kill a snake within a very short time. It is also highly contagious and can race rapidly through an entire collection, often with fatal results.

Contributory factors include temperatures that are too low and drinking water that is unsanitary and polluted with feces.

Treatment must be begun as early as possible. The vet will begin to administer doses of amoebicides such as Flagyl, and may also provide fluids to fight dehydration.

Another common intestinal problem is the presence of worms or internal parasites. These cannot be detected by an external examination of the snake, but their presence can be indicated if the snake eats normally yet never seems to gain weight, or actually becomes thinner. In very heavy infestations, there may be blood present in the feces, and if you examine an infected snake's feces, you may be able to see tiny threadlike worms present. Worms are most common in wild-caught snakes.

If you suspect that your snake has worms, your vet will need to see a recent fecal sample.

Inclusion Body Disease

Inclusion Body Disease is a very serious (but fortunately somewhat rare) disease that has only been recently discovered among captive snakes. It is caused by a retrovirus and is invariably fatal (no cure or treatment is known). The disease seems to affect only members of the boid family, and, although both boas and pythons are susceptible, boas are more likely than pythons to become "carriers," which harbor the virus but do not show any signs of infection.

The disease affects a variety of internal organs, including the kidneys, pancreas and spleen, but the most damage is done to the central nervous system, producing serious damage to the brain and spinal cord. Infected snakes therefore show bizarre neurological symptoms such as partial paralysis, inability to turn themselves over and jerky or uncoordinated motions. Many infected snakes develop an effect known as "stargazing," in which the muscles of the neck involuntarily contract and pull the head upwards, until it looks as though the snake is looking at the sky. Sometimes the snake

will actually raise itself up until it falls over backwards.

Other symptoms include vomiting and inability to swallow, and infected snakes often cannot shed their skin properly because they cannot control their bodies enough to peel off the old skin. Death comes from paralysis resulting in inability to eat or drink.

Inclusion Body Disease is highly contagious, and appears to be spread through contact with exposed surfaces. The virus may also be spread by snake mites. Infected snakes may not begin to show symptoms until up to six months after exposure. Unfortunately, there is no known way to determine whether a living snake has the infection—the only conclusive diagnosis comes from a microscopic examination of the body tissues after death. The disease can therefore only be diagnosed in

living snakes by the progressive appearance and worsening of the known symptoms.

Researchers at the University of Florida have isolated the virus that may be a causal agent of the disease and have been developing a blood test that may be able to provide a diagnosis, but testing so far has been inconclusive.

Since there is no known cure or treatment for Inclusion Body Disease, it is recommended that any infected snakes be removed immediately and humanely euthanized.

Mites and Ticks

External parasites such as mites and ticks are probably the most commonly encountered health problem among captive snakes. The most obvious signs of infestation are a number of small moving dots on the snake's scales, particularly around the eyes and lips. These are snake mites, which are host-specific to snakes—your snake cannot get them from cats or dogs, only from other snakes or from contact with a surface containing mite eggs. Ticks are a bit larger, and look like small black or brown seeds, which are attached between the scales. Ticks are very common in wild-caught Latin American boids, such as Boa Constrictors and Rainbow Boas. They are also found fairly often in wild-caught Reticulated Pythons. Mites and

Inclusion Body Disease only seems to attack boas and pythons. (Burmese Python)

ticks are both easily transmitted from one cage to another, and may soon spread to infest your entire collection.

Both mites and ticks live by sucking blood from your snake, using their needlelike mouthpieces to pierce the thin skin between the scales. Although this loss of blood will not kill the snake by itself, it does weaken it to the point where it becomes vulnerable to other infections. Ticks and mites themselves can transmit a variety of disease organisms. They should be eliminated as soon as they are detected.

The best way to rid a cage of mites is to use a "no-pest" strip containing the insecticide Vapona. Such strips are readily available at most stores. Place a strip into a cloth bag, remove the water dish from the snake's cage, and place the pest-bag inside for about three days. To kill any newly hatched eggs, this treatment should be repeated a week later.

Ticks are not as vulnerable to the insecticide as are mites, but fortunately tick infestations are not as prevalent. The only way to ensure removal of ticks is to carefully examine the snake, scale by scale, searching for attached ticks. When one is discovered, it should be dabbed with a drop of alcohol to kill it, and then carefully removed with a pair of tweezers. Great care should be taken to avoid pulling

It is not unusual for imported snakes to carry ticks, such as the one shown here on a Ball Python.

the ticks out too roughly, as this may leave their heads and mouthparts still embedded under the snake's skin, where it can lead to an infection.

The best preventative for a mite or tick infestation is to carefully quarantine and examine any new arrivals.

Skin Problems

Most skin problems encountered in snakes will be the result of poor or incomplete shedding. The outer layer of a snake's skin is composed of the protein keratin, which is a dead biological material somewhat like plastic in its properties. Because this outer layer cannot grow, it must be periodically shed in order to allow the snake to get larger, a process called "ecdysis."

Before shedding, the snake will usually stop eating and spend most of its time soaking in its water dish. About three weeks later, its skin will get noticeably darker and its eyes will turn a hazy blue as the old outer layer of skin is separated from the inner layer. This blue color will disappear after a few days. About a week after that, the

All newly shed snakes should be checked to make sure that the eyecaps have been properly shed.

snake will begin to retain fluids in its face, which causes the lips to swell and crack open the old layer of skin. The skin is then pulled off, inside out, in one continuous piece. Snakes will usually shed after having consumed between three and five meals.

Occasionally, snakes have trouble in attaining a complete shed. Boids in particular are prone to peeling their skin off in large flakes instead of one complete piece, which often leaves pieces of old skin still attached. These are excellent breeding places for mites and certain bacteria. They can be removed by spraying the affected areas with a water mister or soaking the snake for several minutes in warm water, and then gently rubbing off the old skin. This problem usually indicates a humidity level that is too low, and it can be prevented by increasing the moisture content inside the cage. It may also mean that there aren't enough rough areas in the cage for the snake to hook its old skin and peel it off. To prevent this, snake cages should be provided with a pile of rocks and/or some gnarled branches for ease of shedding.

Although incomplete shedding is usually confined to boids, any snake can be affected by another fairly common shedding problem. Snakes lack eyelids, and instead have a clear scale over the eye called the brille or eyecap. This is normally

BLISTER DISEASE

Captive snakes are also subject to a form of skin problem that has nothing to do with shedding. This is "blister disease," which takes the form of large fluid-filled blisters underneath the skin, particularly along the belly, which can burst open and become infected. It is most common in garter snakes and water snakes, but is also seen in boids. Usually, blister disease is caused by environmental conditions that are too wet. Treatment consists of placing the snake in drier quarters. If necessary, your veterinarian can provide antiseptics to apply to the blistered areas.

shed along with the rest of the skin during ecdysis. Occasionally, however, the eyecaps become detached from the rest of the skin and are not shed. Once the eyecap becomes detached in one shed, it tends to continue to remain in place during subsequent sheds. Eventually, these caps build up to the point where the snake can no longer clearly see, which can make it become defensive and irritable. They also serve as breeding grounds for bacteria and ectoparasites. For this reason, it is important to check the discarded skin after every shed to ensure that the eyecaps have come off, and are not still attached to the eye.

If the eyecap is still attached, it can be removed by soaking the area with a damp cloth for a few minutes, and then carefully lifting it off with a pair of tweezers. If there are several layers of shed built up over the eye, however, a veterinarian should address the situation, as improper removal can cause serious and permanent damage to the eyeball.

Nutritional Problems

Snakes that are fed a diet of whole rodents, complete with viscera, bones and stomach contents, do not usually suffer from any nutritional deficiencies. However, water snakes are vulnerable to a vitamin B deficiency, which is brought about by a diet consisting solely of fish. This is caused by an enzyme in the fish, called thiaminase, which breaks down vitamin B and makes it unusable by the snake. Advanced deprivation of vitamin B causes tremors and convulsions in the affected snake, and can cause death.

Treatment consists of vitamin injections, which must be administered by a vet. To help prevent this problem, water snakes should be given a variety of other prey in addition to fish, such as frogs and salamanders. Also, fish that are to be fed to water snakes should first be heated for three or four minutes at a temperature of around 150°F, which will destroy the thiaminase enzyme and allow the snake to utilize its vitamin B. The fish should then be allowed to cool to room

Water snakes fed an exclusive diet of fish can develop vitamin deficiencies.

temperature again before feeding to your snake.

Salmonella

This is a potential problem for the snake's owner, not the snake. Many species of the *Salmonella* bacteria are capable of infecting the human digestive tract, where they produce severe symptoms including vomiting, cramps, fever and diarrhea. Because the bacteria readily invade improperly cooked food (especially poultry and eggs), they are one of the leading causes of food poisoning.

Several *Salmonella* species, however, are also commonly found inhabiting the skin and digestive tract of reptiles, including turtles, lizards (particularly iguanas) and snakes. Under natural conditions, the population of this organism never builds up to a level where it

can produce infections, and most snakes, even those that are carriers of the *Salmonella* organism, show no symptoms of disease. In captivity, however, particularly where the cage is not being kept properly cleaned, *Salmonella* bacteria can be

present in high levels in the snake's feces, its skin, its shed skins or its drinking water.

Although the vast majority of human *Salmonella* cases are the result of improper food preparation and handling, the medical community has noted a small but disturbing number of *Salmonella* infections that can be directly traced to captive reptiles. Probably the most common method of infection is from handling a snake or the contents of its cage, and then placing contaminated fingers into the mouth or eyes. The bacteria can also enter through any small cuts or scratches in the skin. In addition, *Salmonella* organisms can live for several weeks on exposed surfaces, and infections can also occur from contact with areas that have been recently touched or

PREVENTING *SALMONELLA*

Fortunately, a few simple precautions can virtually eliminate the danger of contracting a *Salmonella* infection from a captive snake. First, always wash your hands after handling any reptile or anything from a reptile's cage (this includes shed snake skins). Although washing with plain water is ineffective, soap kills the *Salmonella* organism. Second, be sure that your snake's cage is kept clean, that feces are removed promptly and that the water pan is changed often. Third, never allow a reptile to come in contact with any

surface that is used for human food preparation, such as kitchen counters, sinks or food dishes, and make sure you wash your hands before touching any such surfaces yourself. Fourth, always supervise small children when they are near the snakes. Do not let them put their fingers in their mouths while handling the snake, and make sure they wash their hands promptly afterwards. If these simple rules are followed, it is unlikely that you will ever have any *Salmonella* problems with your reptiles.

Always wash your hands after handling any snake to prevent the spread of *Salmonella*.

contaminated by a bacteria-carrying snake. Among those most vulnerable to the disease are small children, pregnant women and those who have suppressed immune systems due to disease or medication. These high-risk people should avoid any direct or indirect contact with captive reptiles.

Incidents of *Salmonella* infection from captive reptiles have not escaped the notice of state and federal authorities. In 1975, the federal government passed laws banning the sale of any turtle with a shell length less than 4 inches, due to outbreaks of *Salmonella* infection that resulted from small children putting turtles in their mouths. It is incumbent upon every responsible reptile keeper to help distribute the information and knowledge necessary to prevent the spread of reptile-

borne *Salmonella*, before public health officials and legislatures are forced to respond with a new series of legal restrictions on reptile keepers.

Record-Keeping

One aspect of snake-keeping that is, unfortunately, often neglected by herpers is record-keeping. There are two different types of records that need to be kept—a health record and legal documentation.

The health record is a complete and current log of the snake's usual activities. The log book should contain the species name of the snake, the place where it was obtained, age (if known) and the name and address of the snake keeper. If possible, it should also contain a current photo of the snake. Every time the snake feeds and sheds, this should be noted in a dated log book. Other things to keep track of include any diseases or unusual symptoms, any refusal to eat or anything else interesting or unusual. Periodically, the snake should be weighed and measured, and this information entered in the log book. Log books can be as simple as a spiral bound notebook that is divided into columns, or as elaborate as a file folder with photos and written notes. Several computer programs are also available, either commercially or as shareware, which can help with the record-keeping process.

The log book serves several useful functions. First, it provides a concise record of how your snake is faring. At a glance, the keeper can determine when the snake last shed its skin, how much and how regularly it has been eating and what its previous health has been. This is particularly useful if you have a large collection, which makes it impossible to remember the details on every snake.

The log book also allows a snake keeper to spot a change in the snake's regular behavior. If, for example, your snake usually defecates four or five days after it eats and then all of a sudden changes this pattern, you can immediately inspect it for intestinal problems and correct the situation before it becomes too serious. If a snake refuses a meal, a quick check in the log book will show if it is entering a shed cycle or if you need to check for a medical problem.

Whenever the snake goes to a vet for a checkup, the log book should go with it. Information on previous sheds, feeding and the like, can be invaluable to a vet in determining if everything is okay. Feeding and health records can also be useful if you ever sell or trade your snake.

As a quick reference, it is also a good idea to tape a 3 × 5 note card to the snake's cage, on which is noted the last two or three times the snake ate and shed.

A PAGE FROM ONE OF THE AUTHOR'S LOG BOOKS:

Species: Boa constrictor imperator

Obtained: 1-14-97 from Pet Care Inc., Allentown, PA

Sex: Male

Keeper: Lenny Flank

Age: Unknown—approximately 2 years

Date:	Notes:	Date:	Notes:
1-12	large male Boa Constrictor, looks Guyanan, active but a bit on the thin side. Recently had an incomplete shed.	3-8	shed skin
		3-11	ate 1 large rat
		3-12	heater failed, watch out for resp infection…
1-16	approximately 5.5 ft	3-19	ate 2 large mice
1-20	ate 1 large rat	4-4	ate 1 large mouse, 1 small mouse
1-24	ate 1 large rat	4-9	ate 1 gerbil
1-28	refused rat	4-20	ate 2 large rats
2-2	eyes blue	4-26	ate 1 large rat
2-10	shed skin	5-2	eyes blue
2-11	ate 2 large rats	5-14	shed skin
2-19	ate 2 large rats, 1 large mouse	5-15	approximately 6.0 feet
2-21	eyes blue		

If you will be captive breeding snakes, much more detailed records need to be kept. In states that require permits for captive breeding of native reptiles, part of the permit requirements include accounting for each egg and young snake. Even if such records are not legally required, however, they are still useful, and should be maintained. The date of the actual mating should be noted, and a detailed description of the mating process should be included. When the eggs are laid, the date should be noted, and the temperature at which incubation takes place should also be carefully noted. The date of hatching for each egg should be recorded, as well as the sex of each hatchling. If young snakes are sold, lost or die, these facts should be noted. Records such as these can provide useful information to other herpers about such things as optimal incubation temperatures, infant mortality figures, intervals between mating and laying, and laying and hatching and mating behavior. Detailed records may even have some scientific value, as for many species there is virtually no data on these matters.

In addition to the health and care information found in the snake's log book, you should also keep a complete record of all legal documentation that pertains to your collection. For each animal in your collection, keep a photocopy of the sales receipt on file. This is particularly important if you are keeping legally protected animals or species that are not native to your state. In the event that any question arises about the legality of your collection, remember that it is incumbent upon you to demonstrate that each and every animal was obtained legally. You will also need to keep copies and originals of all necessary permits (venomous snake permits, for instance, or captive breeding permits where required). If you ever sell or trade any of your animals, get a receipt and keep a copy of it. And if you ever have contact with any state or federal wildlife agency concerning your collection, keep a copy and original of all such correspondence. If your animals are rare or valuable, clear photographs should be taken and kept in a safe place, in case you ever need to identify your snake after a theft.

For safety, the originals and good clear photocopies should be stored at separate locations to prevent loss through fire or theft.

The casual hobbyist with one or two snakes isn't likely to come under the scrutiny of state or federal wildlife officials. But breeders, or people with large collections (particularly if they contain species that are known to be susceptible to smuggling) may find themselves the target of an investigation. Under these circumstances, the ability to produce documentation proving that the animals were legally obtained can spell the difference between keeping your collection and having it seized or confiscated.

PART III

The World of Snakes and Humans

*Legal Protection and Conservation ·
Herpetological Education · Snakes and Human Culture
· Snakebite · In Conclusion*

CHAPTER 11

Legal Protection and Conservation

Until about 30 years ago, there were virtually no laws whatsoever regulating the capture or sale of wild animals. Individuals or businesses were free, within the limits of the "animal cruelty" laws, to capture whatever species they liked, export or import whatever they wanted and sell them to whomever they wished. The unfortunate result was the decimation of many species of wildlife, including reptiles, and the hunting of other species to near-extinction.

In the 1960s and early 1970s, the growing environmental movement made most people aware of the tremendous damage that humans were doing to our world ecosystems, and a number of laws were passed to protect threatened or endangered species and to regulate the sale and possession of many types of native wildlife. More recently, as snake-keeping has become increasingly popular, many local governments have felt a need to pass local laws and ordinances regulating the ownership of these animals, in the interests of public safety.

Because there are so many differing state and local laws, this book cannot serve as a guide to the legalities of snake-keeping. The best I can do is provide a broad overview—it is the responsibility of the individual snake keeper to know and obey all applicable legal restrictions.

Without question, the single most important international agreement affecting snake keepers and hobbyists is the Convention on the International Trade in Endangered Species (CITES), also known as the Washington Treaty, which was signed in 1973 and ratified by the United States in 1975.

Over 120 nations have also signed the treaty.

Under CITES, protected animals are divided into two groups. Animals that are listed under CITES Appendix I are those that are in immediate danger of extinction. It is illegal to import or export any of these animals, except for zoos under special permit.

Animals listed under CITES Appendix II are not yet in imminent danger of extinction but are declining rapidly and must be given protection. All of the boids are currently listed under CITES II, including the Burmese Python, the Ball Python, the Boa Constrictor and the Rainbow Boa. It is illegal to import or export any of these species unless they were captured under a special permit or unless they were captive-bred.

Like all of the boids, the Green Tree Python is protected by the CITES treaty.

The primary purpose of the CITES treaty is to prevent the international smuggling of endangered or threatened animals that have been taken from the wild. Wildlife smuggling is a serious problem; according to some Interpol estimates, illegal wildlife trade is a $10 billion a year business, placing it just behind illegal drug trafficking and just ahead of illegal arms smuggling.

One innovation in the CITES treaty is the great latitude it gives to "Non-Government Organizations" (known as "NGOs"), such as national environmental and wildlife organizations. Every two years, the signatories of CITES meet to discuss adding, removing or upgrading the status of endangered or threatened species, and in these proceedings the participation of various NGOs allows private organizations to enter the debate with field research and statistics that may not be available to governments that are unable or unwilling to carry out such research themselves. This participation by environmental organizations has greatly improved the effectiveness of the CITES process.

There are several serious flaws in the CITES treaty, however. The most serious problem is that CITES depends solely on the exporting and importing countries to catch and punish violators. Most imported reptiles come from impoverished

LACK OF ENFORCEMENT IS A SERIOUS PROBLEM

Rampant corruption and lack of law enforcement resources in many nations also allow reptiles to be smuggled out with virtual impunity. The United States does a fair job of catching violators at this end, but officials here are working with limited resources as well, and the penalties imposed on convicted smugglers are usually little more than a nuisance compared to the enormous profits to be made.

Third World nations, which simply do not have the resources to monitor their exports of wildlife. Under CITES, a nation is not supposed to allow trade in a species unless it can determine, through field work, that such trade will not be detrimental to its population. However, most Third World nations do not have the manpower or the money to carry out such field work, and thus often simply "rubber stamp" a species, with no real idea of how well it may be able to tolerate export.

Another problem is that the CITES treaty is binding only if both the exporting nation and the importing nation have signed it. Many Third World nations have not yet signed the treaty. Thus, one easy way around the law is to ille-gally collect reptiles in one country that has signed the CITES agreement, smuggle them into a neighboring country that has not and then export them "legally." In the past, this tactic made certain African nations among the largest exporters of Ball Pythons—despite the fact that Ball Pythons are not indigenous to those nations. To combat this, the United States now refuses to allow the import of any CITES-covered species without a permit, whether the nation of origin is a CITES signatory or not.

For all of these reasons, snake hobbyists and collectors should absolutely refuse to buy any imported wild-caught snakes, and should not purchase any snake that was not captive-bred here in the United States.

The most important of the federal laws pertaining to the collection and raising of snakes and other reptiles is the Endangered Species Act, which was passed in 1973, shortly after the CITES treaty was signed. The stated purpose of the Endangered Species Act (ESA) is "(1) to provide a means whereby the ecosystems upon which endangered species depend may be conserved, and (2) to provide a program for the conservation of such endangered and threatened species."

Under the ESA, animals (and plants) that are vulnerable to extinction are listed in two cate-gories. The most seriously vulnerable are listed as "endangered species," which are defined as "any species which is in danger of extinction throughout all or a significant portion of its range." It is illegal to disturb, collect, possess or sell any of these species.

Organisms that are not yet endangered but that could become so in the near future are classified as "threatened," which is defined as "any species which is likely to become an endangered species within the foreseeable future throughout all of a significant portion of its range." Threatened species may be collected, captive-bred and sold, but only under stringent permits that specify the legal limits on such collection. Anyone in possession of a threatened species should be able to show that the animal was obtained legally.

Another federal law that may apply to snake keepers is the Lacey

CHECK YOUR STATE'S LAWS

It is entirely possible that any particular species can be listed as "endangered" in one state and only listed as "threatened" or perhaps not even listed at all in another. The corn snake, for example, is a widely distributed snake that is common throughout the southeastern United States, but it also has an isolated population in New Jersey, and is legally protected there.

Act, which makes it a misdemeanor to transport any animal that was obtained illegally across state lines. If you illegally capture a Rosy Boa in California, for example, where these snakes are legally protected, and transport it to Oregon or Nevada and sell it, you are in violation of federal law.

Again, the only way this law is likely to apply to you is if you have captured a snake in the wild and are attempting to sell or give it to someone in another state. If you are going to capture snakes from the wild, you must make yourself familiar with all of the applicable laws and regulations in your state.

State laws affecting reptile-keepers fall into two distinct categories—laws that regulate and control the capture and sale of native species, and laws that regulate or limit the types and number of snakes that may be kept within the borders of that state.

For the most part, laws pertaining to the collection of native snakes

RESIST TEMPTATION! DON'T CAPTURE A WILD SNAKE

The only circumstances under which the Endangered Species Act is likely to apply to most snake collectors is if they capture their own snakes in the wild or if they purchase a snake that is listed as "threatened" or "endangered" from a breeder. Most responsible snake keepers will refrain from collecting wild snakes at all, preferring to keep them in the wild where they belong, and instead buy captive-bred snakes. However, if you nevertheless choose to capture a snake from the wild, be absolutely positive that it is not a species that is protected under the Endangered Species Act. If you purchase a species that is listed under the ESA (Eastern Indigo Snakes, for example, are listed as "threatened," but can be legally captive-bred and sold under license and sometimes appear on dealers' lists), be sure to ask for the appropriate documentation to show that your snake was obtained legally. Any legitimate breeder of endangered or threatened species will do this routinely.

are enforced by the state game or wildlife commissions. Most states follow a classification system similar to that of the federal Endangered Species Act. Animals that are in imminent danger of extinction within the state are classified as "endangered species," while animals that are severely declining in

numbers and could be in danger shortly are listed as "threatened species." In most states, the collection, sale or possession of any endangered species is illegal. The collection and sale of any "threatened" species is illegal without a permit, and possession of any "threatened" species is illegal unless it was obtained legally.

It would be impossible to list all of the various state laws regulating the possession and capture of snakes. The following presents a representative summary, including populous states with very strict laws as well as less-populated states with looser regulations.

Florida has a widespread and varied snake population. There are no state regulations limiting the

In many states, it is illegal to take a native snake from the wild. (Common Garter Snake)

capture of nonprotected native snakes, and individual collectors are free to capture as many snakes as they wish. There are also no state regulations concerning the import of nonnative species. Snake hobbyists in Florida are, however, required to possess a permit before they can obtain or possess any venomous species.

A permit may be required to keep venomous snakes such as this Eastern Diamondback Rattlesnake. In most areas, however, it is illegal to keep such snakes.

In Georgia, all native snakes are legally protected, with the exception of native venomous species. It is illegal to capture or possess any native nonvenomous snake without a permit. In Idaho, the Longnose Snake and the Western Ground Snake are listed as "threatened" and may not be collected or possessed without a permit. Other native snakes can be collected, but a keeper is limited to four individuals of each species. Residents of Missouri are allowed to capture up to five specimens of native snakes for personal use, but these may not be traded or sold. Captive-breeding of native snakes is illegal in Missouri without a permit. In Nevada, no native species of snake may be captured or kept without a permit. New Jersey prohibits keeping or breeding any native snake without a permit, with the exception of the albino form of the corn snake (*Elapha guttata*)—the normally-colored corn snake is, however, listed as "endangered" in New Jersey and is thus legally protected. In Pennsylvania, nonthreatened native snakes may be collected with a valid fishing license, but wild-caught snakes cannot be sold or traded. In Montana, Minnesota, New Hampshire and South Carolina, there are no legal restrictions on the capture or possession of non-threatened native snakes.

California has an aggressive conservation program and some of the strictest state game laws in the country. In California, reptile collectors are required to possess a valid fishing license. Each collector is subject to a "bag limit" on any particular native Californian species. For species that have been listed as "threatened" or "endangered," the bag limit is zero—in other words, they cannot be collected from the

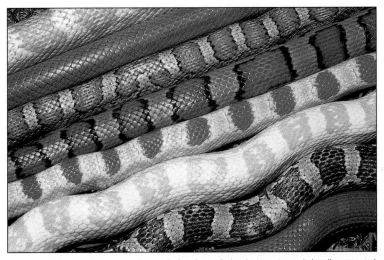

The corn snake is very common, but an isolated population in New Jersey is legally protected (eight variations of corn snake).

wild. For most other species of snake, the bag limit is two specimens per species. For some rare species, such as the California Mountain King Snake, the bag limit drops to one.

Under California law, it is illegal to sell, trade or export any wild-caught native reptiles for commercial purposes. Captive-bred reptiles may be sold or exported, but there are legal limits concerning the species and numbers that may be bred. It is also illegal for any California resident to possess or import any nonnative venomous species of snake.

Very few states have passed laws regulating the possession or import of nonvenomous snakes that are not indigenous to the state. One state that has such a law is Hawaii, and it is a very draconian law indeed. In Hawaii, it is illegal for any person to import or possess a snake of any size or any species. Keeping even a harmless little garter snake on any of the Hawaiian Islands will earn you a rather hefty fine, and

your snake will be confiscated and destroyed.

There is a good reason for such a drastic measure, however. There are no snakes indigenous to Hawaii, which means that none of the state's native bird life has any natural defense to these predators. If a nonnative snake were to be introduced and establish a breeding population, it would quickly wipe out most, if not all, of the unique Hawaiian bird life, much of which is already threatened or endangered. Such an unfortunate scenario has already taken place on Guam, where the Brown Tree Snake, a rather common species from the south Pacific, was accidentally introduced a few years ago. The snake has now spread over the island and has eliminated a number of unique species of birds, and is threatening to wipe out the rest. By outlawing the importation of snakes, Hawaii is hoping to avoid a similar event.

While federal and state laws deal largely with conservation

issues, and thus regulate the collection and sale of snake species, local municipal and county governments tend to be more concerned with public safety issues. A large number of county or municipal governments have local ordinances that may place limits on the type of snakes that hobbyists may keep, in the interests of protecting the public.

A large number of local governments will have ordinances banning the possession of venomous species of snakes. Those that do not have such a law usually pass one quickly if anyone makes the news after being bitten by a pet snake. In some of these jurisdictions, exceptions may be made if the snake has been surgically devenomed. In others, however, it is illegal to keep even a devenomed snake.

An increasing number of local governments are also passing laws forbidding the possession of any snake larger than 8 or 10 feet in length, or banning all of the various species of boids, regardless of length. In a few areas, possession of any "constricting snake" is banned, which makes even such harmless species as rat snakes and king snakes technically illegal to own. As with the case of venomous snakes, these laws are usually made in response to public outcry after some incident involving a large snake. Most of these laws are not strictly enforced, however, unless

The Brown Tree Snake was accidentally introduced on Guam, where it has caused considerable ecological damage.

Some overcautious jurisdictions have passed laws banning any constricting snake, which technically makes it illegal to own even a harmless king snake.

somebody complains or unless the snake is involved in an altercation.

Legal problems involving snakes are in reality quite rare. As long as you act sensibly and take ordinary precautions with your snakes—don't collect snakes from the wild, don't buy or sell any snakes you know are endangered or threatened (unless you have certain proof that they were obtained legally), don't take your snakes out in public and above all, don't ever do any stupid macho showing off with your snakes—it is extremely unlikely that you will ever run into any legal troubles because of them.

Snake Smuggling

The CITES treaty leaves it up to each individual nation how best to enforce its provisions and control the export of wildlife from its borders. In the United States, the U.S. Fish and Wildlife Service (USFWS) has legal authority over the export and import of wildlife and wildlife products, and thus has responsibility for enforcing the provisions of the CITES treaty and the Endangered Species Act.

About eighty-five uniformed Wildlife Inspectors are employed by the USFWS at any given time. These inspectors are responsible for inspecting shipments of wildlife into and out of the U.S., verifying permits and keeping records. To help these inspectors in their jobs, the import and export of wildlife in the U.S. is limited to thirteen designated ports of entry. All wildlife products imported to or exported from the U.S. must pass through one of these designated ports,

where they can be inspected by the USFWS.

The USFWS also serves as a law enforcement agency, investigating violations of CITES and the ESA. A forensics laboratory in Ashland, Oregon, uses modern techniques of molecular biology and DNA analysis to identify animal parts, while a staff of biologists are utilized for species identification. In addition, the USFWS Special Operations Branch conducts undercover "sting" operations, targeting suspected smugglers and illegal dealers. The Special Operations Branch also serves as the intelligence clearinghouse for wildlife investigators.

The Fish and Wildlife Service's efforts, however, are hampered by budgetary problems. Wildlife law enforcement is often near the bottom of the list when it comes to funding priorities, particularly when compared to efforts to counter drug smuggling. Los Angeles International Airport (LAX), for example, handles about one-third of all the live animals imported into the United States each year, with almost $4 billion worth of wildlife passing through its inspection station. But the USFWS has only ten inspectors on duty at LAX—nowhere near enough to inspect every shipment.

Despite its shortages in manpower and funding, the USFWS has had some notable successes. In January 1997, one of the largest reptile and amphibian wholesalers in Florida was indicted for illegally importing over 1,000 herps, including snakes, lizards and tortoises, from Argentina over a period of several years. The Florida operation was part of an international reptile smuggling ring that involved people in New York, North Carolina, New Mexico, Indonesia, Australia, the Netherlands and other nations. The charges filed included illegal wildlife trade, fraud and conspiracy.

In February 1997, the owner of a Florida import company was convicted of conspiring to smuggle a large number of reptiles, worth over $57,000, from Peru into Miami International Airport. The illegally imported herps included 141 Peruvian Boa Constrictors, three Green Anacondas and one Rainbow Boa. He was sentenced to two years in jail and a $25,000 fine.

A month later, an Illinois reptile breeder pleaded guilty to smuggling reptiles to and from Spain for a period of almost ten years. Wall lizards and European Ladder Snakes were smuggled into the U.S., while Massasauga Rattlesnakes, Timber Rattlers and Great Plains Rat Snakes were smuggled back to Spain. The reptiles (including the venomous snakes) were sent through the mail in packages marked as "books." During this period, after a three-year investigation, a total of six people were indicted for conspiring to smuggle over 170 Madagascar Tree Boas, Spider Tortoises and Radiated Tortoises from Madagascar to Europe. The scheme involved people in Germany, South Africa and Florida. One courier was caught with sixty-one Tree Boas and four Spider Tortoises concealed in his luggage.

It is difficult to assess the dollar value of the illegal trade in smuggled herps. In Brazil, which accounts for an estimated fifteen percent of the illegal wildlife smuggled into the U.S., smuggled animals have a higher annual profit than gun smuggling, and wildlife trafficking is second only to illegal drug trafficking. In many cases, drug traffickers also moonlight as herp smugglers, and on several occasions shipments of cocaine have been found that also contained live snakes (usually Boa Constrictors), destined for the U.S. pet trade. The U.S. is a source of illegal reptiles as well as a destination for them—the endangered Bog Turtle, found in the northeastern United States, is the third most valuable wildlife product in international trade, exceeded only by rhino horn and tiger bones. Smuggled Bog Turtles may sell for as much as $10,000 each to foreign collectors.

The vast amount of money that can be made in the illegal wildlife trade has led to rampant corruption and bribery. Australian writer Raymond Hoser has documented widespread involvement of several Australian police departments in the illegal export of reptiles, including instances of bribery, beatings and other violence. Some other nations are notorious for turning a blind eye to illegal wildlife trade. Taiwan, long a major source of smuggled animals, passed a Wildlife Conservation Law in 1989, and even formed a Wildlife Task Force in 1993, but its efforts at controlling the illegal animal trade were so inadequate that they were heavily criticized by CITES

This Collett's Snake is found in Australia—be sure that any imported snake you obtain is brought into the country legally.

LEGAL IMPORTATION

Each year, between 1.5 and 2.5 million live reptiles are legally imported into the U.S., consisting of several hundred different species. Another 2 to 6 million reptile products are also brought into the country every year. Around eighty-five percent of the reptile products imported into the U.S. are snake skins for the leather trade, most of which come from Argentina, Japan, Indonesia, the Philippines, Singapore, Taiwan, Thailand and Venezuela. (Some 150,000 Reticulated Python skins are imported into the U.S. each year for use as leather.) Gucci, Chanel and Saks Fifth Avenue all do a thriving business in python leather accessories such as shoes and wallets. In all, the legal reptile trade is worth as much as $10 billion a year.

officials in 1994, and the U.S. imposed a temporary ban on trade in animal products. Taiwan has since tightened up its enforcement efforts, but remains a major source of illegal wildlife. Thailand and Indonesia are also notorious for their laxity in enforcing CITES provisions.

In the former Soviet Union, the collapse of governmental authority and the lack of resources for law enforcement have led to widespread corruption and organized crime rings, many of which are involved in smuggling. The Russian or Horsefield's Tortoise, for example, has become popular in the U.S. pet industry, and many thousands are now being exported from the former Soviet Union. A high proportion of these are being exported illegally.

Smuggled Russian Tortoises were at the center of an incident that aroused widespread condem-nation in October 1996. A shipment of 1,000 Horsefield Tortoises arrived at Arlanda Airport in Sweden without proper documentation. Swedish officials promptly seized the turtles, which were crammed fifty to a crate, and placed them in a warehouse. Under CITES provisions, the turtles should have been legally confiscated and placed in the care of a rehabilitator, or returned to their country of origin. Instead, Swedish officials killed all 1,000 of them by turning off the heat and freezing them to death in the warehouse where they were being kept. The incident provoked a storm of outrage from wildlife and herpetological organizations all over the world, with several groups calling for a boycott on all Swedish products.

The extraordinary rise in popularity of reptile keeping and breeding that occurred in the 1990s has also led to a new breed of domestic wildlife criminal—professional thief rings. At least six commercial reptile breeders, from New York to Arizona, have been robbed over the past few years, with losses totaling over $100,000. In each case, the burglary appeared to be the work of well-prepared professionals. In two cases, sophisticated security systems were breached, and in each case, only specific animals were taken—exceptionally valuable rarities (including, in one case, albino Ball Pythons worth over $10,000 each), usually pregnant females or breeding pairs. None of these burglaries has been solved. Most likely, these animals were smuggled to other nations after being stolen, where the offspring can be sold at enormous profits.

YOU CAN HELP

It is up to every responsible reptile keeper to help end the illegal trade in smuggled reptiles. The best way to do this is to refuse to buy any imported or wild-caught animal, and to obtain only snakes that have been captive-bred here in the United States. If you do obtain an imported animal, ask for documentation to show that it was obtained and imported legally. And if you are ever offered an animal that may have been imported illegally, be sure to inform law enforcement authorities.

CHAPTER 12

Herpetological Education

Fortunately, there are now a number of people fighting to preserve our snake and reptile biodiversity, along with the rest of our endangered ecosystems. And, as the pet trade has traditionally been a primary offender in driving many species to the brink of extinction, it seems only fitting that today's responsible pet owners and snake keepers should have important roles to play in herp conservation. As a responsible snake keeper, you too are part of a worldwide community that must involve itself in the protection and conservation of these creatures.

Herpetological Organizations

The bulk of all herpetological education and conservation work in the United States is done, either directly or indirectly, by national, state and local herpetological societies. These are nonprofit bodies that are formed by groups of private citizens for the express purpose of furthering public education about reptiles and amphibians and promoting the conservation of wild herps. Herpetological societies also act to promote responsible keeping and captive breeding of snakes and other reptiles and amphibians.

To help them meet these goals, herpetological societies carry out a number of tasks. Many herp societies carry out annual "field surveys," in which volunteer teams will comb wildlife habitats to take a census of the local reptile and amphibian populations. This allows researchers to study population trends of various species, and may provide advance warning if populations of certain species are beginning to drop. It also helps state and federal officials monitor the populations of animals that are listed as threatened or endangered.

Herp society members also monitor local pet shops, ensuring that any reptiles and amphibians that are offered for sale are being kept in adequate conditions.

The most visible work of herpetological societies, however, is in the area of public education. Most herp societies sponsor talks and shows for the public where reptiles and amphibians are exhibited and people are educated about the vital roles that reptiles play in various ecosystems. Speakers are usually made available for school classrooms, Scout troops and other groups or organizations that are interested in reptile and wildlife conservation. State and local herpetological societies may also provide witnesses and information for lawmakers and legislatures that are considering regulations and laws affecting reptiles and their keepers.

Herpetological societies also work hard to ensure that all reptiles that are kept in captivity are done so safely, responsibly and in a way that does not endanger any wild populations. Through newsletters, meetings, guest lecturers and other methods, herp societies disseminate a large amount of information and advice concerning the captive care and breeding of a wide variety of snakes and other reptiles and amphibians. Many local herp societies also work closely with local veterinarians, and run "adoption" services that can provide good

Exhibitions are a great way for the public to learn more about reptiles. Your herpetological society may decide to sponsor a booth.

JOIN YOUR LOCAL HERPETOLOGICAL SOCIETY

I cannot encourage you strongly enough to join your local herpetological society. Membership in a herpetological society can cost between $15 and $35 per year, and it is an investment that is well worth making for any snake enthusiast or hobbyist. Not only do you gain access to a rich source of experience and advice, but you will be helping to play an important role in maintaining and protecting these fascinating and unique creatures.

homes to herps that have been abandoned, confiscated or seized by local law enforcement or humane society officials, or simply given up for adoption.

Habitat Preservation

One of the most successful defenders of reptile habitat has been the Center for Ecosystem Survival (CES). The CES, based in San Francisco, is a nonprofit consortium of zoos, aquariums, science museums and conservation organizations that raises money to purchase critical areas of habitat around the world, setting these areas aside as wildlife refuges and ensuring that they will never be developed or destroyed. The Center was founded by the American Association of Zookeepers, the American Zoo and Aquarium Association and The Nature Conservancy.

The primary work of the CES is carried out through the "Adopt an Acre" program. Under this plan, individuals can donate a sum of money that is then used by the CES to purchase targeted pieces of land in biologically sensitive areas. Each donor is given an honorary deed for a parcel of land, according to the size of the donation. People who contribute $15, for example, receive an honorary deed for one-tenth of an acre of rain forest. People who contribute $65 receive an honorary deed for a half acre, and a contribution of $130 is enough for the purchase of one acre of critical habitat. The CES works with the governments of these nations to incorporate the purchased land into the national park system, where it is permanently protected.

The CES has so far helped to protect over 11 million acres of tropical habitat, in areas including the Maya Biosphere Reserve in Guatemala, the Rio Bravo Conservation Area in Belize, the Pacaya-Samiria National Reserve in Peru, the Panama Canal Watershed in Panama and the Amboro National Park in Bolivia. A companion program called "Adopt a Reef" helps protect endangered marine environments in Palau, Micronesia, the Komodo National Park in Indonesia and Parque del Este in the Dominican Republic. In addition to snakes, other species that have been aided by the programs include spectacled bears, poison arrow frogs, red-fronted macaws, manatees and dugongs, bottlenose dolphins, sea turtles, Komodo dragon lizards and countless others.

One of the most active figures in the Center for Ecosystem Survival is Tim Hoen, the president of the Maryland Herpetological Society. To raise money for the CES program, the Maryland Herpetological Society started an annual reptile show, where hobbyists and collectors from all over the country could gather to exchange specimens and information. All of the show's proceeds are donated to the "Adopt an Acre" program.

The first Mid-Atlantic Reptile Show was held in 1993 in Baltimore. In keeping with the goal of conservation and protection, only captive-bred animals were allowed at the show (a policy carried over to all subsequent shows). The show also had the support of much of the zoological community, including Dr. Roger Conant, former director and curator of reptiles for the Philadelphia Zoo and author of the popular *Peterson Field Guide to Reptiles and Amphibians*. Dr. Conant was the keynote speaker at the first

Mid-Atlantic Show. Since then, other luminaries of the herpetological and zoological world have also lent their support. The Maryland Herpetological Society is now the biggest individual contributor to the CES's "Adopt an Acre" program. The money raised over the past five years by the Mid-Atlantic Show has been enough to purchase over 1,600 acres of endangered rain forest habitat.

Talks and Shows

Perhaps the single most important factor in protecting and preserving reptiles and amphibians is public education. No other group of animals on earth have been maligned for so long (and without any good reason) as have snakes. Most people have at best only a vague understanding of these animals, and most of what they do "understand" is negative and usually inaccurate. For this reason, local herpetological societies often sponsor talks and shows for the public, where reptiles and amphibians can be exhibited and displayed, and people can be educated about the vital roles that herps play within various ecosystems. Even if there are no herp societies in your area, however, there is still one resource that can help educate the public about the importance of understanding and protecting snakes. That resource is you.

If you are comfortable with public speaking, a large number of groups and organizations can serve as potential sites for an educational lecture or show about herps. Your local herpetological society probably has an outreach and education program and would be happy to have another lecturer. If there is no herp society in your area, contact the biology teachers in your local school districts, as well as Scout troops, conservation clubs, local environmental organizations and any other group of people that may have an interest in reptiles, the outdoors or ecology and wildlife. Many of these groups have "guest lecturers" at their meetings and would be happy to allow you to speak to their members.

There are two basic formats for any educational show. The first option is the "static display," in which various animals are presented in cages, and the herpetoculturalist sits or stands nearby and is available to answer questions. This format is the easiest to set up and involves the least amount of work on the part of the herpetoculturalist. It may also be best for the hobbyist who isn't comfortable speaking formally in front of a group of people but who doesn't mind talking one-on-one.

Animals to be used in these educational displays must be selected carefully, keeping a number of criteria in mind. To be

attractive to an audience, they should be both visually interesting and readily viewable. As a trip to the zoo will demonstrate, the displays that get the most audience attention are those that contain active animals out in the open; those that simply look like an empty tank are quickly passed by. Snakes that skulk in hide boxes or bury themselves in substrate are not suitable for display, and species that are severely stressed by being exposed to view should also be avoided. Some suitable animals would include corn, king and rat snakes, and many of the boids.

Unless the theme of the show is reptile breeding or the maintenance of captive snakes, only naturally-colored specimens should be used, and specially-bred "morphs" should be avoided. This is particularly true if the animal is native to your local geographic area (I always like to display as many local species as possible). Displaying the natural color schemes not only conveys some information about how that animal lives in nature, it also allows the audience member to recognize it again if he sees it in a photograph or in the wild.

All animals (particularly those that are aggressive or potentially dangerous, such as hot snakes or some of the boids) should be securely caged in a manner that does not allow enterprising audience members to get their fingers in the cage. All animal cages should be securely locked, both to prevent possible escapes and to safeguard the animals from audience members who may attempt to touch or pet them.

Because the attention span of many audiences (particularly of youngsters) is rather limited, the display should be as varied as possible. A good mix of different sizes and colors will keep the display interesting and will add to the attractiveness of the display. You may also want to exhibit some reptiles other than snakes, to demonstrate how snakes differ from their lizard and turtle cousins.

The other, and more common, format for an educational presentation is the "active display," in which the audience is gathered together into a group, with the herpetoculturalist standing in front of

Snakes that may be dangerous, like the Puff Adder, should be kept in a secure cage for display purposes.

them holding and presenting individual animals. I have always preferred this approach, for a number of reasons. It allows me to directly communicate the particular information I want to convey about any specific animal and avoids the problem of endlessly repeating answers to the same questions from different people. From the logistic point of view, it also allows me to

focus all my attention on handling and watching the particular snake I am holding at the time, rather than trying to keep an eye on a large number of tanks and cages. And finally, since I am a bit of a ham, I enjoy the opportunity to speak in front of an audience.

If the snakes are to be actively handled and displayed, some additional considerations must be made. The animals should be large, in order to afford everyone in the audience a good view. Because the snakes will be in close proximity to members of the audience as well as the lecturer, they should be selected for their good temperament and calmness around strangers. It is difficult to convince people that reptiles are harmless and safe after they have just seen a nervous snake aggressively clamp itself onto your fingers.

Hot snakes should generally be avoided in such shows, as they can present serious safety problems for

Audiences will appreciate the directness of the "active display" method of presentation.

both you and the audience. Using hot snakes in a talk or show may also present you with innumerable insurance and liability requirements. It may be possible to use devenomed snakes. If you do so, make sure that everyone involved in the show understands that the snake has been surgically altered.

In all my talks, I prefer to arrange the audience into a semicircle or U-shape, while I have my animals securely bagged at a table behind me (having the animals out of view of the audience allows them to focus their attention on me and the snake currently being displayed, rather than looking anxiously to see what's ahead). I remove each reptile one at a time, giving a short talk about some particular aspect of its biology or lifestyle as I slowly carry it around the semicircle to allow everyone to see it closely. For a one-hour show, I normally use between fifteen and eighteen different animals.

Each talk or show will vary a bit, depending on the age and knowledge level of the audience, the individual animals to be presented, and the particular topic to be emphasized. Each show should be organized around a particular theme—endangered animals, for example, or animals native to a particular geographic area or reptilian biology and lifestyles. The depth of information presented should depend on the makeup of the audi-

ence. A lecture to 6- or 7-year-olds, for example, can give some very basic lifestyle information for each reptile ("it lives in the desert," "it likes to eat worms and small fish"). Older audiences can be given more detailed (and interesting) ecological information ("this snake excretes dry uric acid crystals instead of liquid urine, which helps it adapt to a desert environment").

Your educational talk or show will have a much more lasting impact on the audience if they are allowed to touch or handle at least some of the animals, as opposed to having them passively displayed. Most educators agree that a "hands on" approach is very effective in communicating information, and in any case most people like to interact closely with animals (which is

why zoos have "petting" sections). It also allows you to graphically demonstrate that many of the myths about snakes and reptiles—they are "slimy" and "icky"—are simply not true.

Allowing audience members to touch or handle the reptiles should be done with care, however. Because many people are afraid of snakes, it is important to clearly communicate that it is okay to not touch the animals if you don't want to, or even to move away if the animal's presence makes you uncomfortable. The audience (especially young children) must also be cautioned to avoid making any threatening movements, such as swatting or grabbing, that may scare the animal and lead to a defensive action. In my talks, I always begin by pointing

USING SNAKES AS EDUCATIONAL TOOLS

Several of the animals I use have been specifically selected to allow me to emphasize a particular point. The corn snake, for example, is an animal that is listed as a "threatened" species in the state of New Jersey. Showing a corn snake allows me to talk about the environmental factors that are reducing its population (such as habitat destruction and overcollection), and to point out that endangered and threatened species are part of our environment—endangered animals exist literally in our own back yards. My Bull Snake was rescued from an

owner who didn't take proper care of him, and he is skittish and sometimes aggressive around people (one reason why nobody in the audience is allowed to touch him). Pointing this out gives me the opportunity to talk about proper snake husbandry and the importance of selecting an appropriate animal to keep as a pet. My Burmese Python is a youngster (only a year old) but is already over 6 feet long. Showing her to an audience emphasizes that these snakes are very large, grow rapidly and are not suitable as pets for a beginning snake keeper.

out that, although the snakes I have are accustomed to being around people, they are still wild animals and still have all their natural instincts, and if they feel they are being threatened they will defend themselves. I then ask people to not touch or pet any animal unless I specifically say it is okay to do so.

For security, as well as safety reasons, only one animal should be available for handling at a time. If several audience members are walking around at once with snakes in their hands, it is too easy to lose control of the situation (and perhaps lose some reptiles in the process). I have always preferred to hold the animals myself. If a particular snake is amenable to being touched by strangers, I will allow those who wish to stroke or pet it to do so (warning them to stay away from the animal's head and face) while I maintain control over the animal.

The order in which I present animals is carefully planned. To relax the audience and make them comfortable, I begin with the smallest specimen and move upwards in size until I reach the big boids, thus allowing those who may be initially a bit nervous to become accustomed to them before being confronted with a large, heavy snake.

One of the best ways to gauge the interest of the audience is by the number of questions asked. If the audience is attentive and asks a lot of questions, you are doing a good job of communicating information to them. If, on the other hand, the audience is sitting stone-faced and silent, your talk is not going so well.

Some audience members may be reluctant to ask questions, perhaps out of shyness or a fear of appearing ignorant or uninformed. It may help to "plant" an accomplice in the audience who can ask a few basic questions such as, "What do snakes eat?" or "How long can snakes live?" This opens up further discussion and also lets audience members know that it's okay to ask questions.

Be prepared for all kinds of questions. Some youngsters will surprise you with their detailed knowledge about reptile biology and behavior. Some adults will shock you with their abysmal ignorance about anything reptilian. (The most common question by far, often asked of each and every snake, will be, "Is it poisonous?") Treat all of these questions with equal respect, and do not even give the unconscious impression that a question is "dumb" or "stupid." Point out politely that there are a lot of mistaken stories and inaccurate information about herps.

Giving educational talks and shows to the public is some of the most important work that any reptile hobbyist can do. The fear that many

A GOOD SPEAKER IS RELAXED AND HONEST

Remember that in the eyes of the audience, you are "The Expert" on reptiles and their behavior. Because the audience will take what you say at face value, be sure that your information is accurate, and answer any questions put to you as concisely as you can. If you do not know the answer to a question, admit it and suggest places where the questioner can learn this information himself. At all times, you should appear relaxed and confident—lecturers who appear tense and nervous tend to make their audiences feel tense and nervous, too. The point of your talk is to reduce people's fear and anxiety about reptiles, not to add to it.

people have of snakes is based largely on ignorance and misconception. Similarly, the various local laws and ordinances that restrict the ownership of reptiles and other exotic animals are usually based on the same lack of knowledge and understanding, as well as the preconceived notion that snake keepers are "strange" and probably a little bit crazy as well. An interesting and informative lecture, by a responsible herper, can go far in improving the knowledge of the public and changing its attitude toward these interesting and beautiful animals.

CHAPTER 13

Snakes and Human Culture

Snakes have several characteristics that have long fascinated humans and have led to superstitions and religious myths. Snakes are one of the few groups of animals on earth that can produce a painful and spectacular death with a single bite.

Their habit of periodically shedding their skin was also noted by most ancient cultures, which viewed this as an act of rebirth and renewal. The staring, unblinking eyes, the fluid legless movements and the cold body and smooth scales were all inspirations for numerous human myths and legends concerning snakes.

The Genesis Serpent

The story of the Genesis serpent is perhaps the best known tale of Western mythology. According to the story, when Adam and Eve were in the Garden of Eden, God warned them not to eat the fruit from the Tree of Knowledge. Satan, however, in the guise of a snake, appeared to Eve and beguiled her to eat the forbidden fruit, and she then enticed Adam to also eat. As a result, God cast them out of the Garden of Eden and cursed the snake, condemning it to crawl on its belly for the rest of its life.

Moses turns his staff into a snake, which then swallows a serpent produced by the pharaoh's magician. An engraving from a nineteenth century Bible.

Satan, in the form of a serpent, entices Adam and Eve to eat the forbidden fruit. A nineteenth century engraving.

Snakes are also mentioned in the biblical tales of Moses. When Moses attempted to persuade the Egyptian pharaoh to release the Hebrews from slavery, Pharaoh's priests threw their staffs to the floor and turned them into snakes. (The ancient Egyptians viewed snakes as gods, and the figure of a rearing cobra was incorporated into the religious headdress worn by the pharaohs.) In response, Moses commanded his brother Aaron to throw down his own staff, which turned into a larger snake and swallowed the Egyptian serpents.

These stories of religious symbolism did have some basis in biology. The deadly Saw-Scaled Viper is common in the Holy Land, and, with its aggressive disposition and powerful venom, it is not surprising that it served as the model for the symbol of evil. Ancient Middle Easterners were also familiar with the fact that some snakes feed almost exclusively on other snakes, including even the venomous Egyptian Cobra. To the authors of the Bible, the image of one of their native snakes swallowing the symbol of the mighty Egyptian

Pharaoh was vivid and compelling, and had its own political and cultural implications.

After the Hebrews left Egypt, they traveled through the Sinai Desert, which is the home of several species of dangerous snakes, including the Saw-Scaled Viper and the Horned Viper. To protect his people, the Bible tells us, Moses fashioned a snake out of brass and carried it on a pole, where it magically cured the victims of snakebite. The "serpent of brass" later became a Christian symbol of victory over death, and during the Middle Ages depictions of such serpents were often present in crucifixion scenes.

Snakes are also mentioned in the New Testament story of the apostle Paul. While preaching on the island of Melita, Paul was bitten by a viper (probably a European Asp), which

was hidden in a bundle of firewood. The "barbarians" all gathered round, expecting Paul to die. Instead, the Bible tells us, "He shook off the beast into the fire, and felt no harm." The Melitans, amazed by Paul's miraculous immunity, were convinced of his divinity. This story, too, has an element of truth to it; it is not uncommon for a molested snake to inflict a "dry bite," from which no venom is injected and no ill effects result.

Another snake legend centers around Saint Dominic de Guzman, the Spanish founder of the Catholic Dominican Order. According to legend, St. Dominic, while preaching the gospel to the Albigenses in central Italy in 1215, was bitten by a poisonous snake and miraculously recovered. (In another version of the legend, the Albigenses, who were

considered heretical, were represented by snakes—Dominic's recovery from snakebite then probably represents a symbol of his resistance to theological heresy.) To commemorate the saint, inhabitants of the village of Cucullo, in central Italy, hold an annual "Procession of the Snakes" on the first Thursday in May. After a Mass in the saint's honor, a wooden statue of Dominic is carried from the church and is draped with local Aesculapian Snakes and Four-Lined Rat Snakes. Each of these is marked with a spot of dye

ST. PATRICK "BANISHED" SNAKES

A famous Christian story concerning snakes revolves around St. Patrick, the patron saint of Ireland. According to legend, Patrick banished all snakes from the island while he banished heresy and evil, and indeed there are no species of snake native to the Irish island. This, however, is more likely the result of geological history than of the divine powers of St. Patrick. During the Ice Age, Ireland and Britain were joined with Europe in one landmass. Because of the cold conditions, snakes and other reptiles found these northern areas uninhabitable. When Ireland "broke off" and formed its own island, it contained no snake species, and has remained serpentless ever since.

The prophet Moses used a brass snake to cure the Israelites of snakebite. Several dangerous species of viper inhabit the Holy Land.

on the top of its head. The statue is then placed on a litter and carried through the streets of the town. The originators of this ritual believed that it gave the village protection from the bite of the mildly venomous European Asp, which is common in the nearby hills. Originally, the snakes used in the ceremony were ritually killed and buried. Today, they are released or sold to tourists.

The choice of the species used for this ritual betrays a knowledge of the natural habits of these snakes. Both the Aesculapian Snake and the Four-Lined Rat Snake are largely arboreal and tend to escape danger by climbing. Thus, they tend to cluster at the top of the statue and stay there during the whole ritual. Other local snakes, such as the European Grass Snake, are more terrestrial and, if placed on the statue, would fall to the ground and attempt a quick getaway—which of course would ruin the festival.

One of the oddest Christian rituals involving snakes centers around a fundamentalist Protestant sect in the Appalachian Mountains in the eastern United States. These people take literally the biblical description of the true believer: "They shall take up serpents." During their church services, they pick up and carry live snakes, usually Timber Rattlesnakes and copperheads, as a testimony to their faith. Although some groups appear

The Copperhead is used in religious services by some Appalachian fundamentalists.

to keep their snakes at low temperatures before the service (which makes the snakes sluggish and less likely to strike), several groups do indeed carry active snakes. If bitten (which appears to happen rather often), the victim usually refuses all medical treatment and depends solely upon the power of God for recovery. These snake-handling services were outlawed several years ago when a number of people died after being bitten.

The Feathered Serpent

Other religions have been less harsh to the serpent than the Christian Genesis story. One of the most famous was the Central American mythology of Quetzalcoatl, the

Feathered Serpent. The Toltec, Mayan and Aztec civilizations all shared cultural and religious continuities, and the rain god Quetzalcoatl was known among them by a variety of names, including Kukulkan, Ce Acatl and Topilitzin. He was always depicted in art and sculpture as a large, fearsome snake, covered completely in feathers and sporting a large pair of wings. In a few examples of Mayan art, rattles are depicted on his tail, identifying him with the Central American Rattlesnake or Cascabel, a large, dangerous serpent that is common throughout Central America. The temple in the Mayan capital Chichen Itza had a large sculpture of a feathered snake running alongside the staircase. Each year at the winter solstice, the shadows cast by the steps fell on the sculpture, producing a sharp triangular design along the snake's back in imitation of the typical diamond pattern found on the Cascabel.

Quetzalcoatl was said to be the son of the mother god Coatlcue, who had snakes for hands and two snake heads for her face.

According to Mayan, Toltec and Aztec mythology, Quetzalcoatl descended to earth in the form of a light-skinned, bearded human, to teach the ancient Toltecs how to plant corn, how to work metal and how to construct buildings. He also taught them basic math and how to construct calendars, based on a long list of names (the Year of Eagle, the Year of Ocelot, the Year of Wind). A particular year would then be known in the Central American calendar as One Ocelot or Three Wind, and together these formed a complicated cycle that repeated itself every 52 years.

After a period of time as ruler of the Toltecs, Quetzalcoatl was challenged by a rival god named Tezcatlipoca. In one version of the legend, Quetzalcoatl was defeated and was forced into exile. In another version, Quetzalcoatl was seduced by an evil woman and, in a self-imposed punishment, set himself afire. In either case, the god left the world of men and disappeared across the eastern sea, vowing to return one day, during the Year of One Reed.

By an amazing historical coincidence, Hernán Cortés and his Spanish conquistadors invaded Aztec territory in 1521, the Aztec Year of One Reed. The Aztec ruler Moteczoma, believing that the serpent god Quetzalcoatl had indeed returned from the eastern sea and had resumed the form of a light-skinned bearded man, was paralyzed by fear and religious dread, and Cortés and his small band of warriors were able to conquer the mighty Aztec Empire in less than two years.

The Hopi Snake Dancers

The "Snake Dance" performed by natives of the American Southwest, is perhaps the most famous of all the Indian rituals. The Hopi tribe of Native Americans, who live in the desert areas of Arizona and New Mexico, viewed the several species of serpent that inhabited their territory as divine messengers, who could communicate to the rain gods dwelling in the underworld.

Once a year, after the corn harvest, the Hopi held a ritual ceremony to ensure that the rains would continue to come to nourish their crops. The ceremony lasted nine days. Over a period of four days, local snakes, largely harmless species such as Bull Snakes but also including a number of rattlesnakes, were hunted and captured by members of two of the Hopi secret societies, the Antelopes and the Snakes. The captured snakes were stored in earthenware pots in an underground religious chamber known as a *kiva*. On the ninth day of the ceremony, the snakes were ritually washed. At sundown, the Antelope priests emerged from the kiva and began to dance in the ceremonial area. Shortly afterward, the Snake priests emerged and were handed live snakes, which were then ritually carried about by the shamans and holy men as they danced. Individual snakes were often carried in the dancers' mouths.

After the dance was completed, the snakes were gathered into a ritual circle drawn on the ground, where they were sprinkled with an offering of corn flour and then released in their burrows, where, it was hoped, they would carry the Hopi prayers to the underworld and speak to the rain gods.

The priests involved in the ritual have always maintained that the rattlesnakes are not defanged, "milked" or rendered harmless in any way. However, no outsider has ever been permitted to view the actual captures, and several snakes that were examined shortly after being released from a dance were found to have had the fangs removed. The practice of removing the fangs may be a recent precaution; in ancient times, the priests probably rendered the snakes temporarily safe by "milking" them and forcing them to eject most of their venom just before the ritual.

The Indian Snake Charmers

A frequent image of India is that of the turbaned snake charmer, or "fakir," sitting cross-legged before a woven basket. As he plays his pipe and sways back and forth, he lifts the lid off the basket, exposing a large cobra, which instantly spreads its hood and rears up into attack position. The cobra sways back and forth, in time to the music, seemingly hypnotized by the sound and rhythm. It may strike at the fakir, but never bites him. After a short time, the snake relaxes back into its basket and the death-defying show is over.

In many nations of southern Asia, snake charmers are professionals, who learn their trade at established schools and who make their living as itinerant entertainers. They receive many years of training before they are allowed to perform on their own. The most commonly used snake is the Asian Cobra. According to Hindu myth, the god Krishna once visited the earth in human form, and fell asleep under a tree. As he slept, a large cobra moved nearby and spread its hood to shade him from the hot sun. After awakening and seeing what the snake had done for him, Krishna placed

A Spectacled Cobra from India.

two fingers on the cobra's back to bless it, producing the spectacle-like pattern on the snake's hood.

In areas where the much larger and more impressive King Cobra is available, it is the snake of choice for charmers.

Contrary to what many people believe, the snakes used for these acts are not devenomed, defanged or altered in any way. Instead, the fakir depends on his encyclopedic knowledge of the habits and behavior of these snakes to escape being bitten.

The music from the pipe is solely for the benefit of the audience; snakes are completely deaf to airborne sounds and cannot hear the fakir's songs. Instead, the snake is merely acting in typical defensive manner towards what it perceives as a threatening object moving

nearby. With its eyes locked onto the moving pipe, the cobra will follow it as it moves back and forth, attempting to stay in striking position. This is what the audience interprets as the snake's "dance."

CHARMERS CAPTURE THEIR OWN SNAKES

It is a matter of pride to most snake charmers that they capture their own snakes. Each snake is utilized for performances for a few weeks, until it begins to become accustomed to humans and doesn't "hood" any more. It is then offered a ritual meal of milk and meat and is released. If the cobra would happen to die before it is released (sometimes the stress of capture and captivity is too much for the snake), it is given a ritual burial.

Usually, the fakir will stay just out of the snake's striking range. He will also move his hands and arms constantly, so the snake is unable to get a good "target lock" on them and is unable to effectively strike at him. Occasionally, though, the fakir will deliberately entice a strike by moving into the snake's zone of defense. Before doing this, he will have carefully watched the snake to determine how agitated it is. Such visual clues as the rapidity of the snake's tongue flicks, the height at which is has reared up, and if its tail is twitching all serve as indications of the snake's aggression level. If the snake does strike at the fakir during the performance, it is usually only a half-hearted effort, as the charmer is very careful not to present a good target. Sometimes the charmer will present his open palm directly in front of the snake, allowing the snake to strike at it. He knows that the snake cannot open its mouth wide enough to sink his fangs into a wide flat object.

The more daring fakirs may conclude their performance with a maneuver called "the kiss of death." This act is usually performed by a young woman. The performer will approach the cobra closely, lean over to it and gently kiss the top of its head three times.

This move requires careful attention to the snake's temperament and behavior. It also takes advantage of a little-known fact about cobras—unlike most other venomous snakes, cobras cannot strike upwards. Instead, they can only bite at an attacker by raising the front of their body as high as possible and then falling forward. As long as the performer stays out of this "danger arc," the snake cannot strike. This is why the snake kisser always approaches from above, where the serpent cannot reach her.

Despite all these precautions, however, a number of snake charmers are bitten and killed every year in Asia. The fakirs consider this a normal risk of employment.

Other Myths and Legends

The myths and stories of many other cultures are sprinkled with references to serpents. Greek mythology tells the story of the Gorgon Medusa, a scaly creature with live venomous snakes for hair. Medusa's appearance was so terrifying that anyone who looked upon her face was turned to stone. Another well-known snake from Greek mythology was Hydra, the many-headed serpent killed by Hercules. And when Hades, god of the underworld, kidnapped Persephone, the daughter of Demeter, Demeter pursued him in a chariot drawn by winged serpents.

The sun god Apollo was said to have killed the serpent-dragon Pythos—from which we get the name of the most widely-known group of modern snakes. Pythos lived inside Mount Parnassus, where he guarded the sacred springs at Delphi from intruders. The serpent-dragon was so fierce that he killed every living thing on the mountain. Eventually, Pythos became so aggressive that he prevented even the gods from entering Delphi, and Zeus sent his son Apollo to kill the snake—a task which took over a thousand of the archer god's silver arrows to accomplish. On that spot was established a temple housing the Oracle of Delphi, a priestess of Apollo who was also known as Pythia.

The Romans adopted much of the Greek mythos, including the references to snakes and serpents. Of particular interest to the Romans was the god of healing, Aesculapius, whose symbol was the coiled serpent. As a part of their worship of Aesculapius, the Romans took the Italian Rat Snake (*Elaphe longissima*) and kept it in their bathhouses across the empire, where the snakes often escaped and established local populations. Today, this snake is known as the Aesculapian Snake, and it still exhibits the disjointed and fragmented range that resulted from the Roman habit.

In Norse mythology, the ocean depths were prowled by Iormungander, the Midgard Serpent, that attacked ships and men until it was killed by the thunder god, Thor.

Iormungander was the offspring of the trickster god Loki and the giant Angur-Boda. Cast into the sea by Odin, the father of the gods, the Midgard Serpent grew until it encircled the globe and could grasp its tail in its mouth. The writhings of its body caused terrible storms. Finally, Thor decided to kill the serpent. The first battle was inconclusive, but at the time of Ragnarok, when the forces of evil attacked the gods at Valhalla, Thor was able to kill the Midgard Serpent with a hammer blow. Iormungander had his final revenge, however—a flood of venom poured out of the dead snake's mouth and drowned Thor.

The Australian aborigines believed that the earth was inhabited by the Rainbow Serpent, which

The Wagler's Viper is felt to be a sacred being by Buddhist monks in Malaysia.

WHAT *IS* AN ASP?

One of the most famous snakebite victims of ancient times was Cleopatra, Queen of Egypt. As her kingdom collapsed under the invading Romans and her situation became hopeless, Cleopatra decided to commit suicide, and had several dozen slaves killed in various ways to determine which of them died with the least pain. Eventually, she chose death by snakebite, and clasped an "asp" (at that time the general term for any poisonous snake) to her breast, was bitten and died. Although some historians have identified the Saw-Scaled Viper as the "asp" that killed Cleopatra, this is rather doubtful since the hemotoxic venom of vipers produces intense pain. It is more likely that the instrument of the legendary queen's death was the Egyptian Cobra, symbol of the ancient pharaohs, whose neurotoxic venom kills quickly and relatively painlessly.

served as the gateway between the world we live in and the dream world.

The Buddhist temple in Penang, Malaysia, keeps large numbers of Wagler's Vipers (*Tropidolaemus wagleri*), which have free run of the building and are often found curled up on tables and altars. They are considered sacred and are not harmed or molested in any way. The snakes, which are also known as Temple Vipers, are venomous but are lethargic and nonaggressive, and seldom try to bite even if they are handled.

Buddhist temples in southeast Asia often carry depictions of the *naga* serpent-guardians, one on each side of the doorway. The *naga* take the form of huge, many-headed cobras. In Javanese legend, the Queen of the Southern Ocean, Loro Kidul, married eight times and killed each husband before dawn. The ninth husband, a holy man, stayed awake

on his wedding night and chanted a prayer. Before the sun came up, a deadly snake emerged from the body of the sleeping queen. When the holy man killed the snake, it turned into a dagger with a wavy blade, known throughout southeast Asia as a *kris* knife. Since then, warriors often wash their *kris* in cobra blood.

Several African tribes worshipped the python, particularly the large African Rock Python, as a god. Unmarried women linked arms and performed a winding dance, in imitation of the python's movements, to ensure fertility and long life. Many villages kept captive Rock Pythons or Ball Pythons as patron deities, and large snakes were often utilized in fertility rites. Harming a python was considered an offense punishable by death.

During the American Revolution, the colonists adopted the rattlesnake as their symbol. Coiled rattlers appeared on colonial currency, official seals and battle flags, often accompanied by the motto "Don't Tread on Me." The Gadsen flag featured a coiled rattler on a yellow background, with the motto "Don't Tread on Me" beneath it. It was flown by the first U.S. Navy ships to put to sea, and was also painted onto the drums carried by the first U.S. Marine units. Throughout the war, American naval vessels also flew red and white striped flags that depicted a rattlesnake stretched from corner to corner.

Modern Folklore

Few animals are the subject of as much misinformation and superstition as are snakes. Some of the folklore told about snakes has a grain of truth buried (sometimes deeply) within it. Most of it, though, is just plain silly.

Probably the most common misconception about snakes is the belief that they are cold and slimy. Since snakes are ectotherms, their body temperature is often lower than that of a human, making the snake feel cool to the touch. When the snake has been basking, it feels warm. Snake skin is very dry and smooth to the touch, and feels much like vinyl or plastic. It is not at all slimy.

One common myth is that of the "hoop snake." According to the story, these snakes are capable of grasping their tail in their mouth and rolling after a person like a bicycle tire. This story probably started from observations of snakes resting in a loose coil.

A corollary to the "hoop snake" myth is the "whip snake." This particular creature is supposed to wrap itself around a human being and whiplash him into submission using its long tail. There is indeed a species of snake known as the Coachwhip, which has a peculiar scale pattern on the end of its tail that looks vaguely like the braids of a bull whip. However, despite the story, no snake ever uses its tail as a whip to defend itself (although some of the lizards, including iguanas and monitors, are quite effective tail-lashers).

Some snakes are said to have venomous stingers hidden in the tips of their tails. This bit of folklore probably refers to the blind and thread snakes, some of which have sharp spines at the tip of their tails that they sometimes push against the skin of the person holding or handling them. These are, of course, completely harmless and contain no stinger or venom. The forked tongue of snakes is also often believed to be venomous or to be capable of stinging. In reality, a snake's tongue is a delicate sensory organ, and snakes are very careful to protect these sensitive organs from injury.

Another common myth is that of the "milk snake," which is supposed to suck the milk from cows at night. This myth was once so prevalent that the species *Lampropeltis triangulum triangulum* is still known by the common name "Eastern Milk Snake."

According to popular myth, the milk snake sucks the milk from cows at night. (albino Eastern Milk Snake)

The "milk snake" story is pure nonsense. Because of the construction of their jaws and teeth, snakes are physically incapable of sucking any sort of liquid, and in any case no cow would ever stand still long enough to allow a snake to get a grip on it with its 200 needle-sharp teeth. This myth may have gotten its start from the fact that many snakes, including milk snakes, can be found prowling in barns and animal pens, where they hunt for rodents.

The "glass snake" is, in modern folklore, said to have the ability to break itself into pieces when attacked. Each piece then crawls off, only to gather later and rejoin to form a complete snake again.

This story has a tiny grain of truth in it. The Eastern Glass Lizard is not a snake, but a legless lizard that looks much like a serpent. Like most lizards, it has the ability to deliberately cast off its tail, which then convulses violently to draw a predator's attention away from the lizard's body. The Glass Lizard's tail is over twice as long as its body; and it often breaks into several pieces, each of which twitches and moves independently. The lizard, after crawling away, regrows a new tail. No snake, however, is capable of performing this trick.

Another myth that appears to be the result of a misobservation is the notion that mother snakes, in time of danger, will swallow their young alive, only to regurgitate them later after the danger has passed. In reality, snakes, even the live-bearers, do not give any parental care to their young and do not make any effort to defend them from predators. (Crocodiles and alligators, however, actually do gather their young into a loose pouch inside their lower jaw.)

The "snakes swallow their young" tale may have arisen when someone killed or came upon a recently dead pregnant female live-bearer and noticed the squirming unborn young inside. The assumption would then be made that the protective mother snake had just swallowed all of the young snakes.

Inasmuch as many snakes eat other snakes, this myth may also have resulted from the observation of a larger snake feeding on a smaller species.

Several bits of folklore center around the snake's methods for catching and swallowing food. One widely held belief is that snakes have the ability to "charm" or "hypnotize" their prey. Once it looks into the eyes of an approaching snake, this story goes, a bird or rodent is paralyzed with fear and thus presents an easy target for the snake. In reality, of course, snakes have no such supernatural ability. Instead, they approach their prey with such stealth that they simply are not noticed by the intended prey until it is too late. The snakes, of course, are also not always suc-

SNAKES DO DIE IN THE DAYTIME

A common bit of folklore states that a snake never dies before sundown, no matter how badly it may have been injured. Snakes, of course, die just as easily as any other animal. However, even a dead snake can exhibit nervous twitching for several hours after death, with even the jaws opening and closing sometimes due to reflex actions. To the frightened and the uninformed, it may appear as though the snake is still alive.

cessful. Like most predators, they have more failures while hunting than successes.

There are several widely known folk methods for determining which snakes are venomous and which are harmless. None are accurate. The only reliable indicator of a venomous snake is the presence of fangs in the front or rear of the jaw, or, in the case of pit vipers, the presence of heat-sensitive pits on each cheek.

According to one bit of lore, however, all venomous snakes have triangular-shaped heads, while harmless snakes have oval or rounded heads. While it is true that the huge venom sacs found in the vipers and pit vipers gives their head a sharp triangular appearance, this is not a reliable indicator. Some harmless snakes, such as hognose and some of the water snakes, can spread their heads when threatened to make them appear larger, which can also give them a triangular appearance. Other lethally venomous snakes, such as coral snakes, cobras and mambas, have venom glands that lie further back along the body and do not bulge out at the cheeks as in the vipers. In the coral snakes, the head is scarcely wider than the rest of the body.

It is also widely believed that if the pupils of a snake's eyes are vertical, like a cat's, this is an indication that it is dangerously venomous, while if the pupils are round, like a human's, it means the snake is harmless. But alas, this is not true either. The pupils are indicative of the habits of a snake, not its venom (or lack thereof). Diurnal snakes, which are active during the day, have round pupils that can be opened or closed to regulate the amount of light that enters the eyeball. Nocturnal snakes, by contrast, have vertical pupils that can be closed down to a narrow slit to prevent much light from entering, or can be opened up widely to allow for maximum light-gathering under dark or dim conditions. Thus, nocturnal harmless snakes, such as Reticulated Pythons, possess vertical pupils, while diurnal venomous snakes, such as mambas, have round pupils.

Even the presence of a "hood," such as that found on the familiar cobra, is not necessarily an indica-

This young lady is checking for vertical pupils in this snake, although this is certainly no reliable method for determining if the snake is venomous or not. (Eastern Hognose Snake)

tion that the snake is dangerous. The American Hognose Snakes can flatten their necks and produce an impressive-looking hood. But the hognoses have only a mild venom.

Nearly all of the American folklore surrounding venomous snakes, not surprisingly, centers around the rattlesnakes, which are the most common venomous snakes in the United States and are unique to the western hemisphere.

Probably the most widely believed tale about rattlers is the assertion that a snake's age can be determined by counting the number of rattles on its tail. While it is true that newborn rattlers have only one (soundless) segment on their tails, (the "button"), and more rattles are added as the snake gets older, it is not true that this is an indication of its actual age in

years. A new segment is added to the rattle every time the snake sheds, and in a good year the snake may shed as many as five or six times. As the rattle gets longer,

THE CUCUMBER MYTH

One myth that is peculiar to the eastern United States is the idea that copperheads (and, according to some, Timber Rattlesnakes) have a strong cucumber smell when they are ready to bite. There is a tiny grain of truth to this story. Copperheads and rattlers, like all snakes, have musk glands near their cloaca that expel a foul-smelling fluid when the snake is threatened. It would, however, require quite an imagination to describe this musk as "smelling like cucumbers."

moreover, it becomes subject to breakage and damage—it is very rare to find a rattler in the wild with a complete rattle. Thus, the size of the rattle is not a reliable indication of the age of the snake.

Another widespread bit of folklore, particularly in the northeast, is that of the "pilot snake." According to this tale, each rattlesnake is accompanied by a Black Rat Snake or Black Racer, which acts as a scout or "lookout" for the rattler. Thus, the story goes, when one encounters one of these pilot snakes in the woods, one should immediately stop and look around for the nearby rattlesnake. In some versions of the myth, the rattler repays the pilot snake for its services by sharing its prey with it. (Inasmuch as snakes swallow their prey whole, this, in reality, would be rather difficult.)

This story is nonsense. It is probably the result of the observation that Black Rat Snakes and Timber Rattlers share the same habitat and can often be found in the same general area. Also, since good hibernation spots may be rare in any given area, these snakes often share a den through the winter, hibernating together until they emerge in spring and go their separate ways.

A closely related myth, prevalent in the western United States, is that of the "crossbreed rattler." When rattlesnakes and Bull Snakes breed, the story goes, the resulting offspring often possess the fangs and venom of the rattlesnake, but the color pattern and lack of rattle found in the Bull Snake. These "crossbreeds" are said to be particularly deadly, because they grow much larger than normal Bull Snakes and strike without rattling a warning.

In reality, these two species cannot interbreed or produce offspring. Bull Snakes, however, do have a color pattern that can be vaguely reminiscent of a rattlesnake (particularly to uninformed persons), and they also hiss loudly and strike vigorously if cornered. Many Bull Snakes are killed every year in the mistaken belief that they are venomous. The "crossbreed" story is probably the result of such a misidentification.

In the eastern states, a similar story is sometimes told of hybrids between the Black Rat Snake and the copperhead.

Another story told about rattlers in some areas concerns their supposedly poisonous breath. If threatened, it is said, the rattler will exhale sharply and eject venom from its fangs, mixing the two to form a deadly poisonous vapor. Although some species of cobras are able to squirt venom over a considerable distance from their modified fangs, no rattlesnake is capable of this feat. The story probably had its source in the rattlesnake's habit of hissing sharply when threatened.

"VENGEANCE" MYTH CIRCLES THE GLOBE

In Africa, it is believed that the mambas always live in pairs of male and female, and that if either is killed by a human, the remaining partner will track down and bite the offending person. The same tale is told of cobras in Asia, and in some parts of the United States, this myth is also attributed to the rattlesnakes. In the cobras, at least, there is a grain of truth to the story—cobras are one of the few snakes that form monogamous pairs at breeding time.

One common story about rattlesnakes (I heard it as a child in South Dakota) goes like this: A man was bitten by a rattlesnake while plowing his field and died shortly after. His oldest son inherited all of his possessions, but shortly afterwards he too died mysteriously—exhibiting all the symptoms of rattlesnake poisoning even though he had not been bitten. A month later, another son also died, again apparently from a rattler and again without having been bitten. A doctor investigated and discovered the truth—the rattlesnake that killed the father had left a fang embedded in the heel of his boot. When each son inherited the boots and tried them on, they were in turn envenomed.

Another variant of this story has a man killing a large rattlesnake and burying the body in his backyard. Years later, while gardening, he accidentally digs up the snake's skull and pokes his finger with a fang, and dies shortly afterwards.

Needless to say, both of these stories are impossible. Although people have been fatally bitten by decapitated snakes, it is impossible for a bare fang, without a venom gland attached, to inject any significant amount of venom.

Finally, there is another story that was once widespread in Texas and the southwest. When a road-runner comes upon a sleeping rattlesnake, the story goes, it gathers branches of thornbush and cactus around it to imprison the snake. Upon waking, the trapped snake becomes so enraged that it bites itself to commit suicide, allowing the bird to feast on the dead snake.

Although roadrunners are a major predator of rattlers (as well as other snakes), no such behavior has ever been observed. No amount of branches would be a barrier to a snake, and in any case, snakes are immune to their own venom.

Rattlesnake Roundups

One of the more sensational (and senseless) interactions between humans and snakes are the so-called "rattlesnake roundups." The first organized rattlesnake hunts were carried out in the American colonies in the 1740s, when a specific day was set aside each year (usually in the spring just after the snakes emerged from their hibernation dens) to hunt for dens and kill all the snakes.

As the years went on, however, the rattlesnake hunts became less a matter of protection and more a matter of showmanship. Prizes were awarded to those who brought in the biggest snake, or who killed the most rattlers. A carnival atmosphere was encouraged, and spectators were charged admission to watch the snakes be killed.

Today, some of the largest rattlesnake roundups occur in areas where there are virtually no snakes to be found, and no danger to either people or livestock. Nevertheless, the roundups have continued, largely as fund-raisers. In Sweetwater, Texas, the largest roundup in the United States, the annual event (started in 1958) is sponsored by the local Jaycees, who raise money through admission tickets and the sale of rattlesnake meat and trinkets made from rattles and skins. The Sweetwater roundup is accompanied by a chili contest, cattle auctions, gun shows and the annual "Miss Snakecharmer" pageant. Other annual roundups are held in Kansas and Pennsylvania.

After being captured and stockpiled for several weeks, the snakes are unceremoniously dumped into "pits," circular structures of brick or stone, with no shade and no food or water. Those that survive this ordeal become the subject of "educational talks." "Snake handlers" display the snakes to a gawking audience, usually accompanied by some patter about the great danger posed by the reptiles. Some of the snakes are used in "contests" such as "sacking," in which teams of handlers attempt to bag the largest number of snakes in the allotted time. Often there is a demonstration in which someone inserts himself into a sleeping bag that has been filled with snakes. Some snakes are milked of their venom, which increases the thrill of the audience and adds to the air of mortal danger. After all of these indignities, the snakes are beheaded with an axe, skinned and deep-fried for sale at the various snack stands. The rattles and skins are made into trinkets such as hatbands, earrings and paperweights. During one sixteen-year period in Sweetwater, almost 71,000 snakes were killed. Almost 18,000 snakes were once killed in a single weekend. Each snake can bring in as much as $75 in meat and trinkets.

The roundups cause tremendous ecological damage. The systematic hunting of snakes in these areas year after year has severely depleted the local populations, and as a result, snake hunters need to travel farther and farther afield in order to gather enough victims for their show. Some of the smaller roundups can't collect any snakes at all, and must import snakes from other areas—including "leftovers" from earlier roundups. In Pennsylvania, where the local Timber Rattlesnake is legally protected, roundup operators must import rattlers from other states. In many areas, repeated raiding of wintering dens has reduced the population such that that the den is no longer used. In addition, the dens are often dismantled and destroyed while the snakes are being gathered, which may make them unusable in future years.

Although the roundup sponsors claim the shows are "educational" and serve a "scientific purpose," in reality they are nothing more than sensationalism and serve no purpose other than making a few quick bucks. Far from encouraging an understanding of the ecology and habits of these animals, rattler roundups do everything possible to

UNCONSCIONABLE ACTS

Particularly harmful is the illegal, but still common, practice of using gasoline as an aid in snake collecting. Rattlesnakes tend to spend the hot daylight hours holed up in rock fissures and burrows, where they are difficult and troublesome to extract. Many rattlesnake hunters solve this problem by using a garden hose and sprayer to squirt gasoline down into the hole. Most of the time, the fumes force the snake out into the open, where it can be captured. Sometimes, the fumes overpower and kill the snake. And in each case, the fumes also force other animals from the den, including tortoises, foxes, and burrowing owls. Gopher Tortoises and Indigo Snakes, both of which are protected under the Endangered Species Act, are often victims of illegal gassing of rattlesnake dens. Excess use of gasoline may also render the den uninhabitable for a number of years.

inspire fear and awe in the eyes of spectators. It is difficult to see what educational purpose is served by a "sacking" contest, or by watching a man wedge himself into a sleeping bag full of snakes. Even the venom that is collected by "milking" dozens of snakes is useless for scientific or medical purposes, because it is not extracted under sterile conditions.

The "handlers," meanwhile, can be incredibly foolhardy with their daredevil antics. At least two deaths are known from rattlesnake bites suffered during a roundup. Many of the handlers have been bitten dozens of times, sometimes as many as one hundred times (some handlers openly brag about the number of bites they have sustained, as if it were a badge of honor rather than a reflection of their inept handling skills). In a particularly silly show of machismo, one person was bitten five times in the face when he attempted to bite the head off a live rattler.

CHAPTER 14

Snakebite

There are about 2,700 species of snake living on the earth today, of which about 400 possess fangs and other venom apparatus. Even the harmless snakes, however, often have digestive enzymes and mild toxins in their saliva. These have a numbing effect on the preferred prey of the snake, and help the snake obtain food. In rare cases, these mild toxins can produce symptoms in humans. Very few people who have had their skin penetrated by common garter snakes, for example, have exhibited signs of mild envenomation, including swelling and pain. For this reason, many snake experts have taken to arguing that there are really no "nonvenomous" snakes—there are only those snakes that have very mild venom and no effective way to administer it to humans.

Only about 200 species of snake are potentially dangerous to humans. Drop for drop, the most powerful venoms among terrestrial snakes belong to the Inland Taipan and the Tiger Snake, both Australian elapids. Among the vipers, the most powerful venom is that of the Saw-Scaled Viper. The sea snakes, members of the elapid family, have even more powerful venom than their terrestrial cousins (they need it as their prey must be killed quickly before it can swim away), but they are only rarely encountered by humans.

Snake venom consists of a large number of components, nearly all of which are proteins manufactured in the snake's venom glands. Among the various types of proteins found in snake venom are proteolysins, which break down cell walls and destroy body tissues and blood vessels; hemorrhagins,

which break open blood vessels and cause internal bleeding; cardiotoxins, which attack the muscles and nerve centers of the heart; and cytolysins, which attack and break down white blood cells.

There are two basic types of snake venom. Hemotoxic venoms contain a high proportion of proeolysins and hemorrhagins, and work by breaking down the capillary walls and destroying body tissues, leading to massive internal bleeding and organ damage. Bites from a hemotoxic snake are extremely painful, and often lead to such tissue damage that amputation of toes or fingers is sometimes necessary in survivors.

Neurotoxic venoms, in contrast, attack the central nervous system by interfering with the transmission of nerve impulses. Because there is little tissue damage, bites from a neurotoxic snake are relatively painless, but produce a deadening effect somewhat similar to alcohol. The victim feels as if he is falling asleep. Death comes when the muscles that power the lungs and heart are paralyzed, asphyxiating the victim.

Both types of toxin are found in most snake venoms. The neurotoxic elements paralyze the prey animal and disable it, while the hemotoxic components serve as "meat tenderizers" that break down the body tissues so that they can be more easily digested. In general, the vipers and pit vipers are predominantly hemotoxic in action, while the elapids are largely neurotoxic. There are exceptions, however—the Mojave Rattlesnake, a pit viper, has venom that is largely neurotoxic, while the Australian Death Adder, an elapid, has hemotoxic venom.

The venom of the Eyelash Viper is not very powerful, but can cause tremendous tissue damage.

Although some species of snake are indeed capable of killing an adult human, for the most part the dangers of snakebite are greatly exaggerated. Almost four times as many people are killed worldwide by bee stings than by venomous snakes. More people are struck by lightning each year than are killed by snakes.

As mentioned before, many venomous snakes will defend themselves with a "dry" bite, in which no venom is injected. On average, about one in three bites is dry. In about one-third of the cases where venom is actually injected, it is such a small amount that no clinical symptoms occur and no damage is done. Even in cases where full envenomation takes place and the bite is untreated, death only occurs on average one out of eight times. If treatment is available, the death rate drops to less than one in sixteen. The rate of recovery, of course, varies with the particular species of snake involved; the Saw-Scaled Viper, for example, produces a death rate in untreated bites of around seventy-five percent, while the copperhead has never been known to have killed a healthy adult human being.

The death rate from snakebite also varies from country to country, depending on the species of snake that are native to the area and on the availability of medical treatment. The area with the high-

More snakebite is caused by cobras than by any other species.

est percentage of snakebite is Okinawa, where a species of pit viper known as the "Habu" bites about 0.2 percent of the population every year. The Habu does not possess a very powerful venom, however, and deaths from its bite are very rare.

The per-capita death rate from snakebite is highest in India and Burma, where about 12,000 people are killed each year by the Asian Cobra and Russell's Viper. Although these snakes have highly potent venom, this high death rate is more easily attributed to the lack of medical care and the large number of people who walk around barefoot at night—making snakebites much more likely. In Latin America, similar circumstances lead to about 2,000 deaths each

year, most from tropical coral snakes and the Fer-de-Lance pit viper. In Africa, about 1,000 people are killed every year by Puff Adders, Egyptian Cobras and Saw-Scaled Vipers.

In industrialized nations where medical treatment is readily available, the death rate drops enormously. In the United States, about 7,000 people are bitten by snakes each year, but only fifteen of these victims die. Most snake bites in the U.S. involve the copperhead, a small pit viper with relatively weak venom. Over two-thirds of all fatal bites are inflicted by Eastern or Western Diamondback Rattlesnakes, with Prairie Rattlers and Timber Rattlers accounting for most of the rest. Coral snakes account for about twenty-five snakebites per year in the U.S. (As a historical curiosity, the first Confederate soldier to die during the Civil War was not

Most snakebite in the United States is caused by the copperhead, which has only weak venom.

shot—he was bitten by an Eastern Coral Snake.)

In Europe, about 1,000 people are bitten each year, usually by the small European Adder. Only about fifteen deaths can be attributed to snakebite, clustered in the southeast area of the continent where the Sand Viper is relatively common. Australia, despite its large number of extremely venomous snakes, only reports five to ten deaths per year, due both to the ready availability of medical treatment and also to the fact that most of the dangerous snakes live in remote areas where they are seldom encountered by people.

Over the years, a large number of "treatments" have been proposed for venomous snakebite. Nearly all of them are ineffective, and some are downright silly. However, since even untreated bites have a relatively low death rate, various folk treatments have persisted in the mistaken belief that they do help.

For years, it was recommended that snakebite be treated by the "cutting and sucking" method. The idea is to restrict the flow of blood by applying a constricting band between the wound and the heart and then, using a razor blade or knife, cutting open the fang marks and using a suction cup to remove the envenomed blood and lymph.

Today, this treatment is recognized as being largely ineffective and sometimes dangerous. The amount

MORE FOLK TALES

Folk remedies for snakebite have ranged from the logical but ineffective to the downright bizarre. One favorite treatment was to place the opened body of a freshly killed chicken over the bite—the intention being to draw the venom into the chicken flesh rather than the victim. Another remedy was to force the victim to consume massive amounts of whiskey—which, while it no doubt made the victim feel much better, actually made things worse by speeding up the flow of blood and helping to circulate the venom more widely. Among the other snake "treatments" found throughout the world are drinking some of the blood of the snake that bit you, allowing a toad to urinate on the bite wound, plastering onion or tobacco paste onto the wound, and inserting the bitten part of the body into a bucket of kerosene. Needless to say, none of these "treatments" has any medical effect whatsoever.

of venom actually removed by this method is minimal at best. In some cases, clumsy attempts to cut open the wounds have led to severe nerve or tendon damage. In other cases, panic-stricken people had caused significant damage by cutting and sucking even though the snake had not injected any venom and no symptoms of poisoning were present.

Another treatment that was given some serious consideration is "cryotherapy," in which the bitten area (usually a hand or foot) is packed with large amounts of ice. The theory is that the cold restricts the flow of blood and slows down the venom. This method has not, however, been proven effective in any clinical tests.

For a time, the use of electric shock was recommended as a treatment for snakebite. When a harmless electric current was applied to

the bite site, it was assumed that the venom would be broken down through electrolysis and rendered harmless. This method has also never been demonstrated to be effective in any medical tests.

Effective Treatment

The only effective treatment for a venomous snakebite is the use of antivenins. These are specific chemical compounds that can bind to the venom molecules and destroy them. Antivenin is usually administered intravenously, and can only be applied by a doctor.

In order to produce antivenin, snakes of a particular species are "milked" of their venom by grasping the snake behind the head and forcing it to bite through a membrane covering a sterilized glass container. The venom glands are gently pressed to squeeze a supply of venom into the container. This is then purified and injected, in small amounts, into an animal—usually a horse. As the amount of injected venom is increased, the horse produces antibodies and becomes more and more resistant to the venom.

After a period of time, the horse will have sufficient antibodies to survive an injection that is several times higher than the normal lethal dose. At that point, a supply of blood is removed from the horse and the serum, which contains the antibodies, is purified as antivenin and packaged in ampules. Antivenins are usually kept refrigerated, and must be periodically replaced as they lose their effectiveness.

Because some people are allergic to horse serum, some pharmaceutical companies use sheep to produce antivenin. Perhaps the most unusual source of snake antivenin is Bill Haast of Florida, whose serpentarium has been supplying pharmaceutical companies with various snake venoms for over fifty years. Haast himself has been bitten over 160 times by numerous species. As a result, his blood has developed antibodies to some of the rarest and most dangerous serpents. Haast's blood serum has so far been used to save the lives of twenty-one snakebite victims.

Some antivenins are manufactured as an antidote to a particular species, and will be effective only against venom from that species. Most zoos maintain stockpiles of antivenin for the species that they keep in their collection. More often, however, the horse will be injected with the venoms of several different species and develop antibodies to them all. This is known as a "polyvalent" antivenin, and it is usually designed to be effective against all of the snakes in a particular geographic area. In the United States, for example, the polyvalent crotalus antivenin is effective against several species of rattlesnake, while in India a polyvalent is produced that treats the bites of Asian Cobras and Russell's Viper.

In the case of snakebite, the victim should be immobilized (movement will speed up the blood flow and distribute the venom more quickly) and carefully watched for signs of envenomation. In the case of elapids or other snakes with neurotoxic venom, the symptoms include drowsiness, slurred speech and tingling in the lips and fingers. Hemotoxic venoms, such as the vipers and pit vipers, produce swelling and discoloration at the site of the bite, followed by swelling of the affected limb and intense pain. Although the bite victim should be transported immediately to a hospital or medical facility, no treatment should be begun until it has definitely been established that venom was injected into the bite.

If medical help can be reached within thirty minutes of the bite, no further first aid is necessary. If medical help is not available, an elastic bandage should be wrapped firmly but not tightly around the bite area. The idea is not to restrict the flow of blood, but to slow down the circulation of lymph. The victim should be transported to medical aid as quickly as possible.

The symptoms and effects of a hemotoxic snakebite will vary according to the size and species of the snake, the amount of venom actually injected, the location of the bite, and the size and health of the person bitten. In general, though, the sequence goes something like this: Most bites occur on the fingers. At the instant of the bite, there is a sharp, burning pain at the wound. Within one minute, the finger will be stiff and difficult to move, and discoloration will be noted at the bite site, as the venom begins to break down body tissues and blood vessels. Within ten minutes the whole finger will be black and discolored, and swelling will be noticeable. Within forty-five minutes, the swelling and discoloration will have reached the elbow. The pain by this point will be intense, with severe throbbing and burning. Red streaks may be seen radiating away from the affected area, as the venom continues to travel in the bloodstream. Over the next twenty-four hours, the entire limb will turn black and may swell to over twice its normal size. In some cases, the swelling may be so severe that the skin will burst open and produce large weeping sores. In serious bites, there may be a feeling of weakness and light-headedness, accompanied by a rapid pulse. Blood may drain from the nose, mouth or kidneys, and blood may also be vomited or passed from the intestines.

Once it has been established that envenomation has occurred, the doctor will begin treatment. The first step is to test the bite victim for sensitivity to the antivenin. A small proportion of people are allergic to horse serum, and the administration of antivenin would lead to severe anaphylactic shock, which would be worse than the snakebite and could be fatal. For this reason, no one except trained medical staff should ever administer any snake antivenin.

If no allergic reaction occurs, the serum is administered through an intravenous (IV) tube directly into the bloodstream, where it begins to break down the venom. A severe bite may require as many as ten or twenty ampules of antivenin. Because each ampule may cost as much as $300, depending on the species (antivenin from foreign snakes will cost even more), and because the recovery process will necessitate several days in the hospital, snakebite can be a very expensive as well as a very painful experience.

Preventing Snakebite

Although the chances of being bitten by a venomous snake are roughly akin to those of being

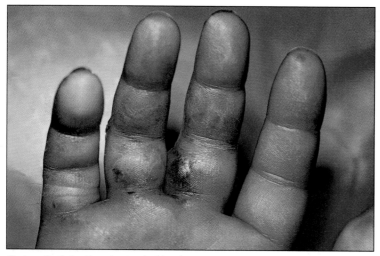

Six days after being bitten by a rattlesnake, this victim's hand still has some healing to do.

EVEN DEAD SNAKES ARE A THREAT

Do not handle dead snakes. Corpses can bite through reflex action for several hours after death. There have even been confirmed cases where people have been fatally bitten while handling the decapitated heads of dead rattlesnakes.

struck by lightning, every state except Hawaii, Maine and Alaska is inhabited by at least one species of venomous snake, and people who spend time in the wilderness, such as hikers, hunters and fishermen, should be familiar with methods of avoiding confrontations with venomous snakes. The incidence of snakebite can be greatly reduced if a few simple safety rules are observed.

The most basic rule is—leave snakes alone. Almost two-thirds of venomous snakebite occur because the human was in some way attempting to interact with the snake, whether to handle it, capture it or kill it. Do not attempt to handle or capture any venomous snake unless you have had sufficient training and have the necessary equipment to do so. People who are simply trying to get a closer look at a snake have been fatally bitten.

Nearly all snakebites occur on the hands or feet, usually when well-camouflaged snakes are unknowingly touched or stepped on. To prevent this, people who spend time in snake-infested areas should wear thick trousers and heavy boots. While hiking in Pennsylvania, I once inadvertently stepped on a young Northern Copperhead who struck several times at my ankle before I could back away. Fortunately for me, the fangs could not penetrate my hiking boots.

Care should be taken when hiking or rock climbing. Never step over a log or rock unless you can see what is on the other side, and do not place your hands or feet into hollow logs, burrows or rock crevices without checking them first. Snakes often lie concealed in such places waiting for prey.

Most snakes are active at night, and thus walking around in the woods during dusk and dawn should be avoided. When camping or hiking, tasks such as gathering firewood or drawing water should be done during daylight.

About half of all snakebites in the U.S. involve children between the ages of nine and fifteen. Young children should be taught to recognize any dangerous snakes in their area and warned to stay away from them.

If you should see a venomous snake in the wild, give it a wide berth and leave it alone. Keeping a distance of at least 5 feet will keep you out of range of even the largest North American venomous snakes.

Do not, under any circumstances, try to capture or kill a venomous snake. Given a chance to retreat, all snakes will back away and leave the scene.

Medical Uses for Snake Venom

Snakes and snake parts have long been important in traditional Asian medicine. One well-known traditional Chinese tonic consists of snake gall bladder and bile. To prepare this "medicine," the snake is stunned and then, while still alive, the body cavity is slit open and the gall bladder extracted. The gall bladder and bile are mixed with wine or whiskey and drunk while fresh. A variation on the same theme is to mix wine or whiskey with snake blood. Snake gall bladder, it is believed, is especially healthful during the winter months while the snake is fattened in preparation for hibernation.

SNAKE SOUP

A traditional Chinese dish is *say gong*, or snake soup. This is prepared by boiling snake bones, adding chopped snake flesh, a dash of snake blood and finally vegetables such as mushrooms, bamboo and onions. Say gong is supposed to increase the circulation, extend life and treat everything from arthritis to an unhappy love life.

In many parts of Asia, snake liquor is a thriving industry. By pickling a venomous viper in a bottle of whiskey, imbibers hope to treat skin disorders and improve their energy circulation.

It is doubtful that any of these traditional concoctions actually have any medicinal value at all. Snake venoms have, however, recently become the object of serious medical research, not only in order to more effectively treat snakebite, but also to utilize the various properties of many snake venom components as human medicines. Doctors today can use a number of pharmaceutical compounds that are extracted from snakes. The pain-killing drug Cobroxin is manufactured from a component found in cobra venom, while another painkiller, Nyloxin, is derived from a different cobra component. A group of drugs known as "beta blockers," used in the treatment of high blood pressure, is manufactured from the venom of Latin American pit vipers, while the anticoagulant Arvin, which helps prevent blood clots, is produced from components of Malayan Pit Viper venom.

There are currently hundreds of potential medical uses for snake venoms and components being investigated by researchers. Neurotoxic venoms are also being investigated for possible use in treating diseases of the human nervous system, including epilepsy and Parkinson's disease. Some snake venoms seem to have antimicrobial or antitumor properties. Before the Salk vaccine was developed in the 1950s, serious research was being carried out on using cobra venom as a treatment for polio. An extract of the venom from the Green Mamba is today being used to study the location and structure of pain receptors in the brain. A group of mamba toxins called dendrotoxins are being used to study the transfer of potassium in nerve cells, which provides useful information on several nervous system diseases. Other components of

mamba venom act as anticholinesterase drugs, and may also be useful in treating neurological disorders.

Bungarotoxin, from the venom of the Asian Kraits, has been used to probe human nicotinic receptors, which play important roles in the human nervous system. Another enzyme, called phospholipase A2, has been extracted from cobra and Cottonmouth venom, and is used to study the symptoms of cardiovascular disease and some forms of allergy.

Several snake venoms have anticoagulant properties, which prevent blood clotting. A few also

have enzymes that dissolve blood clots. One such component, called atroxin, is extracted from the venom of the Western Diamondback Rattlesnake, and has possible uses in treating thrombosis, a serious condition caused by clots in the blood.

Snake products other than venom also have medical uses. A protease inhibitor found in snake blood is being used to help treat AIDS patients. Shed snake skin has been successfully used as a model for testing the effects of drugs and chemicals on human skin.

CHAPTER 15

In Conclusion

Like anything else in life, the recent explosion of interest in the care and maintenance of reptiles in captivity has had both positive and negative results. On the positive side, more people are keeping and studying these animals than at any other time in history. The number of magazines, books and other sources of information devoted to snakes has increased tremendously in the past few years and shows no signs of leveling off any time soon. Our knowledge of the care and behavior of snakes has increased significantly in just the past few years.

On the other hand, the same increase in interest that has led to such knowledge about these animals has played a large role in threatening and endangering them. An enormous number of animals are being taken from the wild to meet the demands of the pet trade. Thousands of animals are being killed every year due to ignorance and improper treatment, and increasing numbers of animals are ending up in shelters and rescue programs, or are released by disillusioned owners into the wild, where they either die or become established threats to native wildlife.

A few trends in herpetoculture will almost certainly continue into the future. The number of people keeping and breeding snakes and other reptiles will continue to increase. As more and more species become available, prices will continue to fall. This will lead to an increasing number of new

"morphs," which will compete for the high-priced end of the reptile trade as more of the rarer and more difficult animals become more widely captive-bred.

The number of veterinarians who specialize in reptiles and amphibians will increase as more and more people begin keeping these animals. And, as the level of information increases, the horrendous death toll caused by improper care and lack of accurate knowledge will decrease.

The extent of government involvement in herpetoculture is also likely to rise. Some of this involvement will center around safety issues, such as regulating the keeping of large constrictors or venomous snakes in captivity. Much government involvement will center around conservation and trade regulation. If our present biodiversity is to be safeguarded and protected for future generations, drastic steps must be taken to prevent the loss of habitat and to combat the illegal trade in live reptiles. Such steps require government resources, but they also require individual action.

By any measure, however, snakes have been an enormously successful group of creatures. Their

unblinking eyes saw the fall of the dinosaurs and the rise of the mammals, including the appearance of a small, hairy, bipedal ape on the African plains a few million years ago. Snakes have been slithering across our planet for over 100 million years, some 500 times longer than *Homo sapiens sapiens,* and have diversified to fill every suitable environmental niche. They have been sometimes feared, sometimes reviled and sometimes worshipped, but they have always fascinated and awed us.

Unfortunately, though, snakes have long been surrounded by ignorance and superstition. As we humans come to dominate our planet more and more, it is vital that we understand the natural system in which we live, and of which snakes and other reptiles are such an important part. Keeping and maintaining reptiles in captivity allows more and more of us to study these animals, admire them and learn about them. The more we understand the natural roles and behaviors of snakes, the more we can appreciate them for what they are, and the more dedicated we can become to preserving these fascinating animals along with the rest of life's diversity.

Scientific Names

Scientific names for the snake species mentioned in this book:

Aesculapian Snake—*Elaphe longissima*

African Horned Viper—*Cerastes cerastes*

African Rock Python—*Python sebae*

African Sand Boa—*Eryx colubrinus*

Amazon Tree Boa—*Corallus enydris enyhdris*

American Sidewinder—*Crotalus cerastes*

Amethystine Python—*Morelia amethistina*

Anaconda—*Eunectes murinus*

Annulated Boa—*Corallus annulatus*

Arafura Wart Snake—*Acrochordus arafurae*

Australian Taipan—*Oxyuranus scutellatus*

Asian Cobra—*Naja naja*

Ball Python—*Python regius*

Beaked Sea Snake—*Enhydrina schistosa*

Black Banded Sea Snake—*Laticauda laticauda*

Black Mamba—*Dendroaspis polylepis*

Black Rat Snake—*Elaphe obsoleta obsoleta*

Blood Python—*Python curtus*

Boa Constrictor—*Boa constrictor constrictor*

Boomslang—*Dispholidus typus*

Brahminy Blind Snake—*Ramphotyphlops braminus*

Brown Tree Snake—*Boiga irregularis*

Bull Snake—*Pituophis melanoleuca sayi*

Burmese Python—*Python molurus bivittata*

California King Snake—
Lampropeltis getula californiae

California Mountain King Snake—
Lampropeltis zonata

Carpet Python—*Morelia spilota*

Cascabel—*Crotalus durrisus*

Cat-Eyed Snake—*Leptodeira septentrionalis*

Chain King Snake—*Lampropeltis getula getula*

Coachwhip—*Masticophis flagellum*

Cobras—*Naja* species

Copperhead—*Agkistrodon contortrix*

Coral Snakes—*Micrurus* species

Corn Snake—*Elaphe guttata guttata*

Death Adders—*Acanthophis* species

Desert Horned Viper—*Cerastes cerastes*

Eastern Diamondback Rattlesnake—
Crotalus adamanteus

Eastern Indigo Snake—*Drymarchon corais couperi*

Eastern Garter Snake—*Thamnophis sirtalis sirtalis*

Eastern King Snake—*Lampropeltis getula getula*

Eastern Milk Snake—
Lampropeltis triangulum triangulum

Egyptian Cobra—*Naja haje*

Elephant's Trunk Snake—*Acrochordus javanicus*

Emerald Tree Boa—*Corallus caninus*

European Adder—*Vipera berus*

European Asp—*Vipera aspis*

European Grass Snake—*Natrix natrix*

Eyelash Viper—*Bothriechis schlegelii*

Fer-de-lance—*Bothrops atrox*

Flying Tree Snake—*Chrysopelea* species

Florida King Snake—*Lampropeltis getula floridana*

Four-Lined Rat Snake—*Elaphe quatuorolineata*

Gaboon Viper—*Bitis gabonicus*

Green Anaconda—*Eunectes murinus*

Garter Snakes—*Thamnophis* species

Green Snakes—*Ophiodryas* species

Green Tree Python—*Morelia viridis*

Habu—*Trimeresurus mucrosquamatus*

Hognose Snakes—*Heterodon* species

Honduran Milk Snake—
Lampropeltis triangulum hondurensis

Horned Viper—*Cerastes cerastes*

Indian Python—*Python molurus molurus*

Indian Wart Snake—*Acrochordus granalatus*

Indigo Snake—*Drymarchon corais*

Jumping Viper—*Porthidium nummifer*

Keeled Green Snake—*Opheodrys aestivus*

Keeled Rat Snake—*Elaphe carinatus*

King Cobra—*Ophiophagus hannah*

King Snakes—*Lampropeltis getula*

Lake Taal Snake—*Hydrophis semperi*

Mangrove Snake—*Boiga denrophila*

Mexican Burrowing Snake—*Loxocemus bicolor*

Milk Snakes—*Lampropeltis triangulum*

Mojave Rattlesnake—*Crotalus scutulatus*

Natal Black Snake—*Macrelaps microlepidotus*

North American Hognose Snake—*Heterodon* species

Northern Copperhead—
Agkistrodon contortrix mokasen

Okeetee Corn Snake—*Elaphe guttata guttata*

Palestine Viper—*Vipera palaestinae*

Palm Vipers—*Bothriechis* species

Parrot Snake—*Leptophis ahaetulla*

Peter's Blind Snake—*Rhamphotphlops unguirostris*

Pine Snake—*Pituophis melanoleuca melanoleuca*

Prairie Rattlesnake—*Crotalus viridis*

Pueblan Milk Snake—
Lampropeltis triangulum campelli

Puff Adder—*Bitis arietans*

Racer Snakes—*Coluber constrictor*

Rainbow Boas—*Epicrates* species

Reticulated Python—*Python reticulatus*

Reuter's Blind Snake—*Typhlops reuteri*

Ribbon Snake—*Thamnophis sauritus*

Rock Python—*Python sebae*

Rosy Boa—*Lichinura trivirgata*

Round Island Boa—*Casarea dussumieri*

Round Island Burrowing Boa—*Bolyeria multicarnata*

Rubber Boa—*Charina bottae*

Russell's Viper—*Vipera russeli*

Sand Boas—*Eryx* species

Sand Viper—*Vipera ammodytes*

Saw-Scaled Viper—*Echis carinatus*

Sidewinder—*Crotalus cerastes*

Sinaloan Milk Snake—
Lampropeltis triangulum sinaloensis

Small-Headed Sea Snake—*Microcephalophis gracilis*

South American Bushmaster—*Lachesis muta*

Southern Copperhead—
Agkistrodon contortrix contortrix

South Pacific Rattlesnake—*Crotalus viridis helleri*

Spitting Cobras—*Naja nigricollis, Naja mossambica,
Hemachatus haemachatus*

Sunbeam Snake—*Xenopeltis unicolor*

Taipan (Inland Taipan species)—
Oxyuranus microlepidotus

Texas Blind Snake—*Leptotyphlops humilis*

Texas Rat Snake—*Elaphe obsoleta lindheimeri*

Tiger Snake—*Notechis scutatus*

Timber Rattlesnake—*Crotalus horridus*

Trans Pecos Rat Snake—*Elaphe subocularis*

Twig Snakes—*Theletornis* species

Wagler's Pit Viper—*Tropidolaemus wagleri*

Water Moccasin (Cottonmouth)—
Agkistrodon piscivorus

Water Snakes—*Nerodia* species

Western Diamondback Rattlesnake—*Crotalus atrox*

Yellow Anaconda—*Eunectes notaeus*

Yellow-Bellied Sea Snake—*Pelamis platurus*

Yellow Rat Snake—*Elaphe obsoleta quadrivittata*

Resources

National Herpetological Societies and Associations

American Federation of Herpetoculturalists
P.O. Box 300067
Escondido, CA 92030-0067
(Publishes *The Vivarium.*)

**American Society of Ichthyologists
and Herpetologists**
Business Office
P.O. Box 1897
Lawrence, KS 66044-8897
(Publishes the quarterly journal *Copeia.*)

National Herpetological Alliance
P.O. Box 5143
Chicago, IL 60680-5143

Society for the Study of Amphibians and Reptiles
ATTN: Karen Toepfer
P.O. Box 626
Hays, KS 67601-0626

Local Herpetological Societies

(This listing is far from complete. If you contact the societies listed below,
they may be able to point you to a local herp society that is closer to you.)

Fairbanks Herpetocultural Society
ATTN: Taryn Merdes
P.O. Box 71309
Fairbanks, AK 99707

Arizona Herpetological Association
P.O. Box 39127
Phoenix, AZ 85069-9127

Arkansas Herpetological Association
ATTN: Glyn Turnipseed
418 N. Fairbanks
Russelville, AR 72801

Northern California Herpetological Society
P.O. Box 1363
Davis, CA 95616-1363

Southern California Herpetology Association
P.O. Box 2932
Sante Fe Springs, CA 90607

Colorado Herpetological Society
P.O. Box 15381
Denver, CO 80215

Southern New England Herpetological Association
470 Durham Rd.
Madison, CT 06443-2060

Delaware Herpetological Society
Ashland Nature Center
Brackenville and Barley Mill Rd.
Hockessin, DE 19707

Central Florida Herpetological Society
P.O. Box 3277
Winter Haven, FL 33881

West Florida Herpetological Society
3055 Panama Rd.
Pensacola, FL 32526

Georgia Herpetological Society
Department of Herpetology, Zoo Atlanta
800 Cherokee Ave. SE
Atlanta, GA 30315

Idaho Herpetological Society
P.O. Box 6329
Boise, ID 83707

Central Illinois Herpetological Society
1125 W. Lake Ave.
Peoria, IL 61614

Hoosier Herpetological Society
P.O. Box 40544
Indianapolis, IN 46204

Iowa Herpetological Society
P.O. Box 166
Norwalk, IA 50211

Kansas Herpetological Society
Museum of Natural History, Dyche Hall
University of Kansas
Lawrence, KS 66045

Central Kentucky Herpetological Society
P.O. Box 12227
Lexington, KY 40581-2227

Louisiana Herpetological Society
Museum of Natural History
Foster Hall, Louisiana State University
Baton Rouge, LA 70803

Maryland Herpetological Society
Natural History Society
2643 N. Charles St.
Baltimore, MD 21218

New England Herpetological Society
P.O. Box 1082
Boston, MA 02103

Michigan Society of Herpetologists
321 W. Oakland
Lansing, MI 48906

Minnesota Herpetological Society
Bell Museum of Natural History
10 Church St. SE
Minneapolis, MN 55455-0104

Southern Mississippi Herpetological Society
P.O. Box 1685
Ocean Springs, MS 39564

St. Louis Herpetological Society
ATTN: Harry Steinmann
P.O. Box 220153
Kirkwood, MO 63122

Northern Nevada Herpetological Society
ATTN: Don Bloomer
P.O. Box 21282
Reno, NV 89502-1282

Association for the Conservation
of Turtles and Tortoises
RD 4, Box 368
Sussex, NJ 07461

New Mexico Herpetological Society
Department of Biology
University of New Mexico
Albuquerque, NM 87131

New York Herpetological Society
P.O. Box 1245
Grand Central Station
New York, NY 10163-1245

North Carolina Herpetological Society
State Museum
P.O. Box 29555
Raleigh, NC 27626

Central Ohio Herpetological Society
217 E. New England Ave.
Worthington, OH 43085

Northern Ohio Association of Herpetologists
Department of Biology
Case Western Reserve University
Cleveland, OH 44106

Oklahoma Herpetological Society
Tulsa Chapter
5701 E. 36th St. N
Tulsa, OK 74115

Oklahoma Herpetological Society
Oklahoma City Chapter
Oklahoma Zoo
2101 NE 50th
Oklahoma City, OK 73111

Oregon Herpetological Society
WISTEC
P.O. Box 1518
Eugene, OR 97440

Lehigh Valley Herpetological Society
ATTN: Rich Rosevear
P.O. Box 9171
Allentown, PA 18105-9171

Philadelphia Herpetological Society
ATTN: Mark Miller
P.O. Box 52261
Philadelphia, PA 19115

Pittsburgh Herpetological Society
Pittsburgh Zoo
1 Hill Rd.
Pittsburgh, PA 15206

Rhode Island Herpetological Association
30 Metropolitan Rd.
Providence, RI 02909

South Carolina Herpetological Society
ATTN: James L. Knight
P.O. Box 100107
Columbia, SC 29230

Texas Herpetological Society
Hutchinson Hall of Science
31st at Canton
Lubbock, TX 79410

Utah Herpetological Society
Hogle Zoo
P.O. Box 8475
Salt Lake City, UT 84108

Washington Herpetological Society
12420 Rock Ridge Rd.
Herndon, VA 22070

Pacific Northwest Herpetological Society
P.O. Box 70231
Bellevue, WA 98008

Wisconsin Herpetological Society
P.O. Box 366
Germantown, WI 53022

Snake Dealers and Breeders

Blue Chameleon Ventures
P.O. Box 643
Alva, FL 33920

Glades Herp
P.O. Box 50911
Fort Myers, FL 33905

Recommended Reading

Behler, John and F. Wayen King. *The Audubon Society Field Guide to North American Reptiles and Amphibians.* New York: Alfred A. Knopf, 1979.

Carr, Archie. *The Reptiles, Life Nature Library.* New York: Time, Inc., 1963.

Conant, Roger. *A Field Guide to Reptiles and Amphibians of Eastern and Central North America.* Boston: Houghton Mifflin, 1975.

Flank, Lenny Jr. *The Snake: An Owner's Guide to a Happy Healthy Pet.* New York: Howell Book House, 1996.

Kauffield, Charles. *Snakes: The Keeper and the Kept.* New York: Doubleday and Co., 1969; Malabar Fla.: Kreiger Publishing Co., 1995.

Mattison, Chris. *The Care of Reptiles and Amphibians in Captivity.* London: Blandford, 1992.

————. *The Encyclopedia of Snakes.* New York: Facts on File, Inc. 1995.

————. *Keeping and Breeding Snakes.* London: Blandford, 1988.

Parker, H. W. *Snakes: A Natural History.* Ithaca, N.Y.: Cornell University Press, 1977.

Riches, R. J. *Breeding Snakes in Captivity.* Miami, Fla.: Palmetto Publishing Co., 1976.

Rosenfeld, Arthur. *Exotic Pets.* New York: Simon & Schuster, Inc., 1987.

Stebbins, R. C. *A Field Guide to Western Reptiles and Amphibians.* Boston: Houghton Mifflin Co., 1966.

Vogel, Zdenek. *Reptiles and Amphibians: Their Care and Behavior.* London: Studio Vista, 1964.

Index

Note: Photograph(s) of a particular snake are represented by italicized page numbers.